THE LOGIC OF INDUCTION

ELLIS HORWOOD SERIES IN ARTIFICIAL INTELLIGENCE
Joint Series Editors: Professor JOHN CAMPBELL, Department of Computer Science, University College London, and
Dr JEAN HAYES MICHIE, Knowledgelink Limited, Edinburgh

Andrew, A.M.	Continuous Heuristics*
Bläsius, K.H. and Bürckert, H.-J.	Deduction Systems in AI*
Boguraev, B.K.	Natural Language Interfaces to Computational Systems*
Bramer, M.A. (editor)	Computer Game Playing: Theory and Practice
Campbell, J.A. (editor)	Implementations of PROLOG
Campbell, J.A., Forsyth, R., Narayanan, A. & Teague, M.	Dictionary of Artificial Intelligence*
Campbell, J. A. & Cox, P.	Implementations of PROLOG, Vol. 2*
Carter, D.	Interpreting Anaphors in Natural Language Texts
Davies, R. (editor)	Intelligent Information Systems: Progress and Prospects
Evans, J.B.	Structures of Discrete Event Simulation
Farreny, H.	Artificial Intelligence Exercise Programs*
Forsyth, R. & Rada, R.	Machine Learning: Applications in Expert Systems and Information Retrieval
Gabbay, D.M.	Programming in Pure Logic*
Gergely, T. & Futó, I.	Artificial Intelligence in Simulation*
Glicksman, J.	Image Understanding and Machine Vision*
Gottinger, H.W.	Artificial Intelligence: The Commercialisation of Intelligent Systems*
Hawley, R. (editor)	Artificial Intelligence Programming Environments*
Hayes, J.E. & Michie, D. (editors)	Intelligent Systems: The Unprecedented Opportunity
Hunter, J.R.W., Gotts, N.M. & Sinnhuber, R.K.E.W.	Artificial Intelligence in Medicine*
Lopez de Mantaras, R.	Approximate Reasoning and Knowledge Acquisition*
Łukaszewicz, W.	Nonmonotonic Reasoning*
Mellish, C.	Computer Interpretation of Natural Language Descriptions
Michie, D.	On Machine Intelligence, Second Edition
Mortimer, H.	The Logic of Induction
Mozetic, I.	Machine Learning of Qualitative Models*
Partridge, D.	Artificial Intelligence: Applications in the Future of Software Engineering
Ramsay, A. & Barrett, R.	AI in Practice: Examples in POP-11
Savory, S.E.	Artificial Intelligence and Expert Systems
Spacek, L.	Advanced Programming in PROLOG*
Sparck Jones, K. & Wilks, Y. (editors)	Automatic Natural Language Parsing
Steels, L. & Campbell, J.A. (editors)	Progress in Artificial Intelligence
Torrance, S. (editor)	The Mind and the Machine
Turner, R.	Logics for Artificial Intelligence
Wallace, M.	Communicating with Databases in Natural Language
Wertz, H.	Automatic Correction and Improvement of Programs
Yazdani, M. (editor)	New Horizons in Educational Computing
Yazdani, M. & Narayanan, A. (editors)	Artificial Intelligence: Human Effects

* *In preparation*

THE LOGIC OF INDUCTION

HALINA MORTIMER
with additional material by
I. CRAIG
Department of Computer Science, University of Warwick
Translator:
EWA SUCH-KLIMONTOWICZ
The Jagellonian Institute, Poland
Translation Editors:
I. CRAIG and A. COHN
University of Warwick

ELLIS HORWOOD LIMITED
Publishers · Chichester

Halsted Press: a division of
JOHN WILEY & SONS
New York · Chichester · Brisbane · Toronto

This English edition first published in 1988 by
ELLIS HORWOOD LIMITED
Market Cross House, Cooper Street,
Chichester, West Sussex, PO19 1EB, England
The publisher's colophon is reproduced from James Gillison's drawing of the ancient Market Cross, Chichester.

Distributors:
Australia and New Zealand:
JACARANDA WILEY LIMITED
GPO Box 859, Brisbane, Queensland 4001, Australia
Canada:
JOHN WILEY & SONS CANADA LIMITED
22 Worcester Road, Rexdale, Ontario, Canada
Europe and Africa:
JOHN WILEY & SONS LIMITED
Baffins Lane, Chichester, West Sussex, England
North and South America and the rest of the world:
Halsted Press: a division of
JOHN WILEY & SONS
605 Third Avenue, New York, NY 10158, USA

This English edition is translated from the original Polish edition *Logika indukcji* published in 1982 by Panstwowe Wydawnictwo Naukowe, Warsaw,© the copyright holders.

© 1988 English Edition, Ellis Horwood Limited

British Library Cataloguing in Publication Data
Mortimer, Halina
The logic of induction. —
(Ellis Horwood series in artificial intelligence)
1. Logic. Induction
I. Title   II. Craig, I.   III. Cohn, A.G.
161

Library of Congress Card No. 88–22962

ISBN 0–7458–0312–1(Ellis Horwood Limited)
ISBN 0–470–21234–9(Halsted Press)

Phototypeset in Times by Ellis Horwood Limited
Printed in Great Britain by Hartnolls, Bodmin

COPYRIGHT NOTICE
All Rights Reserved. No part of this publication may be reproduced, stored in a retrieval system, or transmitted, in any form or by any means, electronic, mechanical, photocopying, recording or otherwise, without the permission of Ellis Horwood Limited, Market Cross House, Cooper Street, Chichester, West Sussex, England.

Table of contents

Editor's preface 7
Introduction 9
  1   The concept of induction and the problem of inductive logic 13
  2   The formal properties of probability 19
  3   Induction and probability 25
  4   Partial interpretation of probability 35
  5   Statistical induction 40
  6   Logical interpretation of probability 47
  7   Henry Kyburg's epistemological conception of probability 72
  8   The subjective interpretation of probability 80
  9   Popper's anti-inductionism and anti-probabilism 90
 10   The inductive rules of acceptance 99
 11   Induction of confirmation 126
 12   Machine learning and induction 154
       Iain D. Craig
Bibliography 177
Index 181

We do not come to the discussion of how we obtain reasonable belief in a scientific hypothesis . . . already knowing what we mean by such a 'reasonable' belief and such a 'valid' inference; in stating the conditions which justify inferences we shall, *ipso facto*, be giving criteria which determine the meaning of the phrases 'valid inference' and 'reasonable belief' in the case of an inductively established hypothesis.

R. B. Braithwaite, *Scientific Explanation,* 1953
(Cambridge University Press, 1955, p. 257)

Editor's preface

The task that was set was to edit this book and to write an additional chapter on machine learning and its relationship to the theories of induction that have been developed in Philosophy.

The editing task proved to be comparatively straightforward at a superficial level. What turned out to be more difficult was handling the style of the translation. The translation was in the form of enormously long sentences that appeared to reflect Polish style rather more than idiomatic English in general, and, in particular the kinds of idiomatic English that one encounters in books on Artificial Intelligence and, perforce, even in Philosophy, these days. Quite obviously, it would have been possible to alter the style so as to reflect the practices and linguistic conventions of the disciplines on which this book is targeted. The problem with that approach was that it entailed that the book be completely rewritten: clearly, this was not possible, given the constraints that were imposed upon the editor.

As a result, the main body of the text has been edited as far as vocabulary and punctuation are concerned and, frequently, some small modifications have been made so that the text reads in a clearer fashion than did the raw translation; in addition, a considerable number of sentences have been reworked so that they read rather more like idiomatic English. The book does, though, read as if it was a translation, but it is hoped that it can be read with considerably greater ease than could the manuscript which was delivered for editing. The enormously long sentences have been considerably reduced in number and some additional paragraphing changes have been made.

The majority of the present text is composed of an analysis of the theories of inductive reasoning that are currently under consideration by philosophers. Induction has been a problem for a considerable time, so the reader should not expect to find any definitive theory in these pages: it is unlikely that any full theory will appear, if ever, within the next few decades — induction draws in so many other philosophical issues. However, the problem of induction does appear to be related to machine learning which is frequently described in terms such as 'inductive inference'. In order to relate the majority of the text to the machine learning literature, an extra chapter (Chapter 12) was added to the original material. As is reported in that chapter, the relationship between computer science and the philosophy is very hard to determine (assuming there is one — it might be argued that machine learning appeals to induction not because it is directly related, but only because there is no other word to summarize its activities as crisply): the machine learning literature is not at all illuminating in this respect. One might conjecture as to the reasons for the apparent neglect of induction theory in the machine learning literature, but such thoughts are probably best left to oneself.

There are many aspects of machine learning for which one can find connections with induction theory. The problem is that they cannot be articulated fully because of the fragmentary nature of machine learning. Also, the enterprise cannot truly be of benefit because one can only engage in it at a very high level at present — that is, at a level of generality which deals only with the area as a whole, but, because of the diversity of machine learning, this could only be a caricature.

Rather than attempt to relate machine learning at a global level to theories of induction (which is probably a task that can only be completed after much effort and which would lead to a separate volume), an alternative strategy was adopted. This alternative amounts to summarizing what has been done and what is currently under attack, but at a rather abstract level. The reader is left to make up his or her own mind about the relationship between the two (arguably very different) activities. It is to be hoped that there are enough pointers into the machine learning literature for the reader to engage in further reading: such additional consultation would appear, though, unlikely to result in any crisp and interesting characterization of the relationship between these two activities.

Warwick, IDC
June, 1988

Introduction

In recent years the interest in the problem of the logic of induction has considerably increased. The literature concerning this subject is enormous. Most of the leading foreign journals dealing with logic and methodology devote a lot of space to the problems of induction. Numerous congresses and international conferences are devoted especially to these problems. At the same time there are so many different conceptions striving to build the logic of induction, and so many difficult problems which, to be solved, need the construction of such logic, that for someone who has not followed systematically the literature dealing with this subject for more than thirty years, it is difficult to become familiar with current literature, estimate the value of particular publications, and understand the discussions which began several years earlier, and in which very controversial views are expressed.

In this situation, it seems necessary to analyse the main trends in solving the problem of inductive logic which are promoted in the literature. Different attitudes concerning the trends of these solutions, trends which have a bearing on the development of research in recent years, were outlined fairly clearly in the years 1950–1970.

The task of this book is simply an analysis of chosen concepts tending to solve certain important problems connected with the logic of induction; concepts which in those years were best known and discussed in logical journals, and which — as it seems — had the greatest influence on the direction of current studies in the field of inductive logic.

In contemporary inquiries into inductive logic, there is a definite dominating tendency to ground the logic of induction on probabilistic criteria. There appear, however, essential discrepancies between the views on what should be this 'inductive probability', i.e. the probability on which inductive logic is to be based. The problems of what this inductive probability should be and by what methods its values should be estimated have undoubtedly the central problems of contemporary studies concerning the logic of induction. With this in mind, a few chapters of this book are devoted to the most important interpretations of probability which appear in literature. In these chapters the various advantages and disadvantages of these interpretations are considered from the point of view of their appropriateness to the logic of induction.

The second essential discrepancy between these viewpoints is connected with the problem of what inductive logic should deal with. Two different opinions on this problem have the strongest influence on contemporary attempts to build such logic.

According to one of them, such logic should establish the criteria of legitimate inference in the strict sense of this word; that is, of the reasonings in which, on the basis of certain premises the conclusion is accepted. It is assumed that it is possible to formulate such criteria for a case when the conclusion does not follow from the premises, that is, for the inductive inference. This view leads to attempts to build inductive logic in the form of rules of acceptance. Chapter 10 is devoted to the discussion of certain types of these rules. Various types of these rules are connected with different views concerning the question of what factors are decisive for the validity of induction.

According to another opinion the criteria of legitimate induction can refer only to confirmation of some sentences by others (or definite degrees of confirmation); however, confirmation of a sentence by some premises from which this sentence does not follow does not allow us to accept this sentence. If one wanted to speak about legitimacy of acceptance by way of induction, one would have to use the notion of acceptance, which would be in some sense graduated and not dichotomic, which appears in the rules of acceptance. This means: some definite degree of confirmation may be treated as the base for a certain corresponding degree of conviction. This view leads to inductive logic in the form of so-called confirmation functions, that is, it leads to the measure of the degree of confirmation of some sentences by others. The penultimate chapter of the book is devoted to the considerations of the criteria of confirmation and certain measures of confirmation propagated in literature.

Chapter 9 is devoted to the criticism of Popper's argument which tends to show that the procedure leading to the acceptance of hypotheses and theories in empirical sciences can be explained without the help of induction. The insertion of this chapter in the book can be explained by the fact that the controversy between Popper and the adherents of the inductive model of empirical sciences has exerted great influence on the studies of inductive logic.

This book does not aspire to present a full classification of views on the problem of inductive logic. The division of the book into the chapters was inspired by the wish to demonstrate the differences of views in the above-mentioned problems, which seem to me particularly important. The differences of views on many other problems are discussed, as well as certain variants of substantially similar attitudes.

Now for some remarks concerning the means of presentation of material covered and the assumed level of the reader's knowledge.

Lack of Polish books devoted to inductive logic induced me to write this book in such a way that it could, besides its main task, which was discussed above, fulfil a certain additional purpose, namely, that it could make a starting point for studies in the logic of induction. I wanted it to be in principle accessible not only for the logicians and philosophers, but also for a wider circle of readers, and especially for students possessing a basic knowledge of logic. The knowledge which this book assumes in the reader is in fact limited to being acquainted with basic notions of logic (particularly a good understanding of the connectives of the sentential calculus, quantifiers, logical structure of sentences, the notions of logical falsehood and truth, and such relations between sentences like logical inference, discrepancy or independence), and with the more important logical tautologies. The reader's knowledge of some simple combinatorial formulas is also assumed (this concerns mostly Chapter 6). It does not mean that this book will be easy reading for everyone who has acquainted himself with elementary logic. From the reader who is not skilful in studying texts on logic or logical methodology, the understanding of many considerations included herein will surely require considerable effort or even the augmentation of his knowledge (for instance in the field of probability calculus).

Taking into account this additional task which the book is to fulfil. I have inserted in it a few chapters in which: the concept of induction and the problem of inductive logic are explained (Chapter 1); the formal properties of probability are characterized (Chapter 2) with special consideration of those which induce the logicians to base inductive logic on probability (Chapter 3); certain typical forms of inductive reasoning are characterized — reductive inference, enumerative induction and inference by analogy (Chapter 3); and very brief information about the theory of statistical induction is presented (Chapter 5).

Concluding the introduction I wish to express my gratitude to those who helped me with the work on the book.

My warmest thanks to Professor Klemens Szaniawski for much valuable advice, hints and explanations; to Dr Grzegorz Lissowski and Dr Włodzimierz Okrasa for extremely accurate and penetrating elaboration of editorial reviews which helped me remove several deficiencies and ambiguities from the book; to Professor Marian Przełęcki for the encouragement to write this book and for numerous discussions over problems connected with its contents.

1
The concept of induction and the problem of inductive logic

Let us begin with a question: What is the logic of induction? This question must be immediately corrected: we should rather ask what the inductive logic 'is to be', and not what it 'is', because in a sense, such a logic does not exist at all, and in another sense its existence is doubtful. It is doubtful whether all non-deductive inferences which lead to the acceptance of hypotheses and theories in the empirical sciences are done according to rules which could be formalized and codified in the form of a logical system. On the other hand it is certain that nobody has ever managed to present a satisfactory system of logic of such inferences. All conceptions and systems of inductive logic which have been presented in methodological literature can be at most treated as attempts to point out certain trends which present a fair chance of creating the logic of induction.

If we have asked the question what the logic of induction is to be, let us first explain in what way the term 'induction' is understood in this question, since this term is clear neither in the common language nor in the writings dealing with methodology.

According to the old philosophical tradition induction was described as a reasoning which led from particular premises to general conclusions; induction understood in this way was opposed to deduction characterized as the reasoning leading from general premises to individual (or less general) conclusions. This characterization of induction and deduction has been rejected because it did not distinguish the class of reasoning which were not sufficiently significant from the point of view of methodology.

The contempory characterization of deduction, which is based on the criterion of the logical entailment of a conclusion from premises, distinguishes deduction as the class of inferences whose methodological validity is indubitable. For the logical entailment of a conclusion from premises consists in the fact that the laws of logic warrant the truth of the conclusion if only the premises are true. It certainly concerns the laws of the 'ordinary', classical formal logic (often called deductive logic), which is usually presented in books on logic. In connection with this guarantee of truth, deductive inferences are called infallible. The above-cited old characterization left beyond the limits of deduction those inferences based on such laws of logic as, for example the principle of transposition or the rule of *modus ponens*, in which both the premises and the conclusion could be equally general or individual or even incomparable in their generality.

The qualification of induction as an inference leading from individual premises to general conclusions which — as it seems — has become quite fixed in the common language, has a similar fault. In methodology the concept of induction is used in a much broader sense, so that, for instance, inference by analogy or the statistical inferences in which the conclusions are not universal statements are, as a rule, classified as inductive inferences.

The concept of induction, however, in contrast to the concept of deduction, is probably not used in contemporary methodology in an unequivocal and commonly accepted way, or at least this concept has no explicit definition. One could think that it is simply used in the sense of a non-deductive and, therefore, fallible inference. In this sense deduction and induction would create a separate and exhaustive division of all possible inferences. The basis for this division — the question of whether the conclusion is ensured by the premises — is doubtless significant from the point of view of methodology.

I tend to believe, however, that this sense of induction is not common in methodology. If, for instance, on the basis of the premise that Monday is the first day of the week someone derived the conclusion that Socrates was a blonde, I do not think that many people would agree that this reasoning was inductive only because it was not deductive. One would, rather, expect that not all non-deductive reasoning is classified as inductive, but only that which possesses certain definite forms which are believed to appear in scientific praxis. Nobody, however, claims to be able to enumerate all these forms.

Therefore, the extension of the term 'induction' is not clearly determined. As a matter of fact, however, for the investigations concerning inductive logic, it is sufficiently clearly determined by the necessary condition which says that induction is a non-deductive inference. For our considerations of inductive logic, we can safely assume that this condition is also sufficient and, hence, that the logic of induction is to be the logic concerning non-deductive inferences.

Let us return to the question what the logic of induction is to be. The problem of the criteria for justification of sentences is considered to be one of the fundamental problems of methodology. The notion of justification is not unequivocal — it is used in a stronger sense and in a weaker one. Logical methodology is mostly interested in the problem of the criteria of the so-called indirect justification of sentences, i.e. justification of sentences by other sentences (assumptions, premises). According to the most rigorous concept of justification — a statement is logically justified by the premises only if it logically follows from them. This concept of justification of sentences is then connected with the guarantee of their truth. This guarantee is certainly treated here as a relative and contingent one; even the most correct, from the logical point of view, reasoning cannot guarantee the truth of the conclusion if the premises are false.

With so rigorous a concept of justification, the problem of the criteria of justification presents no difficulty: these criteria are provided by classical logic. The thing is, however, that such a concept of justification is in conflict with the very common view that the empirical sciences justify their statements (among others, universal statements) on the basis of the sentences which describe the results of observations and experiments from which these statements do not follow at all. This qualification suggests that the concept of justification is also used in the weaker sense which does not require a guarantee of truth.

One can certainly say that in such cases we have to do, e.g., confirmation, and not justification, of statements. This terminology is quite common. Such a change of terminology, however, does not eliminate the problem. The fact is that hypotheses and theories in empirical sciences undergo the procedure of confrontation with the results of observation, i.e. testing, and that testing is considered necessary for the acceptance of those hypotheses and theories. If, however, testing of hypotheses does not consist of deducing them from observational premises, we must accept that non-deductive (i.e. inductive) inferences are applied in the empirical sciences. This situation creates, in the methodology of empirical sciences, the need for a reconstruction of the rules which govern such inferences, and the need to formulate criteria which would allow the recognition, among the non-deductive inferences, of those which could be called correct (i.e. justifying in a weaker sense than deduction), and which are probably used implicitly by the community of practitioners of the empirical sciences.

And so, the logic of induction is to be a theory of such inferences. This theory is expected to characterize such connections between the premises and the conclusion which would make the criteria of correctness of non-deductive inferences. At the same time, it should be stressed that it concerns the connections which exist between the premises and the conclusion with regard to their form (structure, syntax), and not with regard to their content. For instance: the sentences 'every man is a mammal' and 'every mouse is a rodent' are difficult in their contents, but have identical form.

Moreover, it should be emphasized that the very concept of correctness of non-deductive inferences is not clear in itself. As a matter of fact, it is generally accepted that those inferences are correct which lead to the acceptance of statements in empirical sciences, and efforts are made to characterize their form in a clear way. This task, however, is extremely difficult. The difficulty consists primarily of the fact that the inferences actually made in the empirical sciences are, as a rule, enthymemal in their character. They are usually based on so many premises which belong to the current knowledge that no scientist could probably reproduce completely his own reasonings, i.e. enumerate all the premises which those inferences were implicitly based on.

In connection with this, there exists a tendency to interpret certain inferences as only apparently inductive, and factually as enthymematic deductions. Such an interpretation is usually adopted for the so-called eliminative induction, i.e. the inferences described in the nineteenth century by the English logician J. S. Mill [54] in the form of several canons. Namely, it is assumed that the inferences made according to these canons have usually a silent premise in the form of an alternation of a number of n hypotheses; this being so, the observational data which eliminate $n-1$ hypotheses permit the deduction of the hypothesis n: see e.g. [52], [80] and [86]. This deductive hypothesis, however, is impossible to be used for all the inferences in the empirical sciences if we accept that the observational data are the decisive premises for empirical knowledge.

The second essential difficulty in the examination of the actual course of inferences in the empirical sciences is the lack of precision with regard to the question of in what sense one can speak there about acceptance of statements or theories. In this respect, the situation is completely different to mathematics, where only those assertions which are proved by way of deduction from the axioms are accepted. Mathematical statements once they have been correctly proved, cannot ever be refuted, and therefore they can be and really are, accepted with certainty and preemptorily. On the other hand, empirical statements are always exposed to refutation by the results of experience, and this is why they cannot be accepted in an ultimate and irrevocable way. As a rule, in the historical process of development of science, they undergo revision: the statements which were accepted at one time are later refuted or modified. Therefore, acceptance must be understood here in a different, weaker sense.

Vagueness and lack of clarity of the notion of acceptance of the empirical statements must leave doubts concerning the question whether, and which, empirical theorems (theories) are actually accepted in a given period of time. And so the plan to discover what rules actually led to the acceptance of the statements in the empirical sciences (the program of the so-called decriptive methodology) meets with serious difficulties. What is more — as I have already mentioned in the Introduction — one can have doubts concerning the question of whether such rules can be characterized in a formal way, and whether a solution to the problem of inductive logic by means of examination of factual scientific procedures exists at all. All this causes the theoretician of induction — first — to use extremely simplified examples of inferences. Secondly, they try not so much to reconstruct, but rather to create norms of correctness or rationality of inferences which would more or less correspond to what is done in the empirical sciences and in everyday practice.

It should be mentioned that some philosophers and logicians also present views which negate any justifying value of non-deductive inferences. Extremely radical views concerning these matters were pronounced in the eighteenth century by the English philosopher David Hume [38]. He was of the opinion that the existence of inductive inferences could be psychologically explained by the natural tendencies of the human mind to such reasonings. On the other hand, there exists no logic which could present the criteria of correctness for any non-deductive inferences. The acceptance of an inductive conclusion is an act of faith, not knowledge. Fundamental unanimity with Hume's views on induction is declared, for example, by such contemporary philosophers as S. Toulmin [83] or P. Strawson [75].

The best known contemporary representative of the view questioning the existence and the need for inductive logic is Karl Popper [60]. Contrary to Hume, he considers that the empirical sciences do not use any inductive inference at all. According to him the conviction about the inductive character of inferences in these sciences is a dogma which should be simply rejected together with the need to solve any problems connected with the correctness of such inferences. Popper's 'anti-inductionism' is, however, based on a certain misunderstanding concerning the meaning of the term 'induction'; and so, in effect, certain interesting theses of an apparently deductionistic Popperian methodology are at present developed by the supporters of the inductionistic conception of the empirical sciences. In connection with this, Popper's conception will be widely discussed in this book.

Finally, it should be stressed that questioning of the justifying value of inductive inference does not always go hand in hand with resignation from inductive logic. The so-called behaviouristic interpretation of induction introduced by the eminent mathematician Jerzy Neyman [57,58], one of the authors of decision theory, is well known and quite popular. According to this conception the statistical rules are not rules of inductive inference, but only rules of inductive behaviour, i.e. the decision rules act on the basis of data that is insufficient to state with certainty the state of affairs on which the results of actions depend. The supporters of this conception do not question the need or possibility of constructing formal criteria of correctness or rationality of the inductive procedure that is understood in this way; they only deny that induction is an inference.

Traditional logic did not have much to say about validity of induction. Traditional logic courses often cover inductive inference, but it is usually reduced to a description of certain chosen forms of such inference, like, for example, induction by enumeration, induction by elimination, inference by analogy, reductive inference, etc. Certainly, a description like this is not the logic of induction, because such logic is required to present the correctness criteria of reasonings, while the above-mentioned forms of reasoning do not claim validity. As concerns validity, however, there was nothing more than general formulae like the one saying that validity of an inductive generalization depends on the number of the observed cases consistent with this generalization and on their variety.

At present, many logicians deal with the problem of induction; the literature devoted to this problem is enormous; numerous congresses and conferences are exclusively devoted to these problems. In this situation this book cannot claim to analyse everything that has been done in this field. It will be limited only to the analysis of certain basic conceptions which point out the main trends of the modern attempts at creating inductive logic.

A charateristic feature of these modern conceptions is the fact that they are based on the probability of sentences. This has its source in the intuitive conviction that although the truth of the empirical assertions and theories is not certain on the basis of the experiential data, it can be, however, more or less probable. This probability is interpreted in different ways, but as a rule it is treated as a function of numerical values and formal properties which are in conformity with the axioms accepted for probability in mathematics. The tendency to use probability in inductive logic has its source not only in intuition, which I have mentioned above, but also in the fact that the application of the conceptual apparatus of mathematics offers the prospect of precise formulation of the criteria of correct induction. Besides, probability has certain properties which are intuitive for the interpretation of the probability value of the conclusion with regard to the premises: This is the evaluation of the degree of justification of inference.

To enable readers who are unfamiliar with probability theory to read this book, I shall now present a short characterization of the formal properties of probability.

2
The formal properties of probability

In contemporary mathematics the concept of probability is understood in a completely abstract way, which makes it possible to apply it to many different spheres of reality. These spheres, however, must be characterized by a certain, definite formal structure, namely the set of objects for which probability is to be estimated, must compose the so-called Boolean fields.

A Boolean field is a set of any objects (for instance events, sentences or sets) with the following properties: (1) this set includes certain distinguished elements which will be here denoted by the symbols '$\bigvee$' and '$\varnothing$' and will be called the maximum and the zero element: (2) certain operations subject to the laws of Boolean algebra are determined on arbitrarily chosen elements of this set: (3) this set is closed under the results of these operations which means that the results of the operations on the elements are also elements of this set. These operations are called addition, subtraction, multiplication, and complementation, although in mathematics addition and multiplication possess somewhat different formal properties. Boolean addition is usually denoted by the symbol '$\vee$', '$\cup$' or '$+$': multiplication — by the symbol '$\wedge$', '$\cap$' or '$\cdot$', while complementation is denoted by a dash or comma above the element: '$\bar{x}$' or 'x''. The theory of Boolean algebra can be described by the following ten axioms:

(1) $x \vee y = y \vee x$
(2) $x \wedge y = y \wedge x$
(3) $x \vee (y \vee z) = (x \vee y) \vee z$
(4) $x \wedge (y \wedge z) = (x \wedge y) \wedge z$
(5) $x \vee (y \wedge z) = (x \vee y) \wedge (x \vee z)$
(6) $x \wedge (y \vee z) = (x \wedge y) \vee (x \wedge z)$
(7) $x \vee \varnothing = x$
(8) $x \wedge \bigvee = x$
(9) $x \vee \bar{x} = \bigvee$
(10) $x \wedge \bar{x} = \varnothing$

The most important applications of Boolean algebra are the set calculus and the sentential calculus. In the first of these applications the elements of Boolean field are sets among which certain elements are distinguished. The maximum element is the universal set, i.e. the set which includes all the considered sets. The zero element is the empty set, i.e. the set which does not possess any elements. The sum of sets $x \vee y$ is the set of all elements of the set x and all elements of the set y; the product of sets $x \wedge y$ is the set of all elements which belong to both these sets simultaneously. Complementation $\bar{x}$ is the set of all those elements of the universal set which do not belong to the set x. Last but not least, $x=y$ means that the sets x and y have precisely the same elements.

With reference to sentences, it is accepted that one interprets the maximum element as a logically true statement (tautology), the zero element as a logically false statement (negation of tautology), while the identity of the logically equivalent statements is assumed; the sum $x \vee y$ is understood as alternation (it is read: x or y) defined as a statement which is true when at least one of the sentences x, y is true. The product $x \wedge y$ denotes conjunction (read: x and y) defined as a true statement if both x and y are true. The complementation $\bar{x}$ denotes negation of the statement x, and $x=y$ denotes logical equivalence of statements.

It is easy to notice that, in both these interpretations, all the axioms of the Boolean algebra are true for arbitrary sets or arbitrary statements.

The terminology which speaks of probability of events is very popular. This terminology is used in statistics. It should be mentioned, however, that it is not the probability of certain definite individual events which is spoken of there, but the probability of certain types and kinds of events (e.g. the kind of events which consist of getting tails in a toss of a coin). The type of events is interpreted as a set of events of a given type (for instance a set of results consisting in getting tails in a toss of a coin). The application of the probability calculus to events assumes that it is possible to distinguish a universal set of the so-called elementary events which can be individual events (e.g. getting tails in a single throw of a coin). A probability, however, does not refer to those elementary events, but to the elements understood as sub-sets of the universal set of elementary events, i.e. the sub-sets which are elements of a certain definite Boolean field. In this way the interpretation of the elements of the Boolean field as events is reduced to interpreting them as sets. A certain event is treated as a universal set, while an impossible one is treated as an empty set.

Let us now pass to the concept of probability. Probability can be defined as a function of numerical values, whose domain (i.e. the objects for which probability is defined) composes a Boolean field, and which satisfies the theorems of the probability calculus. The probability function is, as a rule designated, by the symbol P. The expression $P(x)$ is the representation of the value of the function P for the argument x (i.e. a number). This way of reading of $P(x)$, however, is inconvenient. This is why, in accordance with the widely accepted habit, we shall usually read $P(x)$ as the probability of x, and say, for instance, that the probability of $x - P(x)$ — is a number, instead of saying that the value $P(x)$ of probability P for x is a number.

The best known sequence of axioms of the probability calculus was presented by the Russian mathematician A. Kolmogorov in 1931 [43]. These axioms impose on the probability function the following condition:

(A.1) for any element $x: 0 \leqslant P(x) \leqslant 1$

(A.2) $P(\vee) = 1$

(A.3) for a finite or denumerable number of pairwise disjoint elements
$x_1, x_2, \ldots$: $P(x_1 \vee x_2 \vee \ldots) = P(x_1) + P(x_2) + \ldots$.

Using the most popular terminology for ascribing probabilities to events, we can explain the meaning of the axioms as follows: Axioms 1 and 2 state that probability of any event is a number from the interval 0 to 1, and the certain event has the maximum probability, i.e. 1. Axiom 3 states that the probability of occurrence of one of the pair-wise disjoint events equals the sum of probabilities of the individual events. Generally speaking, a pair of disjoint elements is understood as two elements whose Boolean product equals the zero element. Therefore, two sets are disjoint if they have no common elements, because then their product is empty. Two statements are disjoint when they are logically discordant, because then their conjunction is logically false. Two elements are disjoint when it is impossible for them to occur simultaneously.

The quoted axioms refer to the so-called absolute probability (which is also called *a priori* probability). With the use of this notion the so-called conditional probability (*a posteriori*) which is a two-argument function, can be defined. The expression $P(x/y)$ which designates the value of the conditional probability for the argument x relative to the argument y, we shall read: the probability of x relative to y (by analogy with the absolute probability). Conditional probability is defined using absolute probability as follows:

(D.1) $$P(x/y) = \frac{P(x \wedge y)}{P(y)}$$

As can be seen this definition determines the conditional probability of x relative to y only for those cases in which $P(y)$ is not zero; if $P(y)$ is zero, the value of $P(x/y)$ is not determined at all. As a consequence of this, all theorems in which conditional probabilities occur lose their significance if those probabilities have no value.

The conditional probability defined by (D.1) satisfies respectively (on the above-mentioned condition) the axioms of the probability calculus, i.e.:

$0 \leq P(x/y) \leq 1$

$P(\vee/x) = 1$

$P(x_1 \vee x_2 \vee \ldots /y) = P(x_1/y) + P(x_2/y) + \ldots$

for the pair-wise disjoint elements $x_1, x_2, x_3, \ldots$
(The condition of disjointness can be reduced to the form: $P(x/y) < P(x)$ and $P(y/x) < P(y)$).

For any finite or denumerable set of elements $x_1, x_2, \ldots$ the following definition of their mutual independence is accepted:

(D.3) $x_1, x_2, \ldots$ are mutually independent $\leftrightarrow$ for any finite number of elements chosen from among them, the equations $P(x_{i_1} \wedge x_{i_2} \wedge \ldots x_{i_k}) = P(x_{i_1}) \cdot P(x_{i_2}) \cdot \ldots \cdot P(x_{i_k})$ hold.

As can be seen, mutual independence in the sense of (D.3) results in pair-wise independence in the sense of (D.2) for any arbitrarily chosen pair of elements. For instance, the results of several successive tosses of a coin are independent in this sense. If by R_1 we designate the results which consist of getting tails in the first toss, by R_2 — getting tails in the second toss, etc., then the assumption about the independence of the results together with the assumption that in one toss the probability of getting the tails is 1/2 leads to the calculation of the probability of getting for example a series of five tails in five successive throws as follows:

$$P(R_1 \wedge R_2 \wedge \ldots R_5) = P(R_1)P(R_2) \cdot \ldots \cdot P(R_5) = (1/2)^5 = 1/32$$

We can also speak of conditional probabilistic independence, namely:
(D.2a) x and y are independent relative to $z \leftrightarrow P(x \wedge y/z) = P(x/z) \cdot P(y/z)$.

Mutual independence in the sense (D.3) can also be relativized in the same way.

With the use of the terms of Boolean algebra which appear in the axioms (1) to (10) we can define a certain relation between two elements, which is usually designated by the symbol '$\subseteq$', namely:

$$x \subseteq y \underset{\text{def}}{\leftrightarrow} x \wedge y = x$$

With regard to sets, this relation is called inclusion, and with regard to sentences it is called inference, i.e.: if x and y are sets, the expression '$x \subseteq y$' means that x is included in y (that is, each element of the set x is at the same time an element of the set y). If, on the other hand, x and y are sentences, then '$x \subseteq y$' means that the sentence y logically follows from x, that is — to put it another way — y is a logical consequence of x.

The above relation satisfies the following theorem:

(T.5) If $x \subseteq y$, then: (a) $P(y) \geqslant P(x)$ and $P(y/x) = 1$. (b) $P(y/z) \geqslant P(x/z)$ and $P(y/x \wedge z) = 1$ for any z.

(T.6) If the elements $x_1, x_2, \ldots$ are pair-wise disjoint, and their sum equals the maximum element $\vee$, then for any element y, the equation $P(y) = P(x_1) \cdot P(y/x_1) + P(x_2) \cdot P(y/x_2) + \ldots$ is satisfied.

This theorem is called the theorem of full probability.

(T.7) $$P(x/y) = \frac{P(y/x) \cdot P(x)}{P(y)}$$

This theorem, called Bayes' theorem, allows us to calculate the conditional probability $P(x/y)$ when the reverse probability $P(y/x)$ and the absolute probabilities of both elements are known. If the elements $x_1, x_2, \ldots$ satisfy the assumption of the theorem T.6, then Bayes' theorem can be presented in the form:

$$P(x_i/y) = \frac{P(y/x_i) \cdot P(x_i)}{P(y/x_1) \cdot P(x_1) + P(y/x_2) \cdot P(x_2) + \ldots}$$

This equation allows us to calculate the conditional probability of the event x_i relative to y if we have the following situation: (1) x_i is one of the events $x_1, x_2, \ldots$ which satisfy the assumption of T.6, i.e. such that the occurrence of one of them is certain while the simultaneous occurrence of any two of them is impossible, (2) both the absolute probabilities of the occurrence of events x_i and their conditional probabilities relative to y are known.

Finally, we shall quote one of the most important theorems of the probability calculus which is called Bernoulli's law of large numbers. We shall present it here in the formulation in which it appears in the textbook by M. Fisz [19], p. 162.

Let us assume that a given variable X_n can take on values k/n, where $k = 0, 1 \ldots n$; we shall consider the events of the form $X_n = k/n$, at the same time we assume that for any n and k, the probabilities of these events are determined by the so-called Bernoulli's (binomial) formula

$$P(X_n = k/n) = \binom{n}{k} p^k (1-p)^{n-k},$$

where p is a number from the interval between zero to one.

The law of large numbers states that: for a number ε tending to 0,

$$\lim_{n \to \infty} P(|X_n - p| > \varepsilon) = 0$$

This means that however small a number ε we choose, e.g. $\varepsilon = 0.0001$, as n increases, the probability of the event that the absolute value of the result of the subtraction $X_n - p$ is bigger than ε decreases to zero; therefore, the probability that the value of X_n is very close to the number p grows to one.

A great role is played in practice by the following application of this theorem. Let us assume that a certain experiment can give us a result A or $\overline{A}$, and that in every such experiment the constant probability of A is determined: $P(A) = p$ (therefore $P(\overline{A}) = 1 - p$). It can be, for instance, an experiment which consists of tossing of a coin, where A = getting the tails and $p = 1/2$. Let the variable X_n represent the relative frequency of the result A in the sequence of n independent experiments, i.e., the proportion of the numbers of experiments with result A to the number n. In this situation, the assumption of the law of large numbers holds because the probabilities of the frequencies are determined by Bernoulli's formula. For instance, for the tossing of an unbiased coin, the probability that in four tosses we obtain three heads and one tail is

$$\binom{4}{3} \cdot (1/2)^3 \cdot 1/2 = 1/4,$$

and the probability that we shall get heads and tails twice each is

$$\binom{4}{2} \cdot (1/2)^2 \cdot (1/2)^2 = 3/8.$$

If we adopt, for instance, $\varepsilon = 0.1$, then in ten tosses the probability that the frequency of heads will be within the limits $1/2 \pm 0.1$ (i.e. we shall get 4 to 6 heads) equals more or less 0.65; for 100 tosses, however, the probability that the frequency of heads will be within the same limits (i.e. 40 to 60 heads) is close to 1. If we adopt a smaller ε, e.g. $\varepsilon = 0.01$, the probability of the frequency of heads within the limits $1/2 \pm 0.01$ for $n = 100$ will be much smaller; it will be closer to 1 only when n is appropriately larger. From the law of large numbers it follows that for ε tending to zero, the probability that A will occur in the set of n experiments with frequency within $p \pm \varepsilon$ can tend to 1, with an appropriately large number of n experiments.

I have presented here the theorems of the probability calculus which the considerations included in the further chapters of this book will refer to.

As we can see from these theorems, probability calculus does not characterize just one function of probability; it characterizes only a definite class of functions, each of which is a probability function. To define one particular probability function, one must establish the set of its arguments and a method of calculating its value for those arguments. The probability calculus itself does not give such a method. It only establishes the value of probability for two distinguished arguments (see (A.2) and (T.1)) and the methods of calculating the probabilities of certain elements — e.g. the sum or product of elements — when the probabilities of certain other elements are known.

In various applications of the probability calculus, the values of probabilities are interpreted as the degree of intensity of certain graduable properties vested in the object which are arguments of this function. According to the property which probability is to measure, we distinguish different interpretations, or different concepts, of probability. One speaks, for instance, about frequential (or statistical), subjective and logical probability. It is clear that the methods of calculating the probability value must be compatible with the interpretation adopted in that particular application.

In the following chapters of this book I shall present various interpretations of probability with which various conceptions of induction and especially different criteria of validity of inductive inference will be connected.

3

Induction and probability

At the end of Chapter 1, I remarked that inductive logic appeals to the concept of probability because of a common intuitive conviction that, although the results of observation do not guarantee the truth of hypotheses and empirical theories, they can endow them with a probability. This prompts logicians to interpret the validity of induction as the probability (value) of the conclusion relative to the premises. And so, for instance Kazimierz Ajdukiewicz in his *Zarys logiki* [Introduction to Logic] formulates the following necessary condition for validity of inference: 'between the premises and the conclusion, there must be a relation which requires that the truth of the premises guarantees the truth of the conclusion or at least makes this conclusion probable'.

It is worth examining a little more closely certain properties of probability because of which this view of the validity of inductive inference became so common. I mean, here, certain formal properties of probability, i.e. the properties determined by the theorems of probability calculus. These theories can be referred to as sentences (if we accept that in place of x, y, etc., appear sentences), because, as we have already learnt, sentential calculus is one of the possible interpretations of Boolean algebra (see Chapter 2).

And so, in particular, on the strength of theorem T.5, the conditional probability of sentences has the following property:

(W.1) if sentence x follows logically from sentence y, then

$$P(x/y) = 1$$

If we accept, then, that the probability value $P(x/y)$ represents the estimation of the inference about the sentence x on the basis of the premiss y, then the highest valuation will be received by the deductive inference in which the conclusion follows logically from premises.

Next, on the strength of (T.1) and (D.1), the conditional probability of sentences possesses the property:

(W.2) If x and y are logically inconsistent (disjoint), then

$$P(x/y) = 0$$

(Conjunction of such sentences is locally false.) The lowest valuation is received by those inferences in which the conclusion is inconsistent with the premise.

Properties (W.1) and (W.2) are, then, consistent with the accepted criteria of valuation of inferences. However, the usefulness of conditional probability for the valuation of inductive inference depends also on the behaviour of the values of $P(x/y)$ in other situations, i.e. in the cases where conclusion x neither follows from premise y nor is inconsistent with it. An interesting discourse on certain qualities of probability for valuation of inductive inferences can be found in Chapter IV of Ajdukiewicz's *Logika pragmatyczna* [Pragmatic Logic] [4]. The author there analyses three popular forms of induction and shows that the criterion of probability of the conclusion relative to premises is consistent with the widespread opinion on validity of inferences which go according to these forms. Ajdukiewicz's work, however, includes certain groundless statements, which are worthy of notice.

One of the types of inductive inference (in the sense adopted in Chapter 1) is reductive inference which consists if this, that the conclusion is a hypothesis H, while the premises are: (1) certain sentences belonging to the body of knowledge W and (2) a sentence E which is a consequence of the hypothesis H and the body of knowledge W: the conclusion, i.e. the hypothesis H, however, does not follow from the premises. A typical example of reductive inference is the procedure of testing hypotheses or theories by their observable consequences which have been proved to be true. Let us assume that we are testing the hypothesis H by an experiment the results of which sentence E (which is a consequence of the hypothesis H and the body of knowledge W) proves to be true.

Let us now observe how the probability values of the hypothesis H relative to the results of the experiment E and knowledge W behave. On the strength of Bayes' theorem (see (T.7) in Chapter 2) the following equality is satisfied:

$$P(H/E \wedge W) = \frac{P(E/H \wedge W) \cdot P(H/W)}{P(E/W)}$$

(Bayes's theorem is here relativized to a certain additional element, namely to W). We have assumed, however, that E is a consequence of H and W, and therefore, on the strength of T.5 (see Chapter 2) we have $P(E/H \wedge W) = 1$, and hence

$$P(H/E \wedge W) = \frac{P(H/W)}{P(E/W)}.$$

If the result of the experiment E were a consequence of the initial body of knowledge W, we would have $P(E/W) = 1$, and hence $P(H/E \wedge W) = P(H/W)$. This equality would be satisfied also if $P(H/W) = 0$ (e.g. if the hypothesis H were inconsistent with the knowledge W). However, in cases when probability relative to the initial body of knowledge W is larger than zero and $P(E/W)$ is smaller than 1 — which can be so interpreted, that E enriches the body of knowledge W in a significant way — the probability of H increases:

$$P(H/W \wedge E) > P(H/W).$$

What is more, the more improbable is E with regard to W, the greater will be the increase. If we wanted to measure the value of a reductive inference by the value of $P(H/E \wedge W)$, the more unexpected will be the result of experiment E relative to the body of knowledge W which we had before the experiment, the better the inference.

In particular Ajdukiewicz stresses the fact that if, given two different consequences of H and W — say E_1 and E_2 — one is a more precise prediction than the other, then, if these predictions prove correct, the more precise one will better confirm the hypothesis (in the probabilistic sense). Let us assume, for instance, that E_1 predicts the eclipse of the sun on a definite day between 10 and 11 o'clock, and E_2 predicts the eclipse of the sun on the same day between 10.30 and 10.31. Since E_1 is a consequence of the more precise prediction E_2, then, in accordance with probability calculus (see (T.5)) $P(E_1/W) \geq P(E_2/W)$. If this inequality is sharp, i.e. $P(E_1/W) > P(E_2/W)$, the value of $P(H/E_2 \wedge W)$ will be greater than the value of $P(H/E_1 \wedge W)$.

Furthermore, Ajdukiewicz writes:

> Hence quantitative statements have a smaller a priori probability than do qualitative statements. Theorems in disciplines which can claim confirmation of quantitative predictions following from those theorems are accordingly more probable than are theorems in disciplines which can claim confirmation of qualitative predictions only.

It is easy to show that this property of probability does not follow from the axioms at all, since the equality

$$P(H/E \wedge W) = \frac{P(H/W)}{P(E/W)}$$

indicates clearly that the conditional probability of the hypothesis H is dependent not only on the probability $P(E/W)$, but also on $P(H/W)$, and the latter dependency is positive: the higher $P(H/W)$, the higher $P(H/E \wedge W)$, and at the same time $P(E/W)$. Let us assume, for instance, that we have two hypotheses from astronomy: H_1 and H_2, and that from the hypothesis H_1 does not follow such precise predictions as does H_2. Let the consequence of H_2 and W be the above-mentioned prediction E_2, and the consequence of H_1 and W, the prediction E_1. Let us now assume that:

$$P(H_1/W) = 0.02, \quad P(E_1/W) = 0.005$$
$$P(H_2/W) = 0.002, \quad P(E_2/W) = 0.01$$

It is clear that

$$P(H_1/W \wedge E_1) = \frac{0.02}{0.05} = 0.4$$

while

$$P(H_2/W \wedge E_2) = \frac{0.002}{0.01} = 0.2$$

i.e. that probability of the more precise hypothesis relative to the body of knowledge and the precise prediction which follows from it is smaller than the probability of the hyphothesis which is less precise relative to less precise prediction. Therefore, if we wanted to interpret the value of confirmation of the hypothesis by the results of an experiment as the probability of the hypothesis relative to this result, we would have to state that in the above case the hypothesis H_1 is better confirmed by its imprecise prediction E_1 than the hypothesis H_2 by its more precise prediction E_2.

It can be seen that the above-cited opinion of K. Ajdukiewicz is not true in general, but only with regard to certain special situations in which, in the light of the initial body of knowledge, the probability of a hypothesis or theory which allows us to draw more precise predictions is not too small in comparison with the probability of a hypothesis (theory) whose predictions are less precise.

I do not think, however, that this should disqualify the probabilistic measure of confirmation, for I do not think that confirmation of hypotheses in empirical sciences should be evaluated in such a way that the hypotheses which allow for more precise predictions are always considered to be better confirmed by the fact that their predictions came true than the hypotheses which give less precise predictions. The tendency of the development of science towards greater precision is unquestionable; I do not suppose, however, that this tendency must be explained by better confirmation of more precise theories. We can accept that science tends to possibly precise hypotheses and theories, and to their possibly strong confirmation by the results of experiments, but this does not mean that these tendencies are identical, i.e. that more precise theories are aimed at because they are (or can be) better confirmed than the less precise ones. This problem will be discussed further, especially in Chapter 9.

Let us now proceed to the second of Ajdukiewicz's analyses, which concerns induction by enumeration. Ajdukiewicz adopts the following characterization of such inference:

Induction by enumeration is any such inference in which a statement of a general regularity is accepted as the conclusion on the strength of accepting statements of particular cases of that regularity.

In the simplest case, it will be an inference stating that every object with the property A possesses also the property B on the strength of the fact that all observed objects A had the property B: for instance, the inference that every raven is black on the basis that all observed ravens have been black.

Let $a_1, a_2, \ldots, a_n$ be (various) observed objects with the property A, and let us assume that the sentences a_1 is A, a_2 is A, $\ldots$, a_n is A belong to the initial body of knowledge W. As result of further observations it was found out that a_1 is B, a_2 is B, $\ldots$, a_n is B. Let E denote the conjunction of these latter sentences, and H — the hypothesis that every A is B. Since E is a consequence of H and the sentences of the form 'a_i is A' which belong to the knowledge W, the probability of the hypothesis relative to the premises and the body of knowledge will, like in the previous case, equal:

$$P(H/E \wedge W) = \frac{P(H/W)}{P(E/W)}$$

Ajdukiewicz points at the following interdependencies:

(1) Let us assume that the further results of observation E_1 have shown that the property B is also possessed by some other objects $a_{n+1}, \ldots, a_{n+k}$ (which have already been known as A, but it was not known that they were B). On the strength of (T.4a) for conjunction (see Chapter 2) we shall have in general:

$$P(E \wedge E_1/W) < P(E/W)$$

An exception can occur only in case when $P(E_1/E \wedge W) = 1$, and therefore, in particular, the case when E_1 follows from E and W, which, as a rule, does not occur in inference based on induction by enumeration. If we, moreover, exclude the cases of $P(H/W) = 0$, the inequality

$$P(H/E \wedge E_1 \wedge W) > P(H/E \wedge W)$$

will always hold, which means that further positive results of observation of particular objects A will increase the probability of the inductive conclusion by enumeration. This is consistent with what is usually said about induction by enumeration: that the confirmation of the conclusion grows with the number of observations consistent with the conclusion. Certainly, if we observed that an object A is not B, no observation compatible with H could confirm such an hypothesis; but then the probability of this hypothesis will not increase either, because from an event E_2 which is inconsistent with H follows the negation of H, and therefore we obtain:

$$P(H/E \wedge E_1 \wedge E_2 \wedge W) = P(H/E_2 \wedge W) = 0$$

(2) Further Ajdukiewicz analyses the dependence of the value of induction by enumeration from the variety of objects to which the premises refer. This analysis, however, must be based on some misunderstanding and, in effect, it does not justify the conclusion which the author draws from it. The misunderstanding concerns the relation between the dependence of the probability of the conclusion upon its generality, and the dependence of this probability upon the variety of objects to which the premises refer. This is testified by the following statement of Ajdukiewicz [4], p. 155:

The less general a conclusion [out of all possible conclusions in a given case], the greater its initial probability, and the greater its initial probability, and the greater its final probability. This condition can also be formulated thus: Given an inductive conclusion in the form 'Every S is P', derived from premises which state about objects $a_1, a_2, \ldots, a_k$ that these are P, the fewer the properties shared by those objects, except that they are S [i.e. the more heterogeneous these objects are, the greater the final probability of the conclusion].

And so the fact of the matter is that the latter of these sentences is not equivalent to the former, and, in general, it concerns a completely different dependency. Ajjdukiewicz's statement which precedes the above opinion does not leave any doubt as to the fact that the first dependency refers to probabilities of different hypotheses relative to the same premises: let us say that $P(H_1/E \wedge W)$ and $P(H_2/E \wedge W)$ where H_1 and H_2 are universal propositions and, what is more, — say — H_1 is a more precise H_2. For instance, let H_1 be a sentence saying that every mouse has a property B, and H_2 a sentence which states that every rodent has the property B. In this situation H_1 follows from H_2, hence, on the strength of (T.5) we have

$$P(H_1/E \wedge W) \geqslant P(H_2/E \wedge W)$$

And so, the first dependence which Ajdukiewicz speaks about in the above-cited text is justified in the probability calculus.

The second dependency is referred by Ajdukiewicz to the situation in which the probabilities of the same hypothesis relative to different premises are compared. Ajdukiewicz formulates it more clearly on page 153 of his book 'The same inductive conclusion "Every A is B", derived from one and the same number of premises, becomes more probable if the objects to which the premises refer are more varied.' And on the same page, the author writes that, although on the basis of the premises which make statements about 1000 mice subjected to examination, that they have a property B, the conclusion that all mice have the property B is more probable than the conclusion that all mammals have the property B. The latter conclusion, however, 'can be made more probable by basing it [. . .] on the examination of one thousand animals which [. . .] include, e.g. mice, dogs, cats, cows, horses, etc. In this formulation one can clearly see what variety and what dependency the author bears in mind. And so, this dependency does not follow from the former one at all, neither does it follow from the axioms of probability. Let us assume that the body of knowledge W includes the sentences that the animals $a_1, \ldots, a_{1000}$ are mice, and sentences which refer to 1000 other animals and state, e.g. that $a_{1001}, \ldots, a_{1200}$ are cats, $a_{1201}, \ldots, a_{1400}$ are dogs, etc. Let E be property B, and E_1 — the sentence saying that $a_1, \ldots, a_{1000}$ have the property P, and E_2 — the sentence that $a_{1001}, \ldots, a_{2000}$ have the property B. The thing is that such assumptions are too weak to prove that the probability of the sentence 'all mammals have the property B' relative to E_2 and W is greater than the probability of this sentence relative to E_1 and W. To prove such an inequality, the assumption that $P(E_1/W) > P(E_2/W)$ would be necessary. We can suppose that Ajdukiewicz makes this silent assumption. A question arises, however, whether this assumption is just, right and natural. In this particular case justness of such assumption depends upon what this property B is, what relation exists between this property or a property of this kind, and the differences between mammals of various species. In general, I think that it certainly is not always natural to accept an assumption that the more varied are the examined objects A with regard to some arbitrary features, the smaller is the probability of a property B common to n examined objects A.

Therefore, it cannot be said that, with enumerative induction, it is always the case that the more varied are the objects which the assumptions speak about, the greater is the probability of the conclusion.

I think, however, that this does not at all disqualify probability as a evaluation criterion for such inferences. I believe that it is too great a simplification to ascribe to scientists or methodologists the view that inductive generalizations are always better when the observed objects are more varied, no matter in what respect they differ and how it refers to the property about which the generalization concerns. I think that scientists are inclined to subject the evaluation of enumerative induction to variety of examined objects only if they know that the more varied are the objects (in a definite sense), the less probable the uniformity with regard to the property to which the conclusion refers. But then the evaluation will be concurrent with the criterion of high probability of the conclusion relative to the assumptions.

One can hold/entertain a view that the diversity of the examined objects is a sort of substitute for randomness of the test. Attention should be paid, however, to the fact that the objects which are divergent in one respect can be homogeneous in another respect and, therefore, *de facto*, the researcher is made to choose the respect in which he considers to be the most important. Incidentally, as a matter of fact, the concept of divergence not relativized to a particular way in which the divergence exists, has no sense.

Other reservations are about the importance which Ajdukiewicz sees in inference by analogy. Ajdukiewicz characterizes inference by analogy as an inference whose premises are the same as in enumerative induction, while the conclusion is not a universal sentence, but a statement that the next object a_{n+1} (of which we know that it is A) has the property B). Ajdukiewicz, avoiding a detailed analysis of such inferences, states that they come close to the induction by enumeration. He writes:

> If there are premises which say about n objects of kind A that they are B, then the more probable is the general inductive conclusion, based on these premises, that every object of kind A is B, the more probable also is the conclusion that the $(n + 1)$-st object of kind A is B. [4], p. 157.

An essential difference between inference by analogy and enumeration induction Ajdukiewicz detects only in the fact that the observations of objects of kind A which are not B do not exclude here a high probability of the conclusion.

However, the basic difference between inference by enumerative induction and inference by analogy consists of the fact that the former is, and the latter is not, a reductive inference; namely, none of the premises of an inference by analogy follows from the conclusion and the other premises (which, in enumerative induction were included in the body of knowledge). From the conclusion 'every A is B' and the premise 'a_i is A' follows the premise that 'a_i is B'. But the conclusion 'a_{n+1} is B' and the premises 'a_{n+1} is A', 'a_i is A and 'a_i is B' for $i \geqslant n$ — are logically independent sentences, i.e. there is no logical implication or logical inconsistency between them.

In connection with this, inference by analogy is not able to prove even that the probability of the conclusion relative to the premises (no matter how numerous) is greater than the initial probability. Since the premises E do not follow from the conclusion H and the body of knowledge W, it is not possible to simplify

$$P(H/E \wedge W) = \frac{P(E/H \wedge W) \cdot P(H/W)}{P(E/W)}$$

to the form

$$P(H/E \wedge W) = \frac{P(H/W)}{P(E/W)}$$

i.e. in the way in which it was possible in the induction by enumeration in view of the fact that the inference of E from H and W gives $P(E/H \wedge W) = 1$. It can be seen from the formula that if $P(E/H \wedge W)$ is smaller than unity, the probability of the conclusion relative to premises E and body of knowledge W can be smaller than the initial probability of the conclusion. It depends upon whether, and how, E is probabilistically dependent on H relative to the body of knowledge W (see (D.2A) in Chapter 2). If it is independent, i.e. $P(E/H \wedge W) = P(E/W)$, then $P(H/E \wedge W) = P(H/W)$. If it is negatively dependent, i.e. $P(E/H \wedge W) < P(E/W)$, then $P(H/E \wedge W) < P(H/W)$. To make the probability of the conclusion relative to the premises increase — as can be seen — positive probabilistic dependence of E on H is necessary, i.e. the inequality:

$$P(E/H \wedge W) > P(E/W)$$

must hold.

If, therefore, we wanted to make the value of the inference that the $n+1$-st A is B dependent upon the number n of the premises about n objects of kind A that they are B, and if we wanted to measure this value by the probability value of the conclusion relative to the premises and the body of knowledge, we would have to possess a probability function which would satisfy these inequalities. Generally speaking, it would concern the inequalities of form

$$P(a_{n+1} \text{ is } B/a_1, \ldots ,a_n \text{ are } B \wedge W) > P(a_{n+1} \text{ is } B/W)$$

(with the assumption that the sentence '$a_1, \ldots ,a_{n+1}$ have a common property A' belongs to W). Imposition on a probability function of the condition that it should satisfy such inequalities for any properties A and B, would certainly be very arbitrary (such an assumption was adopted by Carnap — see Chapter 6.1). On the other hand, however, if one considers that the larger the number of premises, the better is the inference by analogy, one must probably assume some dependence of this kind.

I suspect that the scheme of inference by analogy used by Ajdukiewicz (and many other logicians) is too great a simplification of such inference. I think that the value of inference by analogy depends essentially on knowledge about properties A and B.

Let us, for instance, assume that someone tosses a coin about which he knows that it is unbiased, and he gets the obverse n times running. The conclusion that the result of the next toss will also be the obverse, drawn on the basis of such premises and such knowledge would be equally good (or, rather, bad) as the conclusion that the next toss will give the reverse. If, however, this person knew that — let us say — the coin is heavier on one side, but he did not know on which one, these premises would make an argument for the former conclusion to be considered better than the latter one; the larger the number n, the better the former conclusion.

The imposition on the probability function of the condition that it should satisfy the above-mentioned inequality in the cases where the body of knowledge W includes certain appropriate statements about the dependences between the properties A and B would be no more arbitrary. On the contrary, the values of the conditional probabilities relative to the body ofknowedge W should show this kind of dependency on W if they are to constitute a base for induction.

Concluding, I can say — despite certain reservation concerning the soundness of some of Ajdukiewicz's opinions — that his analysis shows certain formal features of the probability function which incline logicians to attempt the foundation of inductive logic on the probability of a conclusion relative to its premises.

4

Partial interpretation of probability

At the end of Chapter 2, I wrote that the probability calculus itself is of abstract character and gives no method for determining the value of the probability function for its various arguments; such a method must be dependent upon the interpretation of probability applied to a definite domain of reality, i.e. to which objects we wish to ascribe probability and which property of these objects we want to measure by probability.

In fact, only one of the methods discussed in literature is developed well enough that it is commonly applied in various empirical sciences and in practice. It is the method, or rather a set of statistical methods, connected with partial interpretation of probability. Although modern conceptions of inductive logic refer rather to the logical or subjective interpretation of probability (due to various reasons which will be discussed later), the achievements of the statistical theory are of great importance for inductive logic. Since this theory has at its disposal a very precise notional apparatus with the help of which it analyses the results of so-called statistical induction which are used both in science and practice.

Partial interpretation of probability is based on the concept of relative frequency of events, or properties, in a certain finite set of events or objects. If a certain set A has n elements and there are m elements with the property B among them, then the relative frequency of objects B in the set A is m/n. It is easy to notice that if we assume that a complete set V is a finite set, the function determined for every subset of V as a ratio of the number of its elements to the number of elements of V will satisfy the theorems of probability calculus. In most of the interesting instances of the application of the concept of probability, however, this concept cannot be interpreted in such a simple way. Therefore, the interpretation of probability commonly accepted in the theory of statistics, which is called frequential or statistical, or sometimes empirical probability, does not identify this concept with relative frequency, but only associates it in a way with relative frequency.

This interpretation was developed by von Mises — in 1928 [55] — who identified the probability of event A with the limit of its relative frequency in a certain infinite sequence of events. He treated such a sequence, which he called a collective, as an abstract being, namely as an idealization of an empirical sequence of experiments, which can practically be infinite in the sense that it can always be made longer (like, for instance, the sequence of tosses of a coin). In such a collective, he distinguished a subsequence of events of kind A (e.g. of results which consisted of getting the obverse of the coin). The sentence 'the probability of an event A equals p' means in this interpretation that there exists a certain infinite collective (which represents a definite sequence of experiments), and a subsequence of this collective (which represents results of kind A of these experiments), while the limit of relative frequency of the elements of this subsequence in this collective equals p. Von Mises required the collective to be random with regard to the given kind of events. To specify the concept of randomness, however, proved difficult. Von Mises understood randomness as the independence from 'the choice of a place' in the sense that: if we choose a subsequence of a collective in such a way that we include in it every second, every third, every nth element, or, e.g. every element which occurs immediately after an element with a definite property (for instance, every event which follows obtaining the obverse) — the limit of the frequency of the given sequence of events will not change. However, since the limit of the frequency cannot be independent of every choice of place in general, and we can only demand independence from a certain kind of choice; it does not ensure the independence from another kind of choice which can be just as well considered essential for randomness.

Hans Reichenbach in 1934 [65], and then Wesley Salmon [66], who also interpret probability as the limit of relative frequency in a sequence of events, deny the postulate of randomness of this sequence because they believe that, theoretically, it is needless. Instead of the assumption about randomness of the sequence for which probability is defined, they adopt a pragmatic postulate of choice of a proper empirical sequence in each particular application of the theory.

The concept of probability as the limit of frequency is not an empirical concept in the same sense as the concept of randomness itself: frequencies can be directly observed, but their limits cannot. This concept of probability, however, is of an empirical character in a weaker sense in which the relations between probability and the observed relative frequencies; since the collective is treated as an idealization of an empirical sequence of experiments.

Most contemporary mathematicians and staticians have abandoned the statistical interpretation, and they treat probability in a more abstract way. Some of them, like, for instance, H. Cramer [12], regard probability as an 'abstract correspondence' of frequencies observed in a large group of events: it is observed that the relative frequencies of a certain type of events in certain sets of events are more or less constant, and a mathematical model for these regularities is adopted. In a modern statistics, there appears to be a distinct inclination to the view that probability is not conceptually connected with relative frequencies, but only by its practical applications. The concept of probability itself is regarded as a mathematical concept whose sense is simply characterized by axioms.

In connection with the statistical applications of probability, I must stress that although, as a rule, probabilities of events are spoken of there, it does not concern individual events, but certain types of events which can be identified with sets or sequences of events (this problem was mentioned in

Chapter 2). When it is said in statistics that probability of getting an obverse in a toss of an unbiased coin is 1/2, this probability does not refer to any individual event, i.e. to getting an obverse in any particular toss of a coin; it refers to a type (set) of events which consist in getting an obverse in a toss of a coin: this probability characterizes a set of tosses of a coin, and not one particular toss.

This property of the statistical concept of probability is very important and it constitutes a signifiant obstacle in the application of this concept in formulating the criteria of validity of induction. As I have already stated in Chapter 1, the dominating tendency in the modern conception of inductive logic is to make the validity of induction dependent upon the probability of sentences, namely, upon the probability of conclusion relative to some premises. And so, with reference to a great majority of sentences, especially scientific hypotheses, to which inductive logic is to be applied, the partial interpretation of their probability is very difficult. It is generally considered to be unacceptable. An exceptional viewpoint was presented by Reichenbach [65] who was of opinion that the concept 'probability' can be partially interpreted in every context. The context in which the probability of individual events or scientific hypotheses concerning universal regularities or historical facts is spoken of, Reinchenbach treated as elliptical formulations which, in full formulation, refer to sets or sequences of events. For instance, he would think that, while saying 'it is likely to rain tomorrow', we have in mind the fact that in a set of days which follow the days like this one, there often occur rainy days. Saying that a hypothesis is more probable than another, competitive hypothesis, we have in mind the fact that true hypotheses occur more often among those which are similar to the given one than among the hypotheses of the type of the competitive one.

This interpretation of the view on the probability of individual events largely differs from the intuitions which are usually connected with their understanding. No wonder, then, that it has no supporters even among the representatives of the partial interpretation of probability. Statisticians usually share the view of von Mises who is of the opinion that in this kind of context probability has no statistical sense.

Another significant obstacle in usage of probability in the statistical sense as a base for inductive logic is the empirical character of this concept. Von Mises writes in [55] that the theory of probability in the frequential sense

> in its application to reality is itself an inductive science; its results and formulas cannot constitute a base for the inductive procedure as such and, the more so, they cannot determine the numerical value of credibility of the inductive sciences.

The thing is that if the probability values of events are estimated using inductive methods on the basis of the observed frequencies of such events, they are as reliable as the applied inductive method is correct. Therefore, if we wanted to estimate the value of the inductive method by the so-called estimated probabilities, we would get into a vicious circle. A great majority of logicians and statisticians share this view with von Mises. Some, however, like, for instance, Reichenbach and Salmon think that probability theory in the frequential sense can make the base for analysis of inductive procedures in other empirical sciences. They consider that the most efffective approach to the problem of induction is to attempt to formulate the rules for certain special forms of induction. With regard to one of the simpler forms of statistical induction, namely the estimation of probability on the basis of the observed frequencies, Reichenbach promoted the so-called 'simple rule' which prescribes estimating the probability value as equal to the observed frequency, i.e. accepting that $P(A/B) = m/n$, where n is the number of the observed events B, and m is the number of those observed B which have the property A. His argument was as follows: If the limit of the relative frequency of events A in the set of events B does not exist, then no rule can determine it accurately; whereas if it exists, it can be discovered in various ways and its value can even be determined. Only the simple rule, however, gives the guarantee of its accurate determination, and it is so because with a sufficiently large number of experiments, the law of large numbers ensures a high probability that its value is close to the observed frequency.

Reichenbach's idea was widely discussed and criticized. The fact that the simple rule does not ensure good results in a short sequence of experiments was pointed out. Carnap [9] was of the opinion that this rule leads to overhasty inductive conclusions. It was also noticed that Reichenbach's argument for the simple rule recommends to the same extent all the asymptotic rules which prescribe to estimate probability of A relative to B as equal to $m/n+f(n)$, where $f(n)$ is a function of the number of observations n which decreases to zero with the increase of n.

Reichenbach's and Salmon's idea to look for the solution of the problem of induction on the basis of the frequential theory of probability has no interesting continuation in the contemporary literature. Attempts at creating the logic of induction usually refer to probability in the logical sense or in the subjective sense. These concepts will be explained in subsequent chapters. There exist, however, connections between statistical probability, subjective probability and logical probability. In particular, the version of logical probability (presented by Henry Kyburg) which will be discussed in Chapter 7, is very closely related to frequential probability.

A variety of the frequential interpretation of probability is the so-called propensity interpretation propogated by K. Popper [60], [62]. According to this interpretation, probability is a certain dispositional property of objects, which consists of a potential disposition of the objects to particular kinds of behaviour with definite frequencies. Relative frequencies are here treated as external, observable manifestations of this hidden dispositional property. So, for instance, an unbiased coin has a potential inclination to fall on the tails or heads side with the frequency close to 1/2, however, the probability of getting the heads equal to 1/2 is not a property of the set (sequence) of tosses of a coin, but a property of the coin itself, and it is vested in the coin no matter whether it will ever by tossed up or not. Relative frequencies in a series of experiments can testify that the coin has this property, but they are not identical to this property. The difference between this interpretation and partial interpretation is insignificant from the point of view of their possible applications for inductive logic because the method of estimating the value of propensity probabilities is also an empirical method: such probabilities are estimated on the basis of the observed relative frequencies.

5

Statistical induction

The theory of statistical induction is the only theory of induction which is applied in practice. Although this theory refers only to statistical hypotheses, the results of its investigation of inductive rules are of much more universal importance. The rules of statistical induction are characterized by it with regard to various properties which, from the point of view of inductive logic, are very important. Therefore, all attempts at the creation of an inductive logic must take into account the achievements of this theory, and, in fact, they do.

The literature concerning statistical induction is enormous, so a relatively deep discussion of at least the most important achievements of this theory would require writing a separate book. In this chapter I will discuss in an extremely simplified and brief way only those aspects which deserve special attention from the point of view of inductive logic.

Statistical induction includes those inferences whose conclusion is a statistical hypothesis, i.e. a hypothesis concerning probability distribution (in the statistical sense) of a variable or variables — e.g. their dependencies in a certain population. The premises contain numerical data which characterize a particular observed subset of this population, called a random sample. For instance, the conclusion may be a hypothesis which determines the probability value of property A in the population, and the premise — a sentence concerning the observed relative frequency of property A, in the sample from this population. In the simplest instances the random sample is a subset selected from a given population using a method which, when used permanently, leads to the choice of each element of the population with the same frequency.

Two basic varieties of statistical induction can be distinguished: testing of hypotheses and estimation of parameters. We are concerned with testing of hypotheses when, among the hypotheses which constitute possible answers to a given question, one is distinguished in advance as the so-called null hypothesis, H_0. The test is to decide about rejection or non-rejection of such a distinguished hypothesis. The reasons for rejection of the hypothesis H_0 can be different, but it is always required that the probability estimation of the so-called first-order error must be possible for H_0 (this will be explained further below).

We are concerned with the estimation of parameters if we are interested in the problem of what is the value of a given parameter, e.g. what is the probability of a given property in the population. The estimation is to lead to the appraisal of this value, i.e. to the acceptance of a hypothesis concerning the value of a given parameter (such a hypothesis can precisely determine the value of the parameter or the interval in which this value is included).

A statistical test is a rule which prescribes the rejection or non-rejection of the hypothesis H_0 according to the results of a definite experiment. From the point of view of its form, it is a function defined over a set of experimental results which assigns one of two decisions: rejection or non-rejection of H_0 to each result. For instance, if H_0 detemines the probability value of a property in a population, and the experiment consists of examining the relative frequency of this property in an n-element random sample of this population — then the decision to reject H_0 can be assigned to each result where the observed relative frequency of this property is larger (or smaller) than the number p, while the other results can have the decision of non-rejection of H_0 assigned to them. In the literature dealing with statistics the fact is often emphasized that non-rejection of H_0 is not tantamount to its adoption (acceptance).

Tests are required to be able to calculate the probability of an error consisting in the rejection of H_0 when this hypothesis is true. This error is called first-order error; if for a hypothesis and a certain experiment, the probability of such an error cannot be calculated, this hypothesis cannot be tested by the results of the experiment at all (i.e. the rule which would prescribe rejection or non-rejection of such a hypothesis in accordance with the results of such an experiment would not be recognized as a test).

A test can lead to another error, which consists in the fact that H_0 is not rejected despite the fact that it is false; this error is called second-order error. The probability of avoiding the second order error (i.e. non-rejection of H_0 when it is false) is called the power of a test. It is not always possible to calculate the power of a test: it depends upon what the hypothesis competing with H_0 are — in these situations, however, there exist possibilities for comparison of the tests as regards their power.

Let us notice now that the stronger the conditions which the test needs for H_0 to be rejected, the smaller the first order error. In this case, however, the power of the test, i.e. its ability to reject H_0 when this hypotheses is false, will decrease. Let us assume, for instance, that hypothesis H_0 says that the probability of property A in a population is 1/2, while a competitive hypothesis H says that the probability of A is 3/4, and we know that one of these hypotheses is true. Let us now compare two tests based on a four-element sample:

T_1: we reject H_0 when the number of elements with property A in the sample is more than two.

T_2: we reject H_0 when all elements in the sample have the property A.

If the hypothesis H_0 is true, then the probability of getting from the population a random sample of four elements of which three or four would have property A is $(1/2)^4 + 4 \cdot (1/2)^4 = 5/16$; while the probability that four elements would have property A is $(1/2)^4 = 1/16$. Therefore, test T_2 has a much smaller probability of first order error.

If we assume that H_0 is false, then H_1 must be true (we have assumed that one of these hypotheses must be true, which may follow from an adopted theory). And so, if H_1 is true, the probability of getting, at random, four elements with property A is $(3/4)^4 = 81/256$. This being so, the probability of the second order error for the first test is $1 - (189/256) = 67/256$, while for the second test this probability will equal $1 - (81/256) = 175/256$, i.e. it will be much bigger. Therefore we can say that test T_1 is in some respect worse than T_2, but in another respect it is better. This faces us with the problem of choice of test.

A similar problem appears with estimation with reference to the choice of the so-called estimator, i.e. the function which assigns definite values of a certain parameter to the numerical data obtained from observation of the sample. An example of an estimator is Reicshenbach's simple rule which was mentioned in the previous chapter. The estimated parameter is here the probability of a property (event) in a population. The rule requires accepting that the value of $P(A)$ is equal to the relative frequency of A in the random sample. With estimation there is no reason to distinguish the first order, and the second order errors, because no hypothesis is distinguished as H. Instead, the question concerns the error values and their probabilities. The estimation theory examines various properties of estimators which are desirable from this point of view. And so, for instance, an estimator can be convergent to the real value of the estimated parameter when the size of the sample grows infinitely: such an estimator is called a consistent estimator. Another quality of an estimator can be its property that its expected value is equal to its real value, such an estimator is called unbiased estimator. Numerous other desirable qualities of estimators were also distinguished. The problem of choice arises, because it seldom happens that an estimator possesses all desirable qualities simultaneously.

Classical statistics did not make its task the solution of the problem of choice of test or estimator, assuming that such a choice in a particular situation can and ought to be subjected to various pragmatic considerations. Only the characterization of various aspects of rules which could play a role in the choice was considered to be the task of a theory, while the evaluation of which properties of rules are important or more important than the others in particular instances was to be included in the practical applications of a theory.

There exists, however, a trend within statistics which goes further than classical statistics towards evaluation of rules of statistical induction. It is statistical decision theory. Pragmatic considerations are, there, a significant element of the characterization of inductive rules. Inductive rules in the decision theory, however, are essentially different from the rules examined by classical statistics, for they are not formulated as rules of rejection or acceptance of an hypotheses, but as the rules for undertaking an action. Obviously, acceptance (or rejection) of an hypothesis is also a sort of action; decision theory, however, refers its rules to those actions only whose usefulness is calculable, i.e. determined by numbers. Therefore, application of these rules to actions which consist in the acceptance of hypotheses in science requires the assumption of a measure of usability of these actions. Certain attempts at application of these rules to the decisions of hypothesis acceptance in science will be discussed in Chapter 10.3.

The rules considered in decision theory refer to the situations in which the decision is to consist of undertaking a certain action d_i from a set D. The usefulness of each of these actions depends on the present state of affairs. The possible states of affairs are represented by the set H of competitive hypotheses h_j of which exactly one is true. It is assumed that for each pair d_i, h_j, the usefulness of action d_i is determined by the assumption that hypothesis h_j is true. This usefulness can be conceived as the losses resulting from undertaking of the action d_i when h_j is true. The decision rules subject the choice of action to the results of a certain experiment, and the assumption is made that the probabilities of the results of this experiment, relative to hypotheses from set H, are given. Each rule is a function assigning a decision to undertake an action d_i to each results of a given experiment.

The problem consists in the choice of a rule, since (like in classical statistics) different rules can lead to different decisions, though the results of the experiment may be the same. And so, the adopted assumption allows one to calculate the expected value of the loss for each rule if the truth of the individual hypotheses h_j is assumed.

The expected value $E(X)$ of the variable X (in this instance loss) is the total of all possible values X_i of the variable X weighted by the probabilities of those values, i.e. $E(X) = \sum_i X_i P(X_i)$. The calculation of the expected value of a loss for each rule in the instances of validity of particular hypotheses makes it possible to eliminate certain rules as decidedly worse than others, namely, the so-called dominated rules: they are rules which in certain conditions can give a bigger loss than others, but in no circumstances do they guarantee smaller loss. In general, however, there are few rules which are not dominated by any others. In this situation, the least controversial solution would probably be the choice of the rule for which the average value of loss is the smallest (the so-called Bayes' criterion of choice). Yet, a serious shortcoming of this criterion is its limited possibility of application. To calculate the average loss, the values of probabilities of particular competitive hypotheses are necessary; whereas in actual situations of decision making such probabilities are usually not determined. In the literature dealing with statistics various other choice criteria of a rule from among the non-dominated ones are given, for instance the principle of minimizing the average loss (called Laplace's criterion), the principle of minimization the maximum risk (the so-called minimax), etc. Different choice criteria usually lead to making different decisions in the same circumstances.

To illustrate this fact let us return to the above-considered example in which two hypotheses came into play: H_0 which stated that $P(A) = 1/2$ and H_1 which stated that $P(A) = 3/4$.

Let us assume that person X must decide whether he is to undertake action D or not, for instance, buy the goods which the hypotheses H_0 and H_1 refer to, or not, while the value of the goods depends upon which of these hypotheses is true. Assume that X evaluates the effects of actions D and $\overline{D}$ with the use of the values of losses expressed in certain units. For instance, if H_0 is true X will suffer the loss of 150 units if he undertakes action D, and 50 units if he does not undertake this action. If, on the other hand, H_1 is true, action D will cause loss equal to 0, while $\overline{D}$ the loss of 100 units. If X knew that H_1 was true, he would undertake action D; if, on the other hand, he knew that H_0 was true, he would not undertake this action. However, X knows only that one of these hypotheses is true, but he does not know which one. Let us assume that for some reason X must make the decision concerning his action on the basis of examination of a four-element random sample of these goods.

Let us now compare the two rules which advise the choice of D with the same results of the experiment in which the above-mentioned tests T_1 and T_2 prescribed rejection of H_0:

R_1: Undertake action D (e.g. buy the goods), if the number of elements A in the sample is larger than two; undertake $\overline{D}$ if the number is equal to two or less than that.

R_2: undertake D if all four elements are A, undertake $\overline{D}$ if less than four are A.

Let us now calculate the expected values of the losses:

For R_1: (a) if H_0 is true, then the probability of loss equals the probability $P(D)$ of undertaking action D, i.e. the probability (relative to H_0) of getting three of four elements A in the sample; this probability — as we already know — is 5/16. In turn, the probability of the loss of 50 is equal to the probability of $\overline{D}$, which on the assumption of H_0, is 11/16. Therefore, assuming H_0, the expected value of the loss equals:

$$5/16 \cdot 150 + 11/16 \cdot 50 = 81.25$$

(b) if H_1 is true, this value will amount to $189/256 \cdot 0 + 67/256 \cdot 100 = 26.17$.

For R_2: (a) if H_0 is true, the expected loss will equal:

$$1/16 \cdot 150 + 15/16 \cdot 50 = 56.25$$

(b) if H_1 is true, then $81/256 \cdot 0 + 175/256 \cdot 100 = 68.36$

As can be seen, none of these rules is dominated by the other: R_1 will give greater loss than R_2 if H_0 is true, but a smaller one if H_1 is true.

If the probabilities of H_0 and H_1 were given, we could apply Bayes' criterion: i.e. calculate the average values of losses and choose the rule for which this average is smaller. And so, for instance, if $P(H_0) = 1/4$, while $P(H_1) = 3/4$, the average loss will equal:

for R_1: $81.25 \cdot 1/4 + 26.17 \cdot 3/4 = 39.25$ and
for R_2: $56.25 \cdot 1/4 + 68.36 \cdot 3/4 = 65.33$,

so we would choose R_1. If, however, it were the reverse, i.e. $P(H_0) = 3/4$, and $P(H_1) = 1/4$, the average loss for R_1 would be greater, and we would choose R_2.

Now, let us assume that we do not know the probabilities of competing hypotheses, which is a typical situation. Let us compare now two other criteria of choice:

(1) Minimalization of the average loss: for R_1 the average loss equals $81.25 \cdot 1/2 + 26.17 \cdot 1/2 = 53.71$, and for R_2 it amounts to $56.25 \cdot 1/2 + 68.36 \cdot 1/2 = 62.30$. Then, if we adopt this criterion, we shall choose rule R_1.
(2) Minimalization of maximum risk: the rule R_1 causes us to sustain the loss of 81.25, while R_2 at most of 68.36 — in view of which, if we accept this criterion, we will choose rule R_2.

In certain circumstances, the rules R_1 and R_2 led to the same decisions: for instance, if all four elements in the sample have the property A, then both rules prescribe action D; if there are less than three elements in the sample, both rules prescribe $\overline{D}$. If, however, there are exactly three elements A in the sample, R_1 prescribes D, while R_2 recommends $\overline{D}$. Thence, it can be seen that the acceptance of different choice criteria of a rule can lead to different decisions concerning action on the basis of the same result of an experiment.

In the literature dealing with statistics, no convincing arguments can be found which speak in favour of one of these criteria. Such arguments usually consist of this: that certain conditions of rationality for a decision are formulated, which, according to more or less common intuitions connected with the notion of rationality, should be satisfied by rational decisions, and then it is shown that the given criterion of choice of a rule leads (or does not lead) to decisions which are rational in the same sense of conformity with these criteria.

A perfectly elaborated, clear and concise survey of the most important criteria of choice of the rules and arguments for them can be found in the article by Klemens Szaniawski 'Współczesne ujęcie procedur indukcyjnych' [Contemporary formulation of inductive procedures] [82]. The author points out the fact that the controversies about rationality reveal the inconsistency of conditions imposed on rational decisions.

It appears, unfortunately, that a criterion which would satisfy all the postulates of rationality does not exist. It is so for the simple reason that these postulates are inconsistent. Hence, a conclusion can be dawn that our intuitions concerning a rational criterion for decision making are 'too rich', i.e. that we demand too much at the same time from the principle of taking decisions which we would agree in regarding as rational. In this situation, there appears a necessity of choice of such a set of conditions of rationality which would be consistent. However, this can be done in many ways, and therefore the choice must inevitably be arbitrary.

Finally, attention should be drawn to a special way in which statistical theory characterizes the rules of induction. All the qualities considered for these rules are connected with the probabilities of definite results of experiments if the truth of the applied statistical hypotheses is assumed. In connection with this, there are advantages from the point of view of their repeated application, and not one particular application, because — as I have already stated — the probabilities considered in statistical theory do not refer to individual events but to sets of events of a given kind. And so, for instance, in the above-cited example of test T_1, the probability of a mistaken rejection of H_0, i.e. the probability of getting a four-element random sample of a population, in which three or four elements are A, with the assumption that H_0 is true, refers to a set of such samples in the set of all possible four-element random samples from this population.

In this connection, it is not out of place to quote a numerical example described by I. Hacking in [21]: let us assume that we have two competitive hypotheses of which one is true, and for which the conditional probabilities of four possible results in random samples E_1, E_2, E_3 and E_4 are determined. The probabilities are as follows: $P(E_1/H_0) = 0$, $P(E_2/H_0) = 0.01$, $P(E_3/H_0) = 0.01$, $P(E_4/H_0) = 0.98$, while for H_1: $P(E_1/H_1) = 0.01$, $P(E_2/H_1) = 0.01$, $P(E_3/H_1) = 0.97$, $P(E_4/H_1) = 0.01$. Hacking takes into consideration two rules:

T_1: reject H_0 when E_1 occurs, and
T_2: reject H_0 when E_1 or E_2 occur.

For T_1 we have the probability of first order error equal to 0.01, and of second order error equal to 0.03, while for T_2 the probability of first order error is also 0.01, but the probability of second order error is 0.98. According to the classical criteria test T_1 is decidedly better because, in a long series of applications, it gives small probability of both errors. Hacking emphasizes the fact that if we consider the application of both tests to the particular situation in which result E_1 has already been observed, the classical criterion obviously fails: in this situation test T_2 should be recognized as better than T_1, because T_2 does not permit of a mistake, while T_1 makes the mistake inevitable in this particular situation. This is so, because T_1 does not permit the rejection of H_0 if E_0 has occurred, although the probability of E_1 relative to H_0 is zero while the probability of E_1 relative to H_1 is greater than zero.

6

Logical interpretation of probability

The so-called logical probability is not a concept with a definite and commonly accepted meaning. With this concept, however, there is the intuition that its value depends on (some) logical relations between sentences. A characteristic feature of logical relations is that they occur between sentences with regard to the logical structure of these sentences, which can be described with the use of notions from the sphere of the so-called logical syntax which is a kind of grammar. Namely, the logical structure of a sentence is determined by the places which are occupied in it by the logical constants (i.e. connectives and quantifiers) and other words which belong to definite categories distinguished by this grammar. A logical relation is, for instance, logical inference which takes place between sentences, because of their structure, and regardless of the sense of extra-logical contents. To find that one sentence follows from another we do not need any knowledge about the objects to which these sentences refer and in particular we do not need any empirical knowledge about such objects.

In Chapter 4 I wrote that if the estimation of probability value required the application of an inductive procedure, probability could not be the basis of validity of such a procedure. Hence, the rejection from partial probability in inductive logic caused by the empirical and inductive character of the method of estimating its value, and hence the natural tendency to search for such interpretation of probability with which a logical method of estimating of its value would be possible.

The first detailed theory of logical probability was developed by J. Keynes in 1921 [42]. His theory, however, did not supply a method of estimating numerical probability values for particular sentences. Keynes thought that logical probability is not definable, and that some of its basic values must be based on intuition. He believed that these intuitions should be based on the so-called principle of indifference. This principle originated from the first, classical conception of probability (c. 17–18) which was connected with the analysis of games of chance. It consists of the assignment of equal probabilities to those events which do not give cause to expect that they have unequal chances of occurrence. In many cases this principle led to paradoxical results. Let us take the following example: we have a box containing coloured balls, of which we are to choose one ball at random. Having no reason to expect that the choice of a white ball has greater chances that the choice of a ball of another colour, we should think that both of these events have probabilities equal to 1/2. Neither do we have reason to expect that the choice of a green ball has greater chances than getting of a non-green one; therefore, according to the principle of indifference we should assign probabilities of 1/2 to these events. The same will refer to the choice of balls of other colours, but in this way our probabilities will be inconsistent with the axioms, because, for instance, the probability of choosing a white or green or red ball will be greater than one.

In connection with this, Keynes advised limiting the application of the principle of indifference to some sentences only, for instance to the sentences of a particularly simple structure.

A crucial achievement in the theory of logical probability are the works of Rudolf Carnap dating from 1950s [9], [10]. Carnap is the first logician to invent a method which allows effective estimates of the values of logical probability for all sentences of a given language in accordance with the axioms of probability. For Carnap, these values are dependent on the logical structure of sentences which is in accordance with the above-mentioned postulate concerning logical interpretation of probability.

Carnap's idea was continued by J. Hintikka who, in the 1960s, developed a very interesting modification of Carnap's method [31], [32], [34].

These two theories will be now discussed in detail.

6.1 CARNAP'S THEORY

Two basic works of Carnap on the theory of logical probability are *Logical Foundations of Probability* from 1950 [9] and *The Continuum of Inductive Methods* from 1952 [10]. In these books, Carnap describes methods for calculating probability of sentences for languages with an extremely simple structure. To describe this method I must first characterize such languages.

For the logical constants which appear in such language the following symbols are generally used:

For the connectives:

$\sim p$ negation of sentence p (read: not p).
$p \wedge q$ conjunction.
$p \vee q$ alternation (at least one of the two: p or q).
$p \rightarrow q$ implication (if p then q): the meaning of implication can be defined with the use of alternation and negation as follows: $p \rightarrow q \stackrel{\text{def}}{=} \sim p \vee q$.
$p \leftrightarrow q$ equivalence (p if and only if q)

$$p \leftrightarrow q \quad (p \rightarrow q) \wedge (q \rightarrow p)$$

For the quantifiers:

$\bigwedge_x$ universal quantifier (for every x)

$\bigvee_x$ existential quantifier (there is such an x)

The language for which Carnap defines probability, apart from connectives and quantifiers, included the following logical constants:
(1) Individual names of all objects which belong to the universe (i.e. to the set of objects which the given language refers to) Carnap assumes that each object has one name in a language, so if the universe is an infinite set, then the language has infinitely large number of individual names. Let us denote them with $a_1, a_2, \ldots, a_n, \ldots$
(2) One-place predicates, i.e. the expressions which describe the properties of individual objects like, for instance: x is white, x is a man, etc.

In this language there are no predicates of higher arity, i.e. the expressions which describe relations between objects like, for instance, x is larger than y, x lies between y and z, etc.

One-place arguments can be simple or composed of simple ones with the use of connectives. The assumption says that the number of simple predicates is finite — let us designate it with the symbol r, and the simple predicates with the symbols $P_1(x); P_2(x), \ldots P_r(x)$.

Among the compound predicates a special role is played by the Q predicates. A Q predicate is a conjunction of all simple predicates with no repetitions, in which particular, simple predicates can optionally be preceded by the negation symbol. Q predicates of a given language differ from one another only because of the different distributions of negation signs; the differences in the order of elements of conjunction are not taken into account. This being so, the number k of different Q predicates in a given language is determined by number r of simple predicates as follows: $k = 2^r$. And so, for instance, in the language which includes only two simple predicates, $P_1(x)$ and $P_2(x)$ we shall have the following four Q predicates

$$Q_1(x) \stackrel{\text{def}}{=} P_1(x) \wedge P_2(x) \text{ (i.e. } x \text{ has property } P_1 \text{ and } P_2)$$

$$Q_2(x) \stackrel{\text{def}}{=} P_1(x) \wedge \sim P_2(x) \text{ (} x \text{ has property } P_1 \text{ but not } P_2)$$

$$Q_3(x) \stackrel{\text{def}}{=} \sim P_1(x) \wedge P_2(x)$$

$$Q_4(x) \stackrel{\text{def}}{=} \sim P_1(x) \wedge \sim P_2(x)$$

Let us notice now that Q predicates determine the division of the universe into subsets which are pair-wise disjoint (see Chapter 2), and whose Boolean sum (see Chapter 2) is equal to the universe; for each object must possess one of the properties assigned by the Q predicates, and none can possess two such properties. This can be seen in our example. After Carnap, we will use the symbols $Q_i(x)$ for these Q predicates, and we will call Q-sets those sets formed by them in dividing up the universe.

Let us notice that each predicate $M_i(x)$ of the above-described language, no matter whether it is simple or compound is equivalent to the alternation of certain Q predicates. In the above-cited example, the simple predicate $P_1(x)$ is equivalent to the alternation of two Q predicates: $Q_1(x) \vee Q_2(x)$, while the compound predicate $P_1(x) \to P_2(x)$ is equivalent to the alternation of three Q predicates: $Q_1(x) \vee Q_3(x) \vee Q_4(x)$.

The language thus characterized possesses two important parameters: one is the number k of Q predicates and the other is the number of individual names. The languages with a finite number of names N will be designated by the symbol J_N^k, while the languages with infinite number of names — by the symbol J_∞^k. Given Carnap's assumption that every object has exactly one name, the number of names is, at the same time, the number of objects in the universe.

We shall now concern ourselves with the characterization of certain special types of sentences which play an important role in estimating probability values. These are the sentences called state descriptions and structure descriptions by Carnap.

Every state description in the language J_N^k is a conjunction of N sentences of the form: a_j has property Q_i — in short $Q_i(a_j)$ — and in every element of this conjunction there appears a different name a_j. As can be seen, such descriptions state about each object from the universe that it belongs to a definite Q set. These descriptions are considered different if they include the same objects to different Q sets, for instance one description states $Q_1(a_1)$ and another $Q_2(a_1)$: the differences in the order of elements of conjunction are not taken into account. In connection with this, the number of all different state descriptions in the language J_N^k is k^N. If $N = 3$ and $k = 4$, one state description will, for instance, be the sentence:

$$S_1 = Q_1(a_1) \wedge Q_1(a_2) \wedge Q_2(a_3)$$

See that each state description informs us of how many objects belong to each Q set. Let the symbol N_i denote the number of objects included in the set Q_i by a given description. In this way, a definite sequence of numbers $N_1, \ldots, N_k$ is assigned to each description. Such numbers Carnap calls Q numbers. The sum of all Q numbers for each description is obviously equal to N. In the above-cited description S_1 we have the following Q numbers: $N_1 = 2$, $N_2 = 1$, $N_3 = N_4 = 0$.

It is easy to see that each state description constitutes a complete characterization of the universe in the language J_N^k. This means that it says about this universe everything that can be expressed in this language; everything in this sense that every possible sentence of the language J_N^k is either inconsistent with the given description or follows from it. Let us take, for instance, the above-cited description S_1 of language J_3^4 in which there are four Q predicates determined by the simple predicates P_1 and P_2. Let us take the sentence: $\bigwedge_x (P_1(x) \to P_2(x))$; it states that there are no such objects which are P_1 and are not P_2, i.e. that no object is Q_2. This sentence is, therefore, inconsistent with the description S_1 which states that the object a_3

is Q_2. Let us take another sentence: $\bigwedge_x P_1(x)$; this sentence follows from S_1, because, according to this description, each object is Q_1 or Q_2, and from the above-cited definition of Q predicates we can see that in the face of this, each object is P_1.

In connection with this, every state description determines a certain logically possible full characterization of the universe (consisting of N objects), i.e. a possible world. Because every two different descriptions are logically inconsistent with each other, the real world must be consistent with one description only. Besides, the real world must be consistent with one description because the set of all descriptions exhausts all logical possibilities concerning the character of this world. So, the number of logically possible worlds (N-element worlds) equals the number of state descriptions, i.e. equals k^N.

Let us now turn to structure descriptions, I have already mentioned that a sequence of Q numbers: $N_1, N_2, \ldots, N_k$ is assigned to each state description. Such an assignment is such that the same sequence of Q numbers can be assigned to different state descriptions. I shall explain this with an example. Let us take the above-cited description S_1 in the language J_3^4:

$$S_1: Q_1(a_1) \wedge Q_1(a_2) \wedge Q_2(a_3)$$

The next two descriptions will have the same Q numbers:

$$S_2: Q_1(a_1) \wedge Q_2(a_2) \wedge Q_1(a_3)$$

$$S_3: Q_2(a_1) \wedge Q_1(a_2) \wedge Q_1(a_3)$$

It is easy to notice that no other state description in the language J_3^4 can have the same Q numbers.

The number of different state descriptions with the same Q number depends on what these numbers are, and is defined by a formula:

$$\frac{N!}{N_1! N_2! \ldots N_k!}$$

In our example we have $3!/2!1!0!0! = 3$.

Now we can define structure description: it is the alternation of all state descriptions with the same Q numbers. For instance, the alternation of the above-cited descriptions $S_1 \vee S_2 \vee S_3$ is a structure description in the language J_4^3. Every structure description is also a characterization of the world, although it is not as precise as the state description; it is a statistical characterization. Each sequence of Q numbers determines the statistical distribution of objects into separate Q sets, i.e. for each Q_i it determines the relative frequency of objects with property Q_i in the universe, that is, the proportion N_i/N. The number of all different structure descriptions in J_N^k is obviously equal to the number of all possible statistical distributions of N objects in k Q sets, so it is defined by the formula

$$\frac{(N+k-1)!}{N!(k-1)!}$$

State descriptions will be further designated by the symbol S, and structure descriptions — by symbol the Str. These symbols are used by Carnap.

Let us now consider certain important properties of descriptions. I have already stated that no two different descriptions S can be true at the same time (as they are logically inconsistent), but one of them must be true (as the set of all descriptions S exhausts the set of all logical possibilities of state description in a given language). This being so, the conjunction of any two different descriptions of S is a logically false sentence, while the alternation of all these descriptions, $S_1 \vee S_2 \vee \ldots \vee S_k N$ is a logically true sentence (tautology). Structure descriptions have the same property.

Moreover, state descriptions have one more important property which structure descriptions do not have. Each sentence from language J_N^k is logically equivalent to the alternation of certain descriptions S, namely, all those descriptions S which are compatible with this sentence. And so, for instance, the sentence which states that object a_i is P_j is equivalent to the alternation of all those S which state that a_i is P_j; the sentence: $\bigwedge_x (P_1(x) \to P_2(x))$ is equivalent to the alternation of all those S which do not state, for any object, that it is P_1 and is not P_2 at the same time.

For any sentence Z: the alternation of state descriptions equivalent to this sentence we shall call standard form of sentence Z, and the set of all descriptions S which appear in the standard form Z we shall call (after Carnap) the logical range of sentence Z.

It is easy to notice that if a sentence p follows logically from a sentence q, then the logical range of q is included in the range of p; for if there existed a description S which belonged to the range of q, but did not belong to the range of p, there would exist a logical possibility that q were true while p were false (a possible world in which q is true and p is false), but this is excluded by the fact that p follows from q. If, on the other hand, sentences p and q were logically inconsistent, the possibility of their simultaneous truth would be excluded, and no S could belong to the range of p and q at the same time; the ranges of p and q would be disjoint.

In other cases, i.e. when p and q are logically compatible, but none of them follows from the other, their logical ranges overlap to a greater or smaller extent. This means that there exists a larger or smaller number of descriptions S which belong to the ranges of both these sentences, but there also exists a number of such S which belong only to the range of p, or those which belong only to the range of q. And so, taking into consideration a measure of extent to which the ranges of sentences p and q overlap, we can define various relations between the sentences p and q. Such relations can be considered as logical relations in the sense that they are defined in the terms of logical syntax. It is often thought that these relations can be recognized as generalized, graduable inferences, because they reach their maximum when p follows from q in the strict sense of this word, and their minimum is when p and q are logically incompatible. Between those extremes various intermediate degrees can be found, depending on what part of the range of q is included in the range of p.

And so, Carnap's idea consists of this, that the values of logical probability should be made dependent upon this kind of relation. This means that logical probability is, in his conception, the measure of the degree to which the logical ranges of sentences overlap. Carnap calls this the probability confirmation function and uses symbol C to denote it. The confirmation function C is a conditional probability, because it is to be the measure of the logical relation between two sentences: the value of $C(p/q)$ is to represent the degree of confirmation of sentence p by sentence q determined by the logical relation between p and q.

Let us now explain what the Carnapian method of estimating the value of $C(p/q)$ for individual sentences of the language J_N^k consists of.

It is known that if a function $P(x)$ satisfies the axioms of the probability calculus, the two-argument function $P(x/y)$ defined as $P(x \wedge y)/P(y)$ will also satisfy the axioms. This makes it possible to estimate the value of $C(p/q)$ with the help of a one-argument function $m(p)$ which would satisfy the axioms of probability. Carnap chooses this very way. The measure $m(p)$ can be interpreted as the logical *a priori* probability.

We already know that in the language J_N^k, each sentence is equivalent to alternation of certain descriptions S, which we have called the standard form of a sentence. The descriptions S are pair-wise disjoint, so if we had for each of them the estimated value of the measure $m(S)$, then for each sentence p the value of $m(p)$ would equal the sum of values of $m(S)$ for all S in the standard form of p. We also know that the alternation of all descriptions S in the language J_N^k is a logically true sentence that is, the maximum element in Boolean algebra applied to the sentence. Therefore, to get the measure $m(p)$ determined for all sentences of J_N^k which would satisfy the axioms, it is enough to determine the values of $m(S)$ for all state descriptions S so that each value $m(S)$ is a number in the interval between zero and one, and the sum of all these values is equal to one. It is obvious, however, that it can be done in many ways, so we face the problem of choice.

In the book *Logical Foundations of Probability* [9] Carnap defines a chosen function $m^*(p)$ with the help of which he then defines his famous confirmation function $C^*(p/q)$. Carnap makes the value of m^* for a given state description S dependent on two factors:

(1) from the number s of all state descriptions which have the same Q numbers as S; as we already know the number s is determined by the formula

$$s = \frac{N!}{N_1!N_2!\ldots N_k!}$$

(2) From the number r of all structure descriptions in J_N^k, which is determined by the formula

$$r = \frac{(N+k-1)!}{N!(k-1)!}$$

The definition of the measure m^* is as follows:

(Dm^*) $m^*(p)$ is a function specified for sentences of J_N^k which satisfies the axioms of probability calculus and which, for each state description S, has the value:

$$m^*(S) = 1/r \cdot s$$

As can be seen, Carnap applies the principle of indifference for structure descriptions: the values of m^* are evenly distributed on all descriptions S which belong to the range of a given Str, which means that the value of $m^*(S)$ is obtained when we divide the value of m^*(Str) for the Str with the distribution in S by the number of all S with the same distribution; i.e.:

$$m^*(S) = \frac{m^*(\text{Str})}{s}$$

In this way Carnap assumes that all statistical distributions of the elements of the universe in separate Q sets have equal a priori probabilities. On the other hand not all state descriptions have equal probabilities, because the values of $m^*(S)$ depend on what the statistical distribution in the world described by S is. It is easy to notice that the more concentrated is this distribution, the greater is the a priori probability of such an S. If, for instance, a description Str includes all objects in one Q set only, i.e. its Q numbers are equal ($N_i = N$ and $N_j = 0$ for all Q_j different from Q_i), there exists only one description S with such Q numbers; such a Str is, then, identical to that S, and the following equality is satisfied for them:

$$m^*(S) = m^*(\text{Str}) = 1/r$$

If, on the other hand, a description Str determines a completely regular distribution which means that all its Q numbers are equal ($N_1 = N_2 = \ldots N_k = N/k$), then it has in its range more descriptions than any other Str; in the face of which the descriptions with such Q numbers have the smallest a priori probabilities.

A question arises as to why Carnap distributes the values of m^* in this way and not in another. We shall return to this question when we finish the presentation of Carnap's method.

The definition (Dm^*) refers to the language J_N^k whose universe is a finite, N-element set. To define the function m^* for the language J_∞^k with on infinite universe, Carnap creates a sequence of languages $J_1^k, J_2^k \ldots$, so that the universe of any language J_N^k from this sequence is included in the universe of the language J_{N+1}^k. For each J_N^k in this sequence, the function m^* is defined by (Dm^*). Therefore, we have a sequence of functions $m_1^*, m_2^*, \ldots$. Speaking in short, we can say that the values of m_∞^* for J_∞^k are defined by Carnap as the limits of sequences of values m_N^* if N grows to infinity.

The thus defined function m_∞^* for J_∞^k has the following properties:

(1) If p is a singular clause or a sentence composed of singular clauses with the help of connectives, then $m_\infty^*(p) = m_N^*(p)$ because the values of m^* for such sentences do not change when the universe is extended to any large denumerable set, i.e. the equalities:

$$m_N^*(p) = m_{N+1}^*(p) \quad \text{are satisfied;}$$

(2) if p is a universal sentence and it is not logically true, then $m_\infty^*(p) = 0$; this is so because universal statements $\bigwedge_x M(x)$ are in successive J_N^k equivalent to longer and longer conjunctions of singular sentences: $M(a_1) \wedge M(a_2) \wedge \ldots \wedge M(a_N)$, and because of this, the value of m_N^* for such sentences decreases as the number N grows.

The values of the confirmation function $C^*(p/q)$ are determined by the function m^* for a given language in a generally accepted way for conditional (DC^*) probability: $C^*(p/q)$ is a function specified for sentences J^k: that $m^*(q) > 0$ satisfies the equalities:

$$C^*(p/q) = \frac{m^*(p \wedge q)}{m^*(q)}$$

Let us now investigate how the confirmation function $C^*(p/q)$ behaves in the situations which are regarded as typical for induction, that is, when in place of q is a report from observation of certain objects, while in place of p is a universal or individual hypothesis.

If H is a non-tautological universal sentence, the value of $m_\infty^*(H)$ in languages J_∞^k will be equal to zero, so for any report from observation E, the equality

$$C_\infty^*(H/E) = 0 \quad \text{will be satisfied.}$$

In languages J_N^k there are no universal sentences in the strict sense of this word because each sentence with the universal quantifier $\bigwedge_x M(x)$ is logically equivalent to the conjunction of singular sentences $M(a_1) \wedge M(a_2) \wedge \ldots \wedge M(a_N)$. For such conjunctions which are in accordance with E and non-tautological, the values of C^* in J_N^k will not be equal to zero; if the N are large, however, they will, as a rule, tend to zero, except for the cases in which the number n of the observed objects with property $M(x)$ is close to N (i.e. when induction by enumeration comes close to the so-called exhaustive induction, i.e. deduction).

In this way the confirmation function C^* is incompatible with the view that the degree of confirmation of universal hypothesis H increases, as does the number of observations consistent with H, if no observations contradict H. If the measure of the degree of confirmation is $C^*(H/E)$, then no non-tautological universal hypotheses (universal in the strict sense, this means: not equivalent to any finite conjunction of singular sentences) will be confirmed by any observations.

Besides, function C^* will not satisfy the theorem T.5 (see Chapter 2), i.e. the equality $C^*(p/q) = 1$ if p follows from q for any non-tautological universal sentence q. For any sentence p and non-tautological sentence q, the value of $C_\infty^*(p/q)$ will never be equal to 1, because it will always be indeterminate in regard to $m_\infty^*(q) = 0$.

These properties of the function C^* for languages J_∞^k do not disturb Carnap because of his special conception of the role of induction in science, which will be discussed in Chapter 11.

Let us now turn to singular hypotheses which ascribe certain simple or compound properties to objects. For an arbitrarily chosen predicate $M_i(x)$ from language J^k, and any object a, the function m^* satisfies the equality

$$m^*(M_i(a)) = \frac{w_i}{k}$$

where w_i is the number of Q predicates whose alternation the predicate M_i is equivalent to (it has already been stated in the description of language J^k). Hence, for Q predicates we have:

$$m^*(Q_i(a)) = 1/k$$

and for simple predicates:

$$m^*(P_i(a)) = 1/2$$

Let us assume now that E is a sentence which states that among the observed objects $a_1, a_2, \ldots a_n$ there are n_i objects with property M_i. For the hypothesis $M_i(a_{n+1})$ about a non-observed object a_{n+1} the value of C^* will be:

$$C^*(M_i(a_{n+1})/E) = \frac{n_i + w_i}{n + k}$$

In particular, if E states that all observed objects have the property M_i, for the hypothesis $M_i(a_{n+1})$ we shall get:

$$C^*(M_i(a_{n+1})/E) = \frac{n + w_i}{n + k}$$

It can be seen that the greater the number of observations n, the larger this value. When n is very large, the proportion w/k is no more important, and we get:

$$C^*(M_i(a_{n+1})/E) \to 1$$

when $n \to \infty$. If we now regard the values of C as the measure of degree of confirmation of the hypothesis $M_i(a_{n+1})$ by the results of observation E, we shall see that the larger the number of the observed objects with property M_i, the better is the degree of confirmation.

The comparison of values of a priori probability $m^*(M_i(a))$ and a posteriori probability $C^*(M_i(a_{n+1})/E)$ shows that C^* gives positive probabilistic dependence of sentences of the form $M_i(a)$. This dependence results from the regular distribution of the values of m^* on structure descriptions.

To realize this, let us take the coin-tossing game. In Carnap's language it can be described as follows: we have one simple predicate — getting tails, and, therefore, two Q predicates: getting tails and not getting tails (getting heads). Let $T(x)$ designate getting tails in the toss x. Let the universe be the set of two tosses of a coin, a_1 and a_2. In this situation, we have four possible descriptions S: $S_1 = T(a_1) \wedge T(a_2)$; $S_2 = T(a_1) \wedge \sim T(a_2)$; $S_3 = \sim T(a_1) \wedge T(a_2)$; $S_4 = \sim T(a_1) \wedge \sim T(a_2)$. The second and the third description have the same Q numbers $N_1 = N_2 = 1$; the first description has $N_1 = 2$ and $N_2 = 0$, while the fourth description is the reverse: $N_1 = 0$ and $N_2 = 2$. Therefore, we have three different structure descriptions: $\text{Str}_1 = S_1$, $\text{Str}_2 = S_2 \vee S_3$ and $\text{Str}_3 = S_4$. According to the definition (Dm^*) we have equal values of m^* for the descriptions Str, namely $m^*(\text{Str}_i) = 1/3$; while for the descriptions S these values are unequal, namely: $m^*(S_1) = 1/3 = m^*(S_4)$, and $m^*(S_2) = m^*(S_3) = m^*(\text{Str}_2) \cdot 1/2 = 1/6$. It can be seen that these values are different from generally accepted probabilities in the heads and tails game. For an unbiased coin, the probability of getting two tails successively, i.e. S_1, is assumed to be 1/4, just like for two heads, S_4; while for one head and one tail $(S_2 \vee S_3)$, the probability is 1/2. These probabilities follow from the assumption about the independence of results in successive tosses: the conditional probability $P(T(a_2)/T(a_1))$ is equal to $P(T(a_2)) \sim \sim T(a_1)$ and equals the absolute probability $P(T(a_2)) = 1/2$, which is connected with equal distribution of probability for state descriptions: $P(S_1 = P(S_2) = P(S_3) = P(S_4) = 1/4$; whereas equal distribution of m^* for structure descriptions gives the dependence:

$$C^*(T(a_2)/T(a_1)) = \frac{m^*(T(a_2) \wedge T(a_1))}{m^*(T(a_1))} = \frac{m^*(S_1)}{m^*(S_1 \vee S_2)}$$
$$= \frac{m^*(S_1)}{m^*(S_1) + m^*(S_2)} = 2/3$$

while $C^*(T(a_2)/\sim T(a_1)) = 1/3$ and $m^*(T(a_2)) = m^*(S_1 \vee S_3) = 1/3 + 1/6 = 1/2$. This means that the probability of getting tails in the second toss relative to tails in the first toss is, according to (Dm^*) greater than relative to heads for the first toss, and greater than the absolute probability of getting tails on any toss.

It can be seen, then, that by regular distribution of the values of m^* on structure descriptions, Carnap assumes positive probabilistic dependence of sentences which assign the same properties to different abjects. Let us see what Carnap says to justify this assumption, and, consequently, the choice of confirmation function C^* from all confirmation functions which can be received by different distributions of measure m on descriptions S.

In his book *The Continuum of Inductive Methods* [10], Carnap presented a definition of a class of such functions $C(P/q)$ which, according to him, can claim to be treated as confirmation functions. These functions differ from one another in the value of a certain parameter designated by the symbol $\lambda(k)$ which is a function of the number k of Q predicates. The values of these functions can be any prositive real numbers. Estimation of the value of the function $\lambda(k)$ determines the value of the so-called characteristic function $G(k,n,n_i)$ according to the following definitions:

(DG) $\quad G(k,n,n_i) = \dfrac{n_i + \lambda(k)/k}{n + \lambda(k)} = C(Q_i(a_{n+1})/E)$

E represents here a description of a set of n objects in which there are n_i objects with property Q. The values of function G together with the axioms for probability univocally characterize the functions $C(p/q)$ and $m(p)$ for all sentences; this means that for each value of $\lambda(k)$ there is only one function $C(p/q)$ which is in agreement with the axioms and values of $C(Q(a_{n+1})/E)$ defined by (DG), and one function $m(p)$ defined as $C(p/t)$ where t is a logically true sentence. We get the functions m^* and C^* by determining $\lambda(k) = k$.

We have already seen that for $n_i = n$ (i.e. when all objects described by E have the property Q_i) the value of $C^*(Q_i(a_{n+1})/E)$ grows to one as n increases. If $n_i < n$, the value of $C^*(Q_1(a_{n+1})/E)$ will tend to n_i/n as n increases which means that the degree of confirmation of the sentence $Q_i(a_{n+1})$ by the sentence which states that in a set of n objects relative frequency Q_i is n_i/n, will tend to this relative frequency.

We get the limiting functions of the system λ at $\lambda(k) = 0$ on one side and $\lambda(k) = \infty$ on the other. It can be seen from (DG) that at $\lambda(k) = 0$ the characteristic function assumes the value

$C(Q_i(a_{n+1})/E) = n_i/n$

and we get the so-called simple rule of confirmation C^+ which is characterized by the equation:

$$C^+(Q_i(a_{n+1})/E) = 1/k$$

As can be seen, the degree of confirmation of the sentence $Q_i(a_{n+1})$ by the sentence E, measured by C^+, is absolutely independent of what is stated by E, and always equal to $1/k$. And so, the function C^+ determines the function m^+ whose values are regularly distributed over the state description S. Such a distribution is, then, tantamount to the absolute independence of sentences in the form $M(a_1)$, $M(a_2)$ ... for any predicates M. All other functions C of the Carnapian system λ are between these extremes. Values of $C(Q_1(a_{n+1})/E)$ which characterize these functions are influenced by two factors: n_i/n, which can be called the experiential or a posteriori factor, and $1/k$ which can be called language or a priori factor. The lower $\lambda(k)$, the greater the role played by the experiential factor; at $\lambda(k) = 0$ the language factor has no influence on the value of the characteristic function. On the other hand, the higher $\lambda(k)$, the greater is the role of the language factor and the lesser the role of the experiential one.

According to Carnap, neither of these extremes is good: use of a simple rule means too hasty transference of the results of observations on unobserved objects, even when the observations concern a very small number of objects. And so, for instance, when E states that one observed object, say a_1, is Q_i. then, for an unobserved object a_2 we get $C(Q_i(a_2)/Q_i(a_1)) = 1$, which means that observation of one object Q_i gives maximum degree of confirmation of the sentence that an unobserved object is also Q_i. On the other hand, function C^+ is a priori in the extreme: observations do not increase, here, the degree of confirmation of the sentence $Q_i(a_{n+1})$ about an unobserved object; this degree is always equal to the value of $m^+(Q_i(a_{n+i})) = 1/k$, i.e. it depends only upon the number of Q predicates in the language.

After rejecting these two extreme confirmation functions as inadequate, Carnap faces the problem of the choice of one function from among the others. And so, Carnap justified the choice of C^* with the fact that from the point of view of calculation it is the simplest of these functions.

This argument, however, is subject to serious objections. If C^* is to represent logical probability, its value choice should be based on some considerations of logical character. And so, for instance, an argument that logical relations whose measure is C^* represent the relation of partial inference better than the relations measured by other functions of the λ-system would be convincing. The concept of partial or generalized inference has no strictly determined meaning, but, only and at most, some intuitive sense. And so, the question of what properties are connected with intuitions concerning partial inference should be settled first.

Anyway, the condition that the maximum degree of partial inference should be inference in the strict sense seems natural. We have seen, however, that the function C^* does not always have a maximum value in the cases of inference because for a universal sentence q, the values of $C^*_\infty(p/q)$ are not determined. All functions of the Carnapian system have the same property because all these functions are defined in J_∞^k like C_∞^*; namely, by the limits of the values of sequences of functions m in successessive languages J_N^k. In connection with this, all functions m of the system have in J_∞^k a null value for non-tautological universal sentences.

Certain other intuitions are also connected with partial inference. And so, for instance, in his review of the above-mentioned works by Carnap, W. Salmon [67] expresses the view that if probability is to be a measure of partial of the inference, then logical independence of sentences should correspond with probabilistic independence. For instance, the simple sentences of the form $M(a_1), M(a_2)$, where M is an arbitrary predicate and a_1, a_2 are names of two different objects, are logically independent. This being so, the confirmation function should satisfy the condition: $C(M(a_1)/M(a_2)) = m(M(a_1))$. C^*, however, does not satisfy this condition, because it assumes positive dependence of such sentences. From among all functions of the λ-system only the function C^+ is based on a regular distribution of measure m^+ on state descriptions which causes probabilistic independence of such sentences, satisfies this condition. According to Salmon, detecting logical relations between such sentences is an illusion; the dependence between them can be only statistical, that is empirical. In connection with this, the rejection of the function C^+ completely rules out the idea of founding the function of confirmation on partial inference.

The intuition according to which such relation between two sentences should depend only on the logical structure of those very sentences is also connected with the concept of logical relation. Meanwhile, the functions of the λ-system have values which are dependent not only on the structure of particular sentences, but also on the number of predicates in the language. Let us assume, for instance, that in a certain language are two simple predicates P_1 and P_2; let us take the sentence $E = P_1(a_1)$ and $H = P_1(a_2)$. In this language we have four Q predicates, and each simple predicate P_i is equivalent to an alternation of two Q predicates that is, we have $k = 4$ and $w = 2$ for simple predicates. Therefore, we get:

$$C^*(H/E) = \frac{1 + w_1}{1 + k} = 3/5.$$

If, however, we introduce into this language a new simple predicate P_3, in a language thus enriched we shall have $k = 8$ and $w_i = 4$ for simple predicates, in which case for the same sentences H and E we shall have $C^*(H/E) = 5/9$. The more simple predicates appear in the language in addition to P_1, the lower the value of $C^*(H/E)$, although only the predicate P_1 appears in the sentences H and E.

H. Kyburg in [45] remarks that the dependence of values of the function C^* on the number of predicates in the language is so strong that even when their number is comparatively small, the influence of E on the value of C^* (H/E) becomes doubtful. If, for instance, there are thirty simple predicates in a language (which is a comparatively small number) the number k of Q predicates is over a milliard (billion). In this situation the experiential factor

n_i/n loses its influence on the value of

$$C^*(M_i(a_{n+1})/E) = \frac{n_i + w_i}{n + k}$$

which tends to the value of language factor w_i/k. The number of observations n required to increase the degree of confirmation of sentence $M_i(a_{n+1})$ becomes practically unattainable. In this way it appears that the function C^* is not much better than C^+ in this respect which was decisive for the rejection of C^+ by Carnap.

It is beyond doubt that the choice of the function C^* is not based on logical criteria and that the possibility of finding such a criterion for any function from a λ-system, except, maybe, C^+ is doubtful to say the least. Every such function is based on an assumption about the probabilistic dependence of logically independent sentences. The acceptance of such an assumption for all predicates of the language J^k cannot be explained — as Salmon justly stated — by the reasons of a logical nature.

Later Carnap gave up the choice of a single confirmation function as proper logical probability and was inclined to accept the view that inductive logic should confine itself to offering a set of possible confirmation functions to science: the choice should be left to scientific practice and should depend upon reasons of a pragmatic and not logical nature. In his article 'The Aim of Inductive Logic' from 1962 [11] Carnap expressed the opinion that the choice of confirmation function, which is tantamount to the choice of a particular inductive logic, does not belong to logic any more. This choice should be a matter for a normative theory of rational decisions, and should be based on the postulates concerning the rationality of decisions. The above-cited critical arguments have shown, however, that all functions of Carnapian λ-systems have several faults which impair the possibility of treating them as measures of logical relations which could constitute the base for inductive logic. Another drawback of Carnap's conception is the oversimplicity of languages J^k for which Carnap defined his confirmation functions. No scientific theory uses so simple a language in which only names and one-place predicates appear.

6.2 HINTIKKA'S THEORY

In the 1960s Jaakko Hintikka developed a method for estimating the value of logical probability which avoids one fundamental drawback of Carnap's system, namely, it does not lead to the assignment of null probabilities to universal statements. Hintikka presented this method in a few different works, and finally, in his work 'A Two-dimensional Continuum of Inductive Methods' [32] he presented a characterization of a certain class of confirmation function which includes all Carnap's λ-functions. In this way Hintikka's system is a generalization of Carnap's system.

Hintikka's method is based on Carnap's idea that a set of logical possibilities which exclude one another, i.e. the so-called possible worlds, is distinguished. However, the starting point for Hintikka are different logical possibilities, and thence, different descriptions of possible worlds. The essence of Hintikka's idea is the rejection of the assumption that the probability values of universal statements should be determined on the basis of a previous determination of the probability of state descriptions since this was what led to null probabilities of universal statements with infinite universe. In connection with this, Hintikka rejects the construction of probability function for J_∞^k on the basis of a sequence of functions for successive languages J_N^k.

Hintikka's method refers to the same languages as Carnap's method; this means that apart from connectives and quantifiers, only one-place predicates and individual names can appear in these languages. The number of simple predicates is here finite too, and the difference in language consists in the fact that the existence of names for all elements of the universe is not assumed, and therefore, in this language there are no state descriptions of the universe. To determine the value of a probability function Hintikka uses a formal trick similar to Carnap: namely, he uses a kind of standard form for sentences. The standard form which includes quantifiers, but does not contain names is defined as an alternation of certain sentences called 'constituents' by Hintikka. These constituents are descriptions of possible worlds which are formulated without use of names. Here they will be designated — after Hintikka — by symbol the C.

A constituent C describes the universe so, for about each Q set, it states whether it is empty or non-empty. Let us assume, for instance, that in J^k we have $k = 2$, i.e. we have two Q predicates: $Q_1(x)$ and $Q_2(x)$. This being so, we have four possible different constituents:

$$C_1 = \bigvee_x Q_1(x) \wedge \bigvee_x Q_2(x)$$

$$C_2 = \bigvee_x Q_1(x) \wedge \sim \bigvee_x Q_2(x)$$

$$C_3 = \sim \bigvee_x Q_1(x) \wedge \bigvee_x Q_2(x)$$

$$C_4 = \sim \bigvee_x Q_1(x) \wedge \sim \bigvee_x Q_2(x)$$

(by way of digression, the constituent C_4 cannot be regarded as a description of a possible universe; it is a logically impossible sentence — when the assumption states that the universe is not empty — because the alternation of all Q predicates is logically true). Generally speaking constituents are sentences in the form:

$$(\mathrm{DC}) \pm \bigvee_x Q_1(x) \wedge \pm \bigvee_x Q_2(x) \wedge \ldots \vee \pm \bigwedge_x Q_k(x)$$

where $\pm$ means that the sentence $\bigvee_x Q_i(x)$ may optimally be preceded by the sign of negation. The number of such constituents which are different fron one another is 2^k (it is assumed that the order of elements of conjunction does not make difference between constituents.). Each constituent can be formulated in a logically-equivalent way as a conjunction of sequences, as follows:

$$(\mathrm{DC'}) \bigvee_x Q_{i_1}(x) \wedge \bigvee_x Q_{i_2}(x) \wedge \ldots \wedge \bigvee_x Q_{i_w}(x) \wedge \bigwedge_x (Q_{i_1}(x) \vee \ldots \vee Q_{i_w}(x))$$

where at the beginning we have all existential sentences of constituent C without negations, and instead of a conjunction of negated sentences an adequate universal sentence appears.

Constituents C have properties similar to Carnapian descriptions S and str: they are pair-wise disjoint and the alternation of C in J^k is logically true. It is also easy to prove that each sentence g which does not include names is logically equivalent to the alternation of all constituents C which are compatible with it; for every such sentence, g states that certain Q sets are empty, or that some Q sets are not empty, or else, that some are empty and others are not. Let us take, for instance, the sentence $\bigwedge_x (P_1(x) \to P_2(x))$; it states that there are no objects which have property P_1 and do not have property P_2. Thereby, this sentence states that all Q sets which include objects P_1 and not P_2 are empty. Thus, this sentence is incompatible with all constituents C which state that one of those Q sets is not empty. Other constituents C exhaust all the logical possibilities of description of the universe in which our sentence can be true, so it is equivalent to the alternation of all those constituent C compatible with it.

The alternation of constituents C which is equivalent to the given sentence g constitutes its standard form called 'distributive standard form' by Hintikka. Properties of this standard form make it possible to estimate the probabilities of all sentences which do not contain names in J^k by estimating the probabilities of constituents, in a way similar to that of Carnap.

We can see now that to each constituent C we can assign a number w which will be the number of all those Q sets whose non-emptiness is stated by a given constituent — see (DC'). The symbol C_w will designate any constituent which states that the number of non-empty Q predicates is w. Numbers w for constituents C play a similar role to that played by Q numbers for Carnapian descriptions S. They do not characterize the constituents univocally, because different constituents C can ascertain non-emptiness of the same number of Q sets, but different Q sets. The number of constituents C_w with the same number w depends on the numerical quantity of w and is defined by the formula

$$\binom{k}{w} = \frac{k!}{w!(k-w)!}$$

And so, for instance, when $k = 4$ we have one constituent C_0, four constituents C_1, six constituents C_2, four constituents C_3 and one C_4. For example, C_3 constituents will be not only the sentence which states that sets Q_1, Q_2 and Q_3 are not empty while Q_4 is empty, but also those sentences which state that only the constituent C_1 or only C_2 or only C_3 is empty.

The class of confirmation function described by Hintikka is characterized with the help of two parameters, λ and α: every estimation of values of these parameters defines one function of absolute and conditional probability for all sentences J^k. The parameter λ is adopted from Carnap's work and it plays the same role in Hintikka's system: it modifies the values of conditional probabilities of simple sentences (probabilistic dependences of such sentences.) Parameter α plays a similar role with reference to universal sentences.

Hintikka assumes that the universe of language J^k is an infinite set; he thinks that this assumption is most realistic in the sense that it allows one to estimate the value of a probability function without knowledge of the exact number of objects in the universe which we do not possess. This assumption constitutes a very good approximation for all those cases when the universe is very large. To designate his functions, Hintikka uses the generally accepted probability symbol P. Conditional probability, however, is understood here in the same way as the confirmation function was by Carnap, namely, it is to be the measure of logical relations between sentences.

The method of estimating the value of probability is as follows: a priori probabilities are assigned to constituents C so, that they make up a unit; all a priori probabilities of sentences which do not contain names are defined in this way because each such sentence is in J^k equivalent to a certain alternation of constituents C. Then the probabilities of sentences which do not contain quantifiers is estimated. Every such sentence includes some names $a_1, \ldots, a_n$ and predicates, so it is a description of an n-element set Z_n of objects which belong to the universe. In connection with it every such sentence E is equivalent to the alternation of all those state descriptions S of the set Z_n which are compatible with it. A state description S is similar to that of Carnap — with the difference that it is not a description of all universes, but of its subset Z_n. Therefore, the estimation of probabilities of descriptions S for all sets Z_n gives the values of $P(E)$ for all sentences E without quantifiers which include names $a_1, \ldots, a_n$. A description S of a set Z_n is equivalent to the alternation of pair-wise disjoint conjunctions in the form of $S \wedge C$ for all constituents C consistent with S. Therefore, on the strength of (T.6) the value of $P(S)$ is equal to the sum of values $P(S \wedge C)$ for all those C. The value of $P(C \wedge S)$ for each C and each S consistent with it is calculated from the distribution of values of $P(C)$ on descriptions S of set Z_n according to the given C. This means that the conjunctions $S \wedge C$ for all S consistent with C have probabilities assigned so that they sum up to the value of $P(C)$ which has already been estimated.

The distribution of probability on constituents C and the distribution of value of $P(C)$ on sentences $S \wedge C$ can differ from one another to a great extent: they can be regular or more or less irregular depending on what values will be determined for the parameters α and λ. As the role of parameter λ is the same as in Carnap's system, and it was described in Chapter 6.1, we shall confine ourselves to descriptions of the role of parameter α, assuming that parameter λ is defined like Carnap's function C^*. A priori probabilities of constituents are defined as follows:

$$(\text{P.C}_w) \quad P(C_w) = \frac{(\alpha + w - 1)!}{(w-1)!} \bigg/ \sum_{j=0}^{k} \binom{k}{j} \frac{(\alpha + j - 1)!}{(j-1)!}$$

Different values of α determine different probability functions. The assumption is that α can be any natural number. We get limit functions when $\alpha = 0$ and $\alpha = \infty$. If $\alpha = 0$, the numerator of $P(C_w)$ is reduced to 1, then the dependence of $P(C_w)$ on number w disappears, and we have:

$$P(C_w) = 1 \bigg/ \sum_{j=0}^{k} \binom{k}{j} = 1/2^k$$

2^k is the number of all constituents C in J^k, and so $\alpha = 0$ determines equal probabilities for all these descriptions. By way of digression, positive probability is also assigned to the constituent C_0 which is logically false. For all natural values of α, the postulate (P.C$_w$) assigns different probabilities to the constituents: C_0 has null probability, while the other constituents C_w always have probabilities greater than zero; the greater the probability, the larger the number w. Therefore, all universal sentences which are not logically false have a priori probabilities greater than zero.

The differences between probabilities of constituents C_w increase as does α in the same way that the value of $P(C_k)$ tends to one, while for all $w < k$, $P(C_w)$ tends to zero. The constituent C_k states that all Q predicates are non-empty, so it is a description of the world in which no non-tautological universal statement is true. Therefore, the other limiting case for the class of functions of Hintikka's system are Carnap's λ functions which have null values for non-tautological universal sentences in an infinite universe.

At all values of α, except for $\alpha = \infty$, Hintikka's functions differ from Carnap's only in respect of the values they assign to universal statements. As the absolute probabilities of those sentences are not null (except for the logically false ones), conditional probabilities can also be different from zero depending on the relation between sentences. I shall now quote two of Hintikka's theorems which show these dependences.

Let us notice that a number c of Q predicates represented in S (i.e. ascribed by S to certain elements Z_n) is assigned to each description S of the set Z_n. Let us use the symbol S_c to denote such description. Now we can see that all constituents C_w with the index $w < c$ will be inconsistent with S_c because they will state that certain predicates which S_c ascribes to some elements of Z_n are empty. Therefore, only some constituents C_w with the index $w \geq c$ can be consistent with S_c. We shall use the symbol C_{c+i}, where $i = 0, 1, \ldots, k - c$ to designate them. In Hintikka's system such constituents satisfy the theorem:

(T.1) If $n > \alpha$, then for any two constituents compatible with the description S_c of the set Z_n the inequality:

$$P(C_{c+j}/S_c) > P(C_{c+i}/S_c)$$

is true if and only if $i < j$.

This means that of all constituents compatible with S_c the greatest is the probability of constituent C_c. For a given sentence S_c which describes the set Z_n there always exists exactly one constituent C_c which is compatible with it; the other constituents C_{c+i} compatible with S_c have probabilities which decrease with an increase of i. Consequently, the description C_k which, for Carnap, had the greatest probability (equal to one in J_∞^k) has the least probability relative to S_c. The highest probability, on the other hand, is that of the constituent C_c which states the strongest universal proposition compatible with S. Namely, this constituent states that all Q predicates which do not belong to any element of the set Z_n are empty.

Besides, the constituent C_c compatible with S_c satisfies in Hintikka's system the following theorem:

(T.2) $P(C_c/S_c)$ tends to one if n increases to infinity.

Therefore, no matter how large α is (providing it is finite), we can always find an n, such that the probability of constituent C_c relative to description S_c of the set Z_n will be arbitrarily high. Because the constituent C_c as an element of a conjunction (see (DC′)) includes the strongest universal statement compatible with S_c, at a sufficiently large n the probability of this sentence is close to one.

By way of digression: the fact that the constituent which states the strongest universal proposition compatible with S_c has higher probability than others compatible with S_c (which state weaker universal sentences) does not mean that this strongest universal sentence has higher probability than the weaker universal statements: this would violate the axioms of probability calculus. If the strongest universal sentence which is compatible with S_c has probability close to one, all its weaker consequences have probabilities even closer to one. The fact should be stressed that no constituent is equivalent to a universal statement. Each constituent states a universal proposition, but it also states an existential sentence of the form $\bigvee_x Q_i(x)$ — see (DC′). Constituent C_{c+i} relative to S has probability smaller than C_c because it states the existence of objects with such properties Q_i which are not vested in the elements of Z_n.

Let us now return to the role of the parameter α. Values of $P(C/S)$, and thence the probabilities of general hypotheses relative to the results of observation depend upon the value of this parameter. This dependence on α that the higher is the value of α, the greater the number of n of observations necessary to make the probabilities of the universal statements consistent with observation as high as possible. In connection with this, Hintikka interprets the parameter α as the measure of 'methodological pessimism' understood as the conviction about the incorrectness of the universe. $\alpha = \infty$ represents extreme pessimism: the universe of C_k in which no non-tautological universal statement is true has then a probability equal to one and the results of observation cannot give higher than null probability to a universal statement. On the other hand, $\alpha = 0$ represents extreme optimism: we get a function which, for a general hypothesis H, can have a very high $P(H/E)$ even when E gives an account of a very small number of observations. We can say, then, that α gives for general hypotheses a similar effect to that which λ gives to individual ones: $\alpha = 0$ expresses too great a hastiness in generalizing the results of experiments, while $\alpha = \infty$ expresses a complete lack of confidence in any generalizations.

Hintikka consciously does not make a choice of any particular value of α: it seems that to find a non-arbitrary criterion for such a choice is impossible.

Anyway, for all finite values of α, all Hintikka's functions have non-zero values for universal statements. Thanks to this, if H is a consistent universal statement, then in all instances when a sentence G follows from the sentence H we get $P(G/H) = 1$, while in Carnap's system such probabilities were undetermined. Besides: if sentence E is an account of observation of a set of objects, then the higher is n, the higher the value of $P(H/E)$ of the general hypothesis H compatible with E. Therefore, Hintikka's functions, at least in some respects, can better aspire to the role of logical probability and are more suitable for the evaluation of induction by enumeration.

In Chapter 3, I stressed the fact that according to common opinion, the value of enumerative induction depends not only upon the number of observed objects, but also on their variety. Hintikka discusses this problem in his work [55]. There, he refers to the above-cited theorems (T.1) and (T.2) from which it follows that relative to the results of observation S_c the probability of constituent C_w compatible with S_c increases with the decrease of w, so, it is the highest for the constituent C_c. Consequently, if $w > c$ then the constituent C_w states the existence of objects with non-observed properties (i.e. not ascribed to any of the observed n objects by S_c). If, with increase of number $n + m$ of further observed objects, these properties will not occur either, $P(C_w/S_c)$ will decrease to nought (which follows from the theorem (T.2)). This means — Hintikka states — that if the set of observed objects does not show as much variety as it is allowed by the constituent C_w, the probability of such a description will decrease to zero in spite of the increase of the number of confirming observations. So, the increase of the number of observations compatible with C_w itself does not increase the probability of C_w, whereas, if with a greater number of observations, it appears that there exist objects compatible with C_w with properties which were not observed before, this result will cause an increase of probability of C_w. As soon as we observe all possible properties which are allowed by constituent C_w, i.e. when we get the result of observation S_w, the probability of C_w will grow to one together with the increase of n (T.2). The result of observation S_w is tantamount to the observation of all possible varieties of objects allowed by C_w. Hintikka draws attention to the fact that the dependence of the value of induction on the variety of instances compatible with the conclusion is connected with the eliminative aspect of induction. The point is that the variety of observed objects allows us to eliminate certain competitive hypotheses whose elimination cannot be done in cases when the observed objects are more homogeneous.

In the situation considered by Hintikka the problem appears to be as follows. Let us assume that in the set of observed objects Z_n, only the following Q predicates are represented: $Q_1, Q_2, \ldots, Q_c$, where c is smaller than the number k of all Q predicates. Many different constituents can occur in the language J^k which are compatible with the result of the observation S_c; let us use $\{C_c\}$ to designate the set of these constituents. If further observations of objects $a_{n+1}, a_{n+2}, \ldots$ do not indicate the existence of objects with some other properties Q_i, none of the constituents $\{C_c\}$ will be eliminated. If, however, in further observations, it appears that there exists an object with some other property, say Q_{c+1}, this result of observation will eliminate (falsify) all those descriptions included in $\{C_c\}$ which stated that the predicate Q_{c+1} was empty. This will, among other things, eliminate the constituent C_c which is simpler than any other constituent from the set $\{C_c\}$

in the sense that in the universe described by C_c the variety of objects is less (there are more empty Q predicates) than in the universe described by the descriptions C included in $\{C_c\}$. Let us assume that C_w belongs to $\{C_c\}$ and $w > c + 1$ if further observations are also compatible with C_w and demonstrate that all Q predicates about which C_w states that they are not empty, actually are non-empty, then C_w will be the simplest compatible description of the universe with such observation S_w.

In connection with this, Hintikka expresses the view that the functions defined by him allow an account of both enumerative and eliminative aspects of induction: when the number of observations exceeds $n (n > \alpha)$ the further growth of probability of constituent C_w depends upon whether new observations eliminate certain simpler competitive constituents. As soon as the new observations eliminate all competitive constituents simpler than C_w, the further growth of probability C_w depends only upon the number of further observations compatible with C_w.

In [32] Hintikka stresses the fact that apart from qualitative variety we can also speak of quantitative variety. And so, for instance, if in each of two sets of objects the same Q predicates, say $Q_1, \ldots, Q_c$ are represented, but in one set most objects have property Q_1 while in the other all numbers n_i of objects with properties Q_i are equal, then the qualitative variety is identical in both sets, but the quantitative variety is greater in the second set. Hintikka emphasizes the fact that certain functions from his system (it depends on the estimation of parameter λ) have the characteristic that the value of $P(C/S_c)$ depends not only upon the qualitative variety, but also the quantitative one; namely, the constituent C_w has the greatest probability relative to an experiment compatible with C_w in which all and only those Q predicates are represented whose non-emptiness is stated by C_w, and, moreover, each of these Q predicates is assigned to more or less the same number of observed objects.

The dependence of probability of hypotheses from the variety of objects in the experiment, which is shown by Hintikka, concerns those hypotheses which are constituents (general descriptions of the universe). These descriptions are not universal statements, because they include existential statements as elements of their conjunction as well. Besides, variety was understood here either as the number of different observed Q predicates or as a regular distribution of the observed objects on these predicates. However, when we say that the value of induction by enumeration depends upon the number of observed objects, we refer to universal conclusions in the strict sense of this word, and variety understood in a different way (see Chapter 3). Let us assume, for instance, that in the language J^k we have three simple predicates: P_1, P_2 and P_3, and, hence, eight Q predicates. Compare, now, two results of observations: let S_2 be a description of an n-element set, which states about one half of these objects that they have properties P_1, P_2 and P_3, and about the other half that they have properties P_1 and P_2, but not P_3. Let S_2' be a description of an n-element set which states that one half of the objects in this set have properties P_1, P_2 and P_3, while the other half have P_2, and P_3, but not P_1. Both these results are exactly the same as regards the variety which Hintikka spoke about: in both cases precisely two Q predicates are represented ($c = 2$) and the distribution of objects on the Q predicates is even. Let us now consider the general hypothesis of the form: $\bigwedge_x (P_1(x) \to P_2(x))$; say, that it is the sentence 'each raven is black', and the predicate $P_3(x)$ has the meaning 'x lives in a moderate climate'. In regard to this hypothesis the set of objects described by S_2 is more heterogeneous than the set described by S_2', because in the first experiment the crows are more varied (they live in moderate climate and in other climates as well), while in the second experiment they all come from moderate climate, and the hypothesis H refers to ravens. According to a common belief, the result S_2 should confirm the hypothesis that each raven is black better than the result S_2' just because of greater observed variety of ravens, Hintikka's system, however, does not take this understanding of variety into consideration.

Hintikka's functions (as well as Carnap's functions) do not say anything about the criterion which is usually adopted for inference by analogy. The criterion is that the more properties the observed objects P_1 share, the better is the inference concerning a P_1 object that it also has property P_2 on the basis that the observed objects P_1 had the property P_2. P. Achinstein proves in [1] that none of Carnap's functions can satisfy this criterion. The same concerns Hintikka's functions. M. Hesse in [28] states that it follows from the fact that all Carnap's and Hintikka's functions are symmetrical with regard to Q predicates: $P(Q_i(x)) = P(Q_j(x))$ for any $i \neq j$. In connection with this, the following equalities hold for any Q predicates: $P(Q_1(a)/Q_2(b)) = P(Q_1(a)/Q_3(b))$ no matter how different objects a and b are as regards their simple properties; for instance:

$Q_1(x) = P_1(x) \wedge P_2(x) \wedge P_3(x) \wedge P_4(x)$, $Q_2(x) = P_1(x) \wedge P_2(x) \wedge P_3(x) \wedge \sim P_4(x)$, while $Q_3(x) = P_1(x) \wedge \sim P_2(x) \wedge \sim P_3(x) \wedge \sim P_4(x)$. Hence the premise $E_1 = P_1(a) \wedge P_2(a) \wedge P_3(a) \wedge P_4(a) \wedge P_1(b) \wedge P_2(b) \wedge P_3(b)$ gives the same probability of the conclusion as the premise $E_2 = P_1(a) \wedge P_2(a) \wedge P_3(a) \wedge P_4(a) \wedge P_1(b) \wedge \sim P_2(b) \wedge \sim P_3(b)$, though in the premise E_1 the objects a and b are more similar to each other than in the premise E_2.

Both Hesse and Hintikka announced an attempt at developing a system in which there would be no such symmetry of Q predicates. Hintikka suggested that it might be possible to assume a certain order in the set of simple predicates and thus have the asymmetry of Q predicates necessary for probability functions to show the dependencies from differences and similarities between the objects described in the premises.

A proper modification of the system would probably allow eliminating these drawbacks (from the point of view of intuitivity) which have just been discussed. Much more difficult is the problem of generalization of these systems to more complex languages.

In [31] Hintikka presented a form of description of the universe to which all statements of the language of first order logic, i.e. the language which includes predicates with any number n of arguments, can be reduced.

However, there is no effective method which would make possible the calculation for a given language of a number of those descriptions which would be compatible. The lack of this method results from the undecidability of the first order logic. Hintikka's work [35] includes also interesting considerations concerning the possibility of definition of logical probability when the number of the so-called layers of quantifiers is reduced which allows the calculation of the number of consistent descriptions. This work also contains an interesting suggestion connected with distinguishing between the so-called obvious contradictions (surface ones, like, for instance, in the sentence $p \wedge \sim p$) and non-obvious contradictions (deep ones) which can be very difficult to find. Well, Hintikka suggests that such a probability function should be constructed which would have null values for obviously contradictory sentences. Although such a function would not satisfy the axioms of probability calculus because it would not have null-values for non-obviously contradictory sentences, according to Hintikka it could constitute the base for inductive logic in the situation in which we do not know all logical tautologies, but only the obvious ones.

Research in the construction of logical probability using Carnap's and Hintikka's methods has been conducted by numerous logicians, especially by the so-called Finnish school. Abundant literature concerning mostly the development of this method for languages which are in many respects similar to the languages of empirical theories is published.

In conclusion, I can state that Carnap's and Hintikka's systems doubtless have numerous drawbacks in common. The most significant one is that they lack some non-arbitrary criterion of choice of confirmation function from among an infinite number of functions which — according to the accepted definitions — are treated as suitable for this role. These definitions determine so large a class of such functions that it includes both those functions which represent extreme 'methodological pessimism' (rejection of induction) and those which represent extreme 'optimism' (too much hastiness in accepting inductive conclusions).

Common disadvantages of these functions are also (so far) their limitation to very simple languages, several of their properties which are non-intuitive from the point of view of their applications to certain forms of inductive inference, and the dependence of the values of confirmation function upon the number of predicates in the language. This dependence was described in the previous section (Section 6.1) on the examples concerning Carnapian function C^*, but it occurs in all of Carnap's and Hintikka's functions.

Adherents of Carnap's and Hintikka's methods do not consider this dependence as a serious drawback. They think that the choice of a language need not be arbitrary, because there may exist certain pragmatic reasons for the choice of this and not another language in specific scientific contexts.

7

Henry Kyburg's epistemological conception of probability

The difficulties in finding some natural measure for the relations of partial inference induce many logicians to think that the values of logical probability should be based on knowledge of frequential probability. One of the adherents of this view in Poland was Kazimierz Ajdukiewicz. In his *Pragmatic Logic* [4] he defines the logical probability of a statement p relative to a statement g as 'the highest degree of the certainty of acceptance of the statement p to which we are entitled by a fully certain and valid acceptance of the statement g'. Such a concept of probability does not indicate any method of computing this probability. According to Ajdukiewicz, however, an assumption can be made that the statistical concept of probability is co-extensional with the logical concept of probability, at least with reference to those statements for which statistical interpretation of their probability exists. And so, for instance, if a sentence p states about an object that it is an element of a set A, and if a statement q states that that object is an element of a set B, then we can accept that the logical probability $P_L(p/q)$ which equals the statistical probability $P_S(A/B)$.

Identification of the values of logical and statistical probability imposes an empirical character on logical probability: in interpretation values must be estimated on the basis of the observed frequencies, i.e. by way of induction, and therefore considering them as the base for induction leads to a vicious circle. I have discussed this in Chapter 4.

Henry Kyburg's conception described in his book *Probability and the Logic of Rational Belief* of 1961 [45] is a very ingenious way out of this situation. His definition of probability is not a relation between two arbitrary sentences; it is a relation between a statement and actual knowledge. For this reason, Kyburg has called his interpretation of probability 'epistemological'. For Kyburg, the value of the logical probability of a statement depends upon knowledge about statistical probabilities, but is not identified with the value of statistical probability.

Kyburg defines logical probability with the help of the notion of randomness to which he gives a special sense and it is relativized to knowledge. In the definition of randomness, Kyburg uses the concept of probability in its frequential sense: namely, he refers to those statements about such probabilities, which belong to knowledge. Kyburg, however, realizes the fact that

HENRY KYBURG'S EPISTEMOLOGICAL CONCEPTION OF PROBABILITY

knowledge about frequential probabilities is seldom precise, usually only the fact is known that probabilities of certain events are included in some numerical intervals. In connection with this Kyburg, expresses the opinion that these intervals can be treated as probability values, and he uses the formula $P(A/B) = (p;q)$, where $p \leq q$ in the sense of a statement that the value of $P(A/B)$ is an interval of numbers between p and q. The statement $P(A/B) = (p;q)$ can be defined as a sentence which states that $P(A/B)$ is equal to a certain number r which satisfies the condition: $p \leq r \leq q$. Therefore, we can see that Kyburg defines randomness (and, thence, logical probability) with the help of knowledge about statistical probability which need not be precise. In the extreme case, when such knowledge is precise, we have $P(A/B) = (p;p) = p$.

For probabilities whose values are numerical intervals, the following obvious dependence occurs: if the interval $(p;q)$ is included in the interval $(p';q')$, then the statement $P(A/B) = (p';q')$ follows from the statement $P(A/B) = (p;q)$ because each number which belongs to the interval $(p;q)$ belongs also to the interval $(p';q')$. Therefore, if a statistical sentence of the form $P(A/B) = (p;q)$ is included in the body of knowledge, an infinite number of weaker statements, i.e. those statements which indicate a broader interval, will also belong to the body of knowledge. For instance, if we know that $P(A/B) = (0.4; 0.6)$, we also know that $P(A/B) = (0.3; 0.7)$.

In connection with this Kyburg must distinguish the strongest statements determining the value of $P(A/B)$ among the sentences which belong to the body of knowledge. It will doubtless be the statement $P(A/B) = (p;q)$ which satisfies the condition: the body of knowledge does not include any statement $P(A/B) = (p';p')$ such that the interval $(p';q')$ is smaller than $(p;q)$.

To avoid confusion I shall use in this chapter the symbol P_L for logical probability and P_S for frequential probability. Kyburg defines randomness as a 4-element relation which occurs between an object a, two sets A and B and the body of knowledge K. The definition is as follows:

(DL) Object a is a random element of the set A relative to its inclusion in the set B with the assumption of the body of knowledge K if and only if the body of knowledge K satisfies the following conditions:

(1) The statement $a \in A$ (i.e. the statement that a is an element of the set A) belongs to the body of knowledge K

(2) The sentence $P_S(B/A) = (p;q)$ belongs to the body of knowledge K

(3) A and B are rational sets

(4) If, for a rational set C, the statements '$a \in C$' and '$P_S(B/C) = (p';q')$' belong to K, and if '$P_S(B/A) = (p;q)$' is the strongest statistical statement of the body of knowledge K which determines the value of $P_S(B/A)$, then at least one of the two possibili-

ties holds: either (a) the statement '*A* is included in *C*' belongs to the body of knowledge *K*, or (b) the interval $(p;q)$ is included in the interval $(p';q')$.

This definition is rather complicated. First, the concept 'rational set' requires explanation. Kyburg does not define this concept; he only explains what sets are to be regarded as non-rational. He wants to exclude such sets which 'are not suitable' as classes of reference for probability, because of certain paradoxes. Kyburg describes two examples.

Let *M* be a set of possible tosses of a coin, and O, a set of those tosses in which the result is tails; let *a* be an arbitrary toss of a coin (whose result is not known), and {*a*}, the set whose only element is *a*. If we now make a sum of sets $MO + \{a\}$, the probability of tails in this set will equal 1. However, although *a* is an element of this set, we have no reason to expect that the results of the toss *a* is tails. The second example is connected with a certain paradox which was discussed by N. Goodman [20]. Let *G* designate the set of all objects which are green before the year 2000 or blue after 2000. The set includes all emeralds which have been observed up to now, because they are green. Goodman writes that on the basis of the premise that all emeralds observed up to now have the property *G*, we cannot draw the conclusion that an emerald observed after the year 2000 will also have the property *G*. The same refers to statistical expectations: for instance, on the basis of the observation that 80% of birds of a certain species had the property *G* we cannot believe that the probability of observation of a bird of this species with the property *G* after year 2000 equals 0.8. Goodman called properties (sets) of this kind 'inprojectible' i.e. impossible to foresee.

Kyburg states that relative frequencies of $P_S(B/A)$ which refer to such inprojectible sets *A* and *B* cannot be the basis for the definition of randomness; hence the condition concerning 'rationality' of sets in the definition of randomness. Kyburg ascertains that the formulation of a general definition of rational set is very difficult. Several attempts at defining these inprojectible predicates have been made in the literature but the results are not satisfactory. Kyburg thinks, however, that in every particular case, a sufficient list of simple predicates for a given branch of science can be made, then their negations and conjunctions can be admitted, but not their alternations — which determine those 'artificial' inprojectible properties, and then we can assume that rational sets are the sets determined by those predicates.

Let is now explain the meaning of the condition (4) in the definition of randomness. Let us assume that *A* is a set of Swedes, while *B* — a set of Prostestants. Suppose that we know that a certain man *a* is a Swede, i.e. $a \in A$, and that relative frequency of Prostestants among the Swedes is in the interval (0.8;0.9), and $P_S(B/A) = (0.8; 0.9)$ is the strongest statistical statement belonging to our body of knowledge which determines the value of $P_S(B/A)$. Further, let us suppose that we know about man *a* that he went on a pilgrimage to Lourdes, and that relative frequency of prostestants among such pilgrims is very small, say, it is in the interval (0; 0.1). If by *C* we designate the set of pilgrims in Lourdes, these sentences, which belong to the body of knowledge will be as follows: $a \in C$; and $P_S(B/C) = (0;0.1)$.

In this situation we cannot state that a is a random element of the set of Swedes with regard to the fact that he belongs to the set of Protestants, because the knowledge that he went on a pilgrimage to Lourdes has an essential influence on the estimation of chance that a belongs to the set of Protestants. If, on the other hand, the set C included A, for instance $C =$ the set of Europeans, then the knowledge that a is an European and that — say $P_S(B/C) = (0.2;0.3)$ would not change a's chances of belonging to the set of Protestants. It would be similar in the case of a set C such that $P_S(B/C) = (0.75; 0.95)$. In both these cases we can say that the knowledge that a belongs to C is weaker than the knowledge that a belongs to A, relative to the estimation of a's chances of belonging to the set B.

To put it in other words, the problem is as follows: if, about the object a, we do not know anything except that a belongs to A, then the knowledge of $P_S(B/A)$ is the only base for estimation of a's chances of belonging to B. Then, obviously, a is a random element of A relative to B; but this lack of knowledge is not necessary to recognize a as a random element of A, to do this, it is enough when our knowledge does not include anything that might suggest that $P_S(B/A)$ is not a good basis for estimation of a's chances of belonging to B. This is to be ensured by the 4th condition of the definition of randomness; it is considered to be a specification of the condition that a's belonging to A is the only important thing which we know about the object a — it is important for the conclusion that a belongs to B.

The definition of logical probability of the sentence Z is as follows:

(DP$_L$) $P_L(Z) = (p;q)$ relative to the body of knowledge K — if and only if the body of knowledge K satisfies the following conditions:

(1) there exist such terms 'a', 'A' and 'B' such that a is a random element of A relative to B and the body of knowledge K
(2) K includes the sentence '$P_S(B/A) = (p;q)$' and does not include any stronger statistical statements which estimates $P_S(B/A)$
(3) the statement '$Z \leftrightarrow a \in B$ 'belongs to the body of knowledge K
(4) for any three terms 'a', 'A' and 'B': if the statement '$Z \leftrightarrow a' \in B'$' 'belongs to K and a' is a random element of A' relative to B' and K — then the statement '$P_S(B'/A') = (p;q)$' also belongs to K.

The sense of logical probability is mostly characterized by the first three conditions; condition (4) only ensures the equality of probabilities of synonymous statements. Condition (2) requires that the logical probability should be estimated on the basis of the statistical statement estimating the value of $P_S(B/A)$ which satisfies condition (1) for A and B: this is the strongest of the sentences included in K. According to condition (3), $P_L(Z)$ is determined only for such sentences Z which, on the basis of knowledge, are synonymous to a sentence of the form: $a \in B$. If the knowledge were expressed in a very simple language, condition (3) would constitute a very significant restriction of the applicability of (DP$_L$). Kyburg, however — contrary to Carnap and Hintikka — does not impose any restrictions on the language in which knowledge is expressed. He assumes that knowledge is such as we actually have it, so, in particular, that it includes all logic, set theory and mathematics in which languages are very complex as regards their logical structure. And so, in a sufficiently compound language, for instance, the universal sentence which states that each raven is black can be synonymous with the statement about a set of ravens that each of its elements is a black bird — and this is a sentence whose form is $a \in B$ and states that a set of ravens a is an element of the class of black birds (i.e., a class of sets B such that the element of this class is a sub-set of the set of black birds).

Kyburg interprets the logical probability of the statement that each raven is black as follows. The species of ravens can be a random element of a set of species A, e.g. of northern birds, or a differently distinguished set of species, relative to uniformity of their colour. If according to our knowledge, the relative frequency of species which are homogeneous as regards their colour in this set of species is very high, then — according to the definition — the logical probability of the statement that ravens are uniform as regards their colour is appropriately high; and as each observed raven is black, the logical probability of the statement that each raven is black is high.

The fact should be stressed, that logical probability as defined by Kyblurg is not an empirical concept, although the definition refers to statements about frequential probability and this is of empirical character. The point is that Kyburg does not identify the value of logical probability with actual values of frequential probability, but only with those values of this probability which are estimated according to the knowledge to which logical probability is relativized. If the statement $P_S(B/A) = (p;q)$ is included in the body of knowledge K and a is a random element of A relative to B and K, then the logical probability of the statement $a \in B$ relative to this body of knowledge equals $(p;q)$, no matter whether the statement $P_S(B/A) = (p;q)$ is true or not. If the results of new experiments induce us to change the estimation of $P_s(B/A)$, the logical probability of the statements $a \in B$ relative to K will not be changed, but the body of knowledge K will. The probability $P_L(a \in B)$ relative to this changed body of knowledge — say K' — will be different, but it will be probability relativized to another different body of knowledge. Therefore, the value of logical probability of a statement Z relative to the body of knowledge K is dependent only upon the relation between the structure of the statement Z and the structure of sentences included in the body of knowledge K. This value does not depend upon what reality is like, but upon what the knowledge about this reality is. To estimate the value of logical probability of the statement Z, only a semantical analysis of the statement Z and body of knowledge is required.

Therefore, we could say that Kyburg's logical probability is, through the body of knowledge, related to empirical probability, and this relation causes the values of this probability not to be arbitrary as in the systems of Carnap or Hintikka. At the same time, however, the relativization of this probability to the body of knowledge deprives it of its empirical character.

It may seem doubtful whether Kyburg's logical probability can be the base for inductive logic if the estimation of its value requires some knowledge about frequential probability, and to acquire such knowledge we need induction. Well, Kyburg thinks that this problem can be solved without getting involved in a vicious circle thanks to the fact that certain theorems concerning frequential probabilities are mathematical and not empirical theorems. This allows us to formulate certain empirical theorems concerning frequential probability on the basis of mathematical theorems. Kyburg describes the following example:

Let us assume that a Martian comes to the Earth and finds a machine which, when a lever is pressed, throws out a white or a black ball. The Martian performs an experiment: he presses the lever 1000 times, and, in effect, he gets 400 black balls and 600 white ones. Let the symbol A designate any ball thrown out by the machine, and the symbol B a white ball. Let us assume that the Martian's mathematical knowledge is similar to ours, so, in particular, he knows the law of large numbers. This allows him to compute the lower limit of the probability that in a 1000-element random sample of the set a, the relative frequency of B is close to its frequency in the whole population A. Such a probability is dependent on the real value of $P_S(B/A)$ which the Martian does not know; it is known, however, that it is at a minimum when $P_S(B/A) = 1/2$. Therefore, the calculation of this probability with this worst assumption gives the lowest limit of probability that the relative frequency of B in the random sample is close to the probability of B in the population. Let us call the sample in which relative frequency of B is in the interval $P_S(B/A) \pm \varepsilon$ a representative sample from the set of results A, and designate the set of all representative samples with R, and the set of all 1000-element random samples from A — with the symbol Z.

Say that the Martian has computed: $P_S(R/Z) = p$ — with the assumption that $P_S(B/A) = 1/2$. Because for $P_S(B/A)$ larger and smaller than $1/2$, the probability $P_S(R/Z)$ will be larger than p (for the same extent of the sample and the same number ε) we can assume that the sentence $P_S(R/Z) = (p;1)$ is included in the Martian's body of knowledge. Let us notice that this sentence is not only an empirical hypothesis, but a consequence of the law of large numbers as well.

Further, Kyburg states that if the Martian has no knowledge about the machine apart from the observed results of the experiment, then, according to his knowledge, the sample a of the achieved results is a random element of Z relative to the representative character of R. If he has no knowledge about the machine apart from the results obtained fom the experiment — Kyburg states — then, in particular, he has no knowledge which would be significant to the conclusion that $a \in R$, apart from the knowledge that $a \in Z$ and $P_S(R/Z) = (p;1)$. Therefore, the logical probability of the statement '$a \in R$', i.e. of the statement that the results of the experiment are representative relative to his body of knowledge is equal to $(p;1)$. The statement '$a \in R$' is equivalent to the statement that $P_S(B/A) = 0.6 \pm \varepsilon$, it is an empirical hypothesis about the frequential probability of white balls thrown out by the machine. Kyburg stresses the fact that the number p, which is the lower limit of $P_S(R/Z)$, can be very high; e.g. for a 1000-element sample and $\varepsilon = 0.03$, this number will be close to 0.9, so the logical probability of the statistical hypothesis $P_S(B/A) = 0.6 \pm 0.03$ relative to the Martian's knowledge will be (0.9; 1).

Thus, logical probabilities of certain empirical, satistical hypotheses can be determined only on the basis of mathematical and observational knowledge by way of deduction. The high probability of the statistical hypothesis $P_S(B/A) = 0.6 \pm \varepsilon$, can, in turn, constitute the base for acceptance of this hypothesis by way of induction. Kyburg believes that this kind of simple statistical inference plays a fundamental role in the process of the creation of knowledge; whereas the richer the empirical knowledge, the lesser the use of such induction. According to Kyburg, the enrichment of empirical knowledge is done by addition of empirical statements to the body of knowledge whose logical probability relative to the initial body of knowledge is appropriately high. This, however, is the problem of rules of acceptance by way of induction, which will be discussed in Chapter 10.

As regards the concept of logical probability in Kyburg's system the following remarks should be made. Kyburg's conception reconciles the intuitions about logical probability as the base for induction with the views of those who believe that only frequential probability can constitute a non-arbitrary basis for induction: it does this in an ingenious way. The 'epistemological' conception of probability developed by Kyburg defines probability in such a way that it can be called logical probability in the sense to which the adherents of logical probability attached great importance: $P_L(Z)$ relative to K is the relation between the statement Z and the statements included in K, which depends only on the logical structures of the sentence Z and those in K. At the same time, Kyburg avoids the arbitrariness which is inevitable in the conceptions of Carnap and Hintikka: for Kyburg the values of logical probability are determined by knowledge the appropriate values of frequential probability. Arbitrariness is here reduced only to the postulate that the object a should be regarded as a random element of A relative to B and, therefore $P_L(a \in B)$ should be estimated on the basis of $P(B/A)$, when the body of knowledge does not force another way of estimating $P_L(a \in B)$.

In favour of Carnap's and Hintikka's conceptions we can say that they allow us to estimate the numerical value of probability of every statement; the measure of the degree of confirmation is always precise in those theories. Kyburg's conception does not always allow such a possibility. His logical probability is a function whose values are not numbers but numerical intervals. $P_L(Z)$ can have a numerical value only in the case when $P_L(Z) = (p;p) = p$ which is possible only if a precise statistical hypothesis is included in the body of knowledge. In connection with this, the values of $P_L(Z)$ satisfy the axioms of probability calculus only in such special cases. Strictly speaking, Kyburg's logical probability is not probability, although it is closely connected with probability. This, however, allows Kyburg to avoid the arbitrariness of the a priori probability. Let us assume that we do not know anything about an object a, save the information that it is an element of the set A, and we do not have any experiments to use in estimating

$P_S(B/A)$. In this situation, the strongest statistical sentence which belongs to our body of knowledge and which refers to the sets A and B, is simply a tautology: $P_S(B/A) = (0;1)$. Therefore, the probability relative to this body of knowledge will be $P_L(a \in B) = (0;1)$. So, as can be seen, the a priori probabilities are completely indefinite.

Generally speaking, Kyburg's conception — though it is very complicated — obviously has an advantage of being natural in comparison with the conceptions of Carnap and Hintikka. It also seems to be very close to actual practice of inductive inferences. Some difficulties connected with the conception of acceptance of sentences, which is based on it, will be discussed in Chapter 10.1.

8

The subjective interpretation of probability

In this interpretation the probability of a statement is understood as the measure of the degree of conviction about its truth, and, in connection with this, it is relativized to a person X who has this conviction. A theory of probability understood in this way was first formulated by F. Ramsey in 1926 [64]; it was further developed mostly by B. de Finetti, 1937 [17], L. Savage, 1954 [69] and R. Jeffrey, 1965 [39]. This theory is often called personalism or subjectivism. Convictions are understood here in a behaviouristic way, namely, as definite behaviour in the situations of taking a decision and particulary in the situations of making bets. An experiment which consists in making bets concerning the occurrence of some uncertain event can decide about which convictions are held by the person who makes these bets.

Suppose, for instance, that the person X bets the person Y that one throw of the die will give six, and is ready to make this bet with the odds 1:5, but not more; this means: if Y bets \$10, X is ready to bet \$2 at most. This being so, if the result is not a six, X will lose \$2, but if the result is a six, he will win \$10. Personalism interprets this behaviour of X as the expression of his belief about throwing out a six in the degree 1/6. Generally speaking: if s_y designates the stake of the person Y, while s_x — the minimum stake of X (when Y stakes s_y), then the measure of X's degree of belief is the proportion $s_x/(s_x+s_y)$. The usefulness of the stakes is assumed to be proportional to their value.

In this way the bets determine the so-called function of belief of the person X: the arguments of this function are sentences, say, of a language J and its values are the degrees of belief of X which are measured by the above-described proportion of stakes in the bets concerning these sentences.

Subjective probability, however, is not totally indentified with the function of the actual beliefs of a person X, but only with this function of beliefs which is called 'coherent' by the personalists. If, for instance, somebody is convinced that the event A will occur to the degree 3/5 and that the event A will not occur to the degree 4/5, he will bet that A will occur with odds of 3 to 2 and that A will not occur with odds of 4 to 1. If A occurs, in the first bet X will win, say, \$2, but in the second bet he will lose \$4, so, eventually he will lose \$2; if A does not occur, in the first bet X will lose \$3, and in the second bet he will win $1, so, eventually he will also lose $2. Therefore, if he had such function of belief, he would have to lose, no matter what would happen.

The function of belief which causes negative (debit) balance in the set of bets, no matter what state of affairs occurs, is called an incoherent function. Ramsey and de Finetti have proved the theorem that to make the function of belief coherent, i.e. to make it so that it does not cause negative balance in the set of bets, it is necessary and sufficient for this function to satisfy the axioms of probability calculus. In the above-cited example, the function of belief of X does not satisfy the axioms, because the values of this fucntion for the sentence 'A will occcur' and its negation' A will not occur' — which equal 3/5 and 4/5 — do not add up to make one.

The personalists think the person whose degrees of belief violate the theorems of probability calculus, is in a situation similar to that of a person whose beliefs are logically inconsistent (i.e. the person who is convinced that A will occur and will not occur at the same time). The personalists often express the opinion that satisfaction of the probability axioms of the calculus is the only condition which logic can impose on the function of uncertain beliefs: if somebody's beliefs are incoherent, he should 'somehow' make them coherent so that the axioms could be satisfied. Logic, however, cannot enjoin him to do anything else; it cannot tell him whether he should reduce the degree of belief that A will occur to 1/5, or reduce the degree of conviction that A will not occur to 2/5, or change these degrees in some other way. In particular Ramsey, while criticizing Keynes's conception of probability, strongly opposed his thesis that the principle of indifference could be a principle of logic. A man who possesses no knowledge concerning the question of whether A will occur or not, in his opinion, cannot be forced by logic to accept the belief that A will occur, in the degree 1/2. He can have any beliefs, if only they are coherent. According to the personalists, logics cannot determine a priori beliefs in reference to any sentences, except for the logically true or logically false statements.

This argument of Ramsey is very difficult to disprove; in Chapter 6 we saw that the attempts at estimating of a priori logical probability are likely to be too arbitrary. This argument, however, can easily be turned against personalism. Although personalism does not impose any particular numbers as degrees of a priori beliefs on anybody, it makes one have some a priori beliefs, and, moreover, these beliefs must be precisely determined by numbers. If the function of belief is to satisfy the axioms, it must be determined. Still, it would be difficult to maintain that a man does not know what are the values of his function of beliefs. If he does not know that, it means that his beliefs are not definite. As regards probability, in the frequential sense, we can say that its certain values are definite, but not known, because this probability is objective in its meaning. As regards subjective probability, such a statement would be nonsense, so the personalists do not say anything like this. The logic of coherence which they impose on the function of X's belief simply requires that X should estimate the exact values of this function in any way (as long as it is coherent).

For this reason, but also for some other reasons, numerous logicians consider that the belief functions should not be probabilities. For instance, I. Levi in [50] expresses the view that, while the degrees of rational risk should satisfy the axioms of probability calculus, the probabilistic interpretation of the degrees of belief gives non-intuitive results. For instance, if one has no reason to be convinced that the event A will occur rather than not, then the right measure of the degree of belief both about the occurrence and non-occurrence of A should have null value. (p. 123). Besides, according to Levi, the fact that degrees of belief should satisfy the following postulate (see [50], p. 124), speaks against probabilistic interpretation of convictions.

If the degree of belief concerning the hypothesis H equals p, and the degree of belief concerning hypothesis G equals q, and $q \leq p$, then the degree of belief about the conjunction H and G should equal q. Probability does not satisfy this postulate, because, except special cases, probability of a conjunction is smaller than the probabilities of each of its elements. The same view concerning beliefs is also discussed by K. Popper (see [94], the discussion about Carnap's lecture).

Personalists are often taunted for attributing Macchiavellism to nature. H. Putnam in [63] writes that the personalists' thesis that the rationality of degrees of belief requires satisfying the axioms of probability calculus, is based on the assumption that if our degrees of belief are not probabilistic, the evil forces of nature will involve us in the unfavourable system of bets. If we reject this irrational assumption, writes the author, the personalists' thesis will lose its basis.

H. Kyburg in [45] stresses the fact that the behaviouristic interpretation of belief fails in many cases. For instance the bet about truth of a theory is nonsense, because it cannot be decided. This concerns universal statements as well.

Certain arguments which are set forth against the probabilistic interpretation of beliefs show that different, sometimes contradictory, intuitions are connected both with the psychological concept of degree of belief, and with the normative concept of degree of rational belief. A good example of the discrepancies between these intuitions are the different views about the dependence of the belief about the truth of a conjunction from the belief about the truth of its elements. The above-cited postulate of Levi is probably based on the transfer of certain intuitions connected with the concept of acceptance of the concept of belief. As regards belief it is easy to give examples in which this postulate is clearly inadequate. Suppose, that a person X has certain reasons for being convinced that A will occur, but is not quite sure that A will actually occur. Rationality requires that X should have some positive belief that A will not occur — probably in a lesser degree than the belief that A will occur. However, the same degree of belief that a conjunction will be true, i.e. that A will occur and will not occur at the same time, would be clearly irrational: X should be quite sure that this conjunction is false, because it is logically false. As can be seen, then Levi's postulate fails in regard to uncertain beliefs.

On the other hand, the objections concerning the behaviouristic interpretation of beliefs, i.e. the identification of the degree of belief of a person X with the risk which X is ready to incur making a bet or understanding some other action connected with a risk of material loss, seem justified. Readiness to take a risk undoubtedly depends upon many factors, like, for instance, X's financial situation or his pyschic traits, and not only upon the beliefs about the chances of occurrence of certain events. Probabilistic interpretation of the degrees of belief, however, does not seem to be of necessity connected with their behaviouristic interpretation. Although Putnam is right when he states that the postulate of satisfying the axioms of probability calculus loses its justifying character in the form of the above-cited theorem of Ramsey and de Finetti, but relinquishment of such a justification does not need to ruin the applicability of the theory.

The objection concerning the postulate of exact numerical measure of the degrees of belief, in fact, is not convincing either. It is commonly believed that the assumption that the beliefs of a rational man should be so clear that it should be possible to define them in numbers, is not realistic. Although this statement is doubtless right, it cannot disqualify a theory because such an assumption can be treated as an idealization.

On the other hand, the fact that this assumption concerns — among others — the degrees of a priori beliefs, causes this assumption to become non-intuitive. The problem of the a priori beliefs is probably the most serious difficulty in the theory of subjective probability, just like in the theory of logical probability. In Chapter 7 we saw that Kyburg's conception avoids this difficulty, it does so, however, at the cost of renouncement of satisfying of axioms of probability calculus. The problem of a priori probabilities will be discussed later.

The theory of subjective probability has become very popular since the times of Savage who, in his book *The Foundations of Statistics* [69] presented a conception of its application in the theory of statistical inference. The attractiveness of this application consists of the fact that subjective interpretation of probability opens up the possibility of using of Bayes' theorem (see (T.2) in Chapter 2) to compute the probabilities of hypotheses relative to the definite results of experiments. It often happens in statistics that the conditional probabilities of various results of an experiment relative to various statistical hypotheses are estimated (for instance the probability of getting a series of five tails in five tosses of a coin relative to the hypothesis that the probability of getting the tails in one toss is 1/2 and the results of successive tosses are independent — is $(1/2)^5$). On the other hand, the absolute probabilities are not only unknown, but usually they have no sense in face of the frequential interpretation of probability. This being so, the frequential interpretation of probability does not create, or greatly restricts the possibility of using Bayes' theorem for computing of conditional probabilities of hypotheses relative to definite experimental results.

On the other hand, in the subjective interpretation of probability, this concept, has its sense in reference to all statement which makes it possible to use Bayes's theorem for the above-mentioned aims. Thanks to this, the evaluation of statistical induction can be based on the value of the conditional probability of a hypothesis relative to the experimental results.

The main objection raised against this conception, and against the idea of basing inductive logic on subjective probability in general, is that subjective probabilities a priori are arbitrary, so they can be different for different people. The personalist's answer to this is that the values of conditional probabilities are, in fact, fairly independent of the values of a priori probabilities, in face of which the arbitrariness of the latter is not so significant as to disqualify the theory. Besides, they think that the process of learning on the basis of experiment leads to conformity of beliefs of different people, although their beliefs before the experiment might have been inconsistent.

The way of explaining the change of beliefs and their adjustment also raises several objections.

According to the view which is quite common among the personalists, changes of beliefs in time are made according to a scheme called 'conditionalysing'. The postulate of satisfaction of the axioms of probability calculus imposed on the function of beliefs of X obviously cannot concern X's beliefs at various different periods of time because this would assume unalterability of X's beliefs. Let us designate the function of X's beliefs at time t with the symbol P_{x_t}.

Assume, that the person X in the period of time t has the beliefs $P_{x_t}(H \wedge E) = p$ and $P_{x_t}(E) = q$, and $0 < q < 1$; this being so, according to the definition of conditional probability, X has a 'conditional belief' $P_{x_t}(H/E) = p/q$. Assume further, that in a later period of time X states with certainty (for instance in effect of observation) that E is true. Using the symbol P_{xE} to designate the function of X's beliefs after the discovery that E, we obtain: $P_{XE}(E) = 1$. The personalists think that the function of beliefs P_{XE} for the hypothesis H has the value:

$$P_{XE}(H) = P_{X_t}(H/E) \quad ,$$

which means that the (absolute) degree of belief about the hypothesis H after the observation of E is the same as the conditional degree of belief about H relative to E before this observation.

Such a scheme of the change of beliefs is called the conditionalysing (or Bayes' model) of change of beliefs. It is called Bayes's because the personalists base it on Bayes's theorem, according to which the following equality:

$$P(H/E) = \frac{P(H)P(E/H)}{P(E)}$$

is satisfied.

And so, if $P(E) = 1$, then $P(E/H) = 1$, and then we get the equality $P(H/E) = P(H)$.

Bayes' theorem, however, does not justify the equality $P_{X_t}(H/E) =$

$P_{XE}(H)$, because P_{XE} is a different function than P_{X_t}. Each of these functions can satisfy the axioms, but from this it does not follow that this kind of relation exists between the values of P_{XE} and P_{X_t}. The relation: if $P_{XE}(E) = 1$, then $P_{XE}(H/E) = P_{XE}(H)$, follows from Bayes' theorem, but the equality $P_{XE}(H/E) = P_{X_t}(H/E)$ does not, and, therefore, the equality $P_{XE}(H) = P_{X_t}(H/E)$ does not follow from it either. Many logicians — for instance Suppes, Levi, Kyburg and Hacking — express the opinion that the thesis about the change of beliefs by conditionalysing is not justified on the basis of the theory of subjective probability.

Hacking in [22] calls the scheme of change of beliefs by conditionalysing, a 'dynamic assumption of personalism', and the points out the fact that personalism cannot defend this assumption in the way in which it defends the assumption about satisfying the axioms using the function P_{X_t}, which Hacking calls 'a static assumption of personalism'. As I have already said, satisfaction of the axioms by P_{X_t} is a necessary condition for a situation in which function P_{X_t} does not expose X to the negative (debit) balance in a set of bets.

Hacking demonstrates that violation of the dynamic assumption does not expose X to negative balance. Let us assume — writes Hacking — that in the period of time t, X has beliefs $P_{X_t}(H \wedge E) = p$, $P_{X_t}(\sim H \wedge E) = q$, $P_{X_t}(H \wedge \sim E) = r$ and $P_{X_t}(\sim H \wedge \sim E) = 1 - p - q - r$, while $p + q < 1$. Hence, $P_{X_t}(H/E) = p/(p+q)$. Then X learns that E and changes his beliefs in the following way: $P_{XE}(E) = 1$, $P_{XE}(H) = P_{XE}(H/E) = p + s/p + q + s$, where $s > 0$. In this way, his change of beliefs does not satisfy the dynamic assumption, because $P_{X_E}(H) \neq P_{X_t}(H/E)$. In spite of this, the new function of X's belief can also be coherent: if X, after getting the information that E, cancels all his bets and makes new bets according to the new function of beliefs P_{XE}, he will not be exposed to a certain loss.

It can be seen from this example that X can change his views violating the dynamic assumption and he can have a coherent function of belief again, if only he appropriately changes the conditional beliefs $P_{X_t}(H/E)$.

Hacking suggests that in the personalists argument, there is a silent assumption that $P_{X_t}(H/E)$ represents the degree of X's belief about the truth of H after getting the information that E is true. However — writes Hacking — conditional probability does not represent anything of this kind: it is simply the quotient:

$$P_{X_t}(H \wedge E)/P_{X_t}(E)$$

From the above considerations, we can see that the dynamic assumption of personalism is simply the assumption about the unalterability of conditional beliefs in time: $P_{X_t}(H/E) = P_{XE}(H/E)$. It can also be seen that this assumption is completely independent of the static assumption.

On the basis of the idea that the satisfaction of the probability axioms is the only postulate imposed by logic on the function of beliefs P_{X_t}, it is said that the dynamic assumption is impossible to maintain. The critics of personalism believe that this is a deviation from the fundamental idea of personalism, and a step towards some conception of logical probability. And so, for instance, H. Kyburg in [47] expresses an opinion that although Carnap has a right to say that belief functions should be changed by conditionalysing, a 'true' subjectivist can, at most, say that if one does not want to change the conditional beliefs, he should change his beliefs by conditionalysing.

Here I would like to describe Carnap's view on this problem. In [11] Carnap distinguishes the function of actual belief from the function of rational belief. The former function is of empirical and non-normative character and can be determined by way of experiments (e.g. bets). The latter — which is called by Carnap 'credance function' and designated by the symbol C_r — should satisfy certain norms, in particular the axioms of probability calculus, but also certain additional postulates imposed by the concept (or an ideal) of rationality of belief. Among this kind of postulate, Carnap includes the postulate of the change of beliefs by conditionalysing, which he expresses in the following way.

If in the period of time between t_n and t_{n+1} X received the observation data E and nothing more, then the transition of the function C_{r_n} into $C_{r_{n+1}}$ should be determined only by E, this means:

$$C_{r_{n+1}}(H) = C_{r_n}(H/E)$$

While for Carnap conditionalysing clearly has the character of the norm of rationality, in the personalism theory the status of the thesis of conditionalysing is vague. In the works written by personalists, no clear formulation of this status can be found. Personalism is considered by its representatives to be a theory of rational beliefs, i.e. a normative theory. Therefore, the interpretation of the thesis concerning conditionalysing as an empirical thesis which refers to the psychological mechanism of the change of beliefs seems to be inconsistent with the theory of personalism. Anyway, under this interpretation this thesis would be obviously false. On the other hand, the interpretation of this thesis as a postulate imposed on the rational change of beliefs is incompatible with the explicitly expressed opinion that the axioms of probability are the only postulate of rationality (as this thesis does not follow from the axioms).

The only consistent interpretation of the thesis about conditionalysing on the basis of personalism was developed by R. Jeffrey in [40]. Jeffrey introduces the restriction of this thesis to certain situations which he defines in such a way that the thesis of conditionalysing appears to be a consequence of this definition. Namely, Jeffrey introduces the concept of the so-called observational base as a set of sentences which satisfy several postulates, among others the following one:

(B) For any statement H and any statement belonging to the base E, the conditional beliefs $P_{X_t}(H/E)$ do not change in effect of observation of E.

It is obvious that for so-understood observational statements E the following inequality:

$$P_{X_t}(H) = P_{X_t}(H/E), \quad \text{when } P_{XE}(E) = 1 \text{ holds,}$$

because $P_{X_t}(H/E) = P_{XE}(H/E)$ on the strength of the postulate (B), and, on the strength of Bayes' theorem, $P_{XE}(H/E) = P_{XE}(H)$ when $P_{XE}(E) = 1$.

In the same work Jeffrey generalizes the scheme of conditionalysing for those cases when the result of the experiment does not give absolute certainty for the truth of any statement included in the observational base. The description of this scheme requires mentioning of two postulates imposed on the base:

(1) the statements $E_1, \ldots, E_n$ which constitute the base, are pair-wise disjoint, and their alternation is a statement which X accepts with certainly at the time t which precedes the observation (these statements can, e.g. describe various possible results of certain experiment).
(2) the result of observation determines for all E_i the values of the function of belief $P_{XE}(E_i)$ after the observation. The scheme for the change of beliefs is as follows:

$$P_{XE}(H) = \sum_{i=1}^{n} P_{XE}(E_i) P_{X_t}(H/E_i).$$

Assume now that the base is a set of two statements: E and $\sim E$, while $P_{XE}(E) = 0.6$ and $P_{XE}(\sim E) = 0.4$. Then we obtain

$$P_{XE}(H) = 0.6 \cdot P_{X_t}(H/E) + 0.4 \cdot P_{X_t}(H/\sim E).$$

This scheme is a consequence of the theorem of complete probability (see Chapter 2 — (T.6)).

The applicability of this scheme, however, is limited only to those situations in which the statements $E_1, \ldots, E_n$ constitute the observational base in the sense defined by Jeffrey.

It seems that Jeffrey's conception greatly simplifies Bayes' model of change of beliefs because it does not include the statements which cause the change of conditional beliefs to the base on the strength of the postulate (B). It would be much more interesting to find an answer to the question why — or in what situations — the invariability of beliefs should be considered as rational behaviour.

Carnap could answer this question in a simple way: the degree of a rational belief ought to be coherent with logical probability; because $P_L(H/E)$ is objective and depends only on the logical structure of the statements H and E, the degree of rational belief $P_X(H/E)$ cannot change in time. A personalist, however, cannot use such arguments, since he reduces inductive logic to satisfying of the axioms of probability by the function P_{X_t}.

Personalists attach great importance to Bayes' model of change of belief. As a rule, they refer to this model to refute the charge that the axioms of probability alone leave too much freedom to beliefs. It is said, for instance, that personalism supports the errors of optimism and pessimism: for an optimist a desired event has high probability, while an undesirable event — one with low probability — for a pessimist it is just the opposite. The personalists believe that the mechanism of conditionalysing eliminates this freedom. And so, for instance L. Savage in [70] writes, that a coherent person (i.e. a person who has coherent beliefs in the sense of personalism) will cease to believe that 13 is his lucky number if, for some time he does not win in the roulette while stacking his money on the number 13. In numerous texts written by personalists we meet the view that the mechanism of conditionalysing leads to the adjustment of the degrees of belief of various people in effect of the same experiments, and in this way arbitrariness of the initial beliefs is eliminated.

In his book *The Logic Of Decision* [39] Jeffrey describes the following example:

Consider two hypotheses: H_1 says that a coin has tails on both sides, while H_2 says that this coin is correct. Assume that before the experiment the person X has the beliefs $P_{X_t}(H_1) = P_{X_t}(H_2)$ 1/2, and the person Y has the beliefs $P_{Y_t}(H_1) = 1/3$ and $P_{Y_t}(H_2) = 2/3$. Let us say that the experiment consists in tossing up the coin five times, and the result E means getting a series of five tails. Jeffrey writes that the conditional probabilities of these hypotheses are for H_1: $P_{X_t}(H_1/E) = 32/33$ and $P_{Y_t}(H_1/E) = 32/34$, while for H_2: $P_{X_t}(H_2/E) = 1/33$ and $P_{Y_t}(H_2/E) = 2/34$, so they are nearly equal for X and Y. Therefore, after the experiment which consists in getting a series of five tails in five tosses of a coin, both X and Y will have very similar beliefs as regards the truth of each of these hypotheses. Attention should be paid, however, to the fact, that Jeffrey based his estimation of conditional probabilities on the assumption that conditional beliefs about the results E relative to these hypotheses are equal for X and Y and amount to:

$$P_{X_t}(E/H_1) = P_{Y_t}(E/H_1) = 1$$

and

$$P_{X_t}(E/H_2) = P_{Y_t}(E/H_2) = (1/2)^5 = 1/32.$$

For the hypothesis H_1, we can accept that this conditional probability is a consequence of the axioms, because, if the coin, has tails on both sides, the result of a series of five tails cannot be different than E. But it is not so for the hypothesis H_2. Actual conditional beliefs about the result E relative to H_2 can differ greatly. The postulate of coherence of beliefs requires only that the beliefs $P_{X_t}(E \wedge H_2)$ and $P_{Y_t}(E \wedge H_2)$ should be properly adjusted to $P_{X_t}(E/H_2)$ and $P_{Y_t}(E/H_2)$.

We could say that a conditional belief $P(E/H_2)$ other than 1/32 would be unreasonable or irrational, since it is known that for a proper unbiased coin (objective) probability of getting a series of five tosses is 1/32.

Kyburg, for instance, would agree, because his conception of rational beliefs is based on their coherence with logical probability, and for logical probability he postulates coherence with the knowledge about objective (empirical, frequential) probability. The personalists, however, do not accept this postulate at least explicitly — because they do not accept objective probabilities at all.

The assumption of different conditional probabilities for X and Y before the experiment tells us that Jeffrey's example is not convincing. If the conditional probabilities $P_{X_t}(E/H)$ and $P_{y_t}(E/H)$ were different, conditionalysing on the basis of the experiment would not necessarily lead to the adjustment of X's and Y's beliefs about the truth of H. The same objection concerns all the instances of adjustment of beliefs which were described by personalists — they all make these tacit assumptions.

Therefore, we can say that conditionalysing can, in some cases lead to the adjustment of beliefs, but on the basis of personalist assumptions this result is not necessary but incidental.

And so, the view that personalism has assumptions that are too weak to base inductive logic on them, is fully justified.

In connection with this, I wish to refer to Savage, who explains the reason for adoption of such weak assumptions. In his book *The Foundations of Statistics* [69] and in the article 'Implications of Personal Probability for Induction' [70] Savage writes that the idea of personalism does not assume any fundamental objection against logical probability. According to him such probability could be regarded as the only rational subjective probability of all people; it could be treated as an extreme case of subjective probability, which would consist in imposing on beliefs of so strong criteria of rationality that they would not leave room for freedom of individual beliefs. Such probability — says Savage — would be an excellent thing, but the possibility of its construction seems unreal in the light of our present achievements in this field. And so, Savage seems to speak in favour of the theory of personalism not because he considers the assumptions which are stronger than the postulate of coherence, as inadmissible. He rather thinks that in the face of the difficulties in formulation of stronger assumptions, it is necessary to be satisfied with the weak assumptions of personalism.

As regards frequential probability Savage thinks that the main obstacle in applying it in inductive logic is its too limited range of applicability. The contexts important for science in which the probability of hypotheses (e.g. the probabality that France will become a kingdom in the next decade) is spoken about, are in a frequential interpretation deprived of any sense.

9

Popper's anti-inductionism and anti-probabilism

Karl Popper's book *Logik der Forschung* [60], one of the most famous books in world literature in the field of the methodology of empirical sciences was published in 1934 in Vienna. The book owes its fame mostly (though not exclusively) to the idea of the rejection of the inductive model of empirical sciences. In face of enormous difficulties in solving the problem of induction and serious drawbacks of all attempts at the solution to this problem, the opportunity of substituting the inductive model of empirical sciences for the so-called hypothetico-deductive model, must have been extremely attractive. It appeared, however, that this prospect is based on a fundamental misunderstanding concerning the concept of induction, and the long-lasting controversy between the so-called 'inductionists' and 'deductionists' started. This controversy is of very special character: Popper and his adherents fiercely arraign inductionism as a fundamentally false view which is based on groundless dogmas and which presents a completely inadequate picture of empirical sciences. On the other hand, the inductionists do not question the hypothetico-deductive method propagated by Popper, they only express the opinion that induction is the essential element of this method.

Popper's arguments against inductionism usually seem to be aimed at this conception of induction, whose adherents would be hard to find today, namely, the view that induction is the process of getting to hypotheses in the heuristic sense. According to Popper, inductionism gives the following image of scientific method: first, various observations are made, and then universal statements are 'drawn' from the collected results of observation. 'Drawing' is here meant as guided discovery of hypotheses, because Popper criticizes inductionism as a manifestation of psychologism in logic and methodology, and he accuses the inductionists of not distinguishing the problem of the source of knowledge from the problem of testing of knowledge. If there exist any psychological laws of getting to hypotheses — writes Popper — they are descriptive laws and they have nothing to do with methodology. According to Popper, inductionism gives a false picture of research procedure, because, in science, hypotheses precede observations; observations are not collected in a chaotic and random way, but they are planned in the way which is suitable for the testing of particular hypotheses which were formed earlier.

This kind of criticism can be considered as relevant only with reference to some grotesque version of inductionism. It would be difficult to quote an example of a contemporary inductionist who could be accused of psychologism. All known attempts at creating an inductive logic refer to the problem of justification, to the problem of the criteria for correct acceptance of hypotheses, and not to the problem of where the ideas of hypotheses in the mind of a research worker come from.

Another difference, which Popper seems to detect between the inductive method and his hypothetico-deductive method is the fact that the former, according to Popper, tends to verification of hypotheses, while the latter to their falsification. In his opinion, the theory of induction is a theory of the incorporation of new theorems into existing knowledge, while his theory is a theory of selection, and of rejection. The falsification of hypotheses is done by way of deduction from the so-called basal statements; namely, if the truth of a basal statement is ascertained, and this statement appears to be incompatible with the hypothesis or theory, the hypothesis is falsified because it is its negation which logically follows from such a statement. For instance, the hypothesis that each object with the property A has the property B will be falsified by a basal statement saying that in a certain space-time region, there exists an object which has the property A, but does not have the property B.

We will not discuss here the Popperian conception of basal statements. It is enough to explain that they are the statements which state that there exists an object with certain observable properties, or some observable event takes place in a certain space-time region, e.g. the sentence: a black bird is sitting on this tree.

Popper's hypothetico-deductive method does not confine itself to refuting theories by deduction. In his conception, a significant role is played not only by the concept of falsification, but also by the concept of corroboration. The thing is, that to accept a hypothesis or a theory, the fact that it has not been actually falsified (which might happen, e.g. because it was not tested at all) is not so important as the fact that it has not been refuted although 'rigorous' tests aimed at its refutation have been conducted. The degree of confirmation of an hypothesis is to be based, amongst other things, on the degree of severity of the tests which the non-falsified hypothesis underwent. In the supplement to his *Logik der Forschung* [60] and in his other works (e.g. [61]) Popper lists several postulates which should be satisfied by the measure of the degree of confirmation, and several particular suggestions concerning this measure. In [60], p. 331 of the Polish translation Popper states that the result of subtraction

(T) $\qquad P(E/H) - P(E)$

is essential for the measure of the degree of confirmation of the hypothesis H by the premise E. It is simply the measure of severity of the test. A test is good for the hypothesis H if a result of its E has low a priori probability $P(E)$, and high (close or equal to one) conditional probability $P(E/H)$: with the help of (T) Popper defines the measure of the 'elucidating force' of the hypothesis H relative to E in the following way ([60], p. 322 of the Polish translation):

(W) $\quad W(H/E) = \dfrac{P(E/H) - P(E)}{P(E/H) + P(E)}$

Popper regards (W) as a way of normalization of (T) (p. 331). As can be seen, since both these measures are based on the probabilistic dependence of the statements H and E (see chapter 2), they have null value when H and E are probabilistically independent, and positive (or negative) values when H and E show positive (or negative) dependences. With the help of (W) Popper defines the measure of confirmation of H by E as follows:

(C) $\quad C(H/E) = W(H/E)(1 + P(H)P(H/E))$

On p. 322 ([60] — Polish translation) Popper writes that the degree of confirmation is to

> exert influence on whether a hypothesis H should be accepted or chosen even if only temporarily; a high degree of confirmation is to be a characteristic of a 'good' (or 'acceptable') hypothesis, while the lack of confimation is to characterize a 'bad' hypothesis.

In connection with this conception of the degree of confirmation, the inductionists accuse Popper that his anti-inductionism is of a purely verbal character, because, since Popper does not explain the acceptance of hypotheses in science in terms of observation and deduction only, but refers also to confirmation of hypotheses by the results of tests (which these hypotheses do not follow from), then he refers to induction. If confirmation leads to acceptance without a guarantee of truth it has — according to the accepted terminology — the character of inductive inference. Popper admits that the acceptance of hypotheses and theories in the empirical sciences is temporary and revocable in character, but this does not make a difference between his conception and the inductionistic one, either. No inductionist states that the acceptance by way of induction is permanent and definitive.

And so, Popper's conception — despite the declarations of its author — does not avoid the problem of induction. Popper's answer to this objection is very odd. Popper denies that he treats his measure $C(H/E)$ seriously. In the supplement to his *Logik der Forschung* (pp. 344 and 337) he writes, that $C(H/E)$ can be interpreted as

> the degree of confirmation of H — or the degree of rationality of our belief in H in the light of tests — only if E is an account of the results of

genuine attempts at falsification of H and not attempts at verification of H.

Further, Popper writes that 'if E is not an account of the results of genuine attempts at falsification of H, then we simply deceive ourselves thinking that $C(H/E)$ can be interpreted as the degree of confirmation or something like this. According to Popper, the fundamental difference between inductionism and the hypothetico-deductive method is that 'the inductionist desires confirmation of his hypothesis' while Popper's method demands striving to falsify it. In connection with this, Popper states that 'the concept of confirmation of hypotheses cannot be formalized, because the requirement of genuineness cannot be formalized'.

Popper and his adherents seem to attach great importance to the postulate of 'genuine' striving to falsify hypotheses. This postulate, however, is in conflict with Popper's conception of methodology. Popper greatly emphasized the need of clearing methodology of all elements of psychologism and subjectivism. The postulate of genuineness is a postulate which refers to the psychological attitude of the researcher and not the objective qualities of research work. It must be obvious to each reasonable man that even the most genuine efforts at doing something will be worth nothing from the point of view of methodology if those efforts are ineffective.

The postulate of genuineness is an ethical rather than methodological postulate.

We could try to interpret this postulate in such a way as to endow it with a methodological interpretation. For instance, it can be treated as a postulate of subjecting hypotheses to such tests which give a high chance of falsification. If we assume that those experiments for which results that falsify the hypothesis are highly probable, or have a good chance of falsifying the hypothesis, this postulate would require making such experiments.

In this form, the postulate of striving to falsify hypotheses is quite familiar to inductionists. What is more, we can say that in a way it is parallel to that of striving for confirmation in the common interpretation of the degree of confirmation of H by E as the conditional probability $P(H/E)$. In Chapter 3 we saw that the smaller $P(E)$ is (and, hence, the bigger is $P(\sim E)$), the bigger $P(H/E)$ is. Therefore, striving to achieve a high degree of confirmation of H requires striving for such premises E whose a priori probability, or probability relative to some initial body of knowledge, is very small.

The measure of confirmation $C(H/E)$ suggested by Popper demonstrates the 'severity' of the test (considering the chances of falsification of a hypothesis) $P(H/E)$ better than the measure; this problem will be discussed in Chapter 11. It seems, however, that this measure does not satisfy Popper either, if he thinks that its value cannot always be identified with the degree of confirmation of H by E.

Anyway, whatever Popper would require of the confirmation of H by E — no matter whether this condition can be formalized — if he does not require of H that it follows from E, such a confirmation must be of inductive, and not deductive, character.

Popper's second fundamental thesis which became no less famous is the thesis that the acceptance of theorems in the empirical sciences cannot be based on their high probability. Let us use the name 'probabilism' for the view that the higher $P(H/E)$ is, the better justified is the hypothesis H by the premises E. According to Popper, probabilism is connected with the view that the only aim of science is the pursuit of truth: because it is impossible to attain certainty that the hypotheses and theories of empirical sciences are true, their high probability is believed to be the best that can be achieved in the pursuit of truth.

However, the view that the only aim of science is the pursuit of truth is false. In Popper's opinion, the pursuit of truth is an aim of science, but it is not the only one. If it were the only aim, the sciences would have to confine themselves to tautologies, and so this aim could not explain what is really done in science. The theory of science must take into consideration the fact that in science the solutions of definite problems are striven for, and such solutions, as a rule, require theorems with rich information content. Seeking information is parallel with the aspiration to formulate the theorems in as precise a way as possible and to allow explaining a comparatively large number of facts, i.e. the theorems which are to a large extent universal. And so, the smaller is the probability of hypotheses or theories, the larger the extent in which they possess all these qualities. This follows from the formal properties of probability: if the statement p follows the statement q, then $P(p) \geq P(q)$. So, since less general hypotheses follow from the general one, then the more general the hypothesis, the smaller its probability. The same refers to precision: for instance the hypothesis that the eclipse of the sun will take place on a definite day follows from a more precise hypothesis that the eclipse will take place at a definite time of that day. This also concerns information content: the tautologies, whose probability is the highest, do not give any non-trivial information. It is usually accepted that the more logical possibilities the given statement excludes, the larger its information content. In connection with this, the values which are inversely proportional to the probability of p, e.g. $1 - P(p)$ are adopted as the measure of information contained in the statement p.

Popper remarks that all these qualities of hypotheses and theories are usually connected with their high degree of falsifiability which increases with the growth of the set of potential falsifiers of the hypothesis. The set of the potential falsifiers of a hypothesis is the set of basal sentences which are inconsistent with the hypothesis. If we take into consideration two empirical hypotheses H_1 and H_2, such that H_1 follows from H_2, and not the other way round, then each basal statement which is inconsistent with H_1 will also be inconsistent with H_2, but certain statements which are inconsistent with H_2 will be consistent with H_1. Therefore, the set of potential falsifiers will be bigger for the stronger hypothesis which can be either more general or more precise. For instance, the statement that at 12 o'clock on a given day the sun will shine, can falsify the hypothesis that at 1 o'clock of that day the eclipse of the sun will take place, but cannot falsify the less general hypothesis which only states that on that day the sun eclipse will take place between 10 a.m. and 2 p.m. On the other hand, each sentence which falsifies the second hypothesis will also falsify the first one. For tautologies, the set of falsifiers is empty, but it is so not only for tautologies; such a set is empty also for all those statements which have no observational consequences, e.g. for metaphysical statements.

Although Popper's remark that striving for information makes us value the hypotheses with low probability is right, the criticism of probabilism based on it is not as crushing as we might at first expect. One of Popper's critical arguments is based on the suggestion that if someone believes that the higher $P(H/E)$ is, the better justified is the hypothesis H by E, he must also believe that the probability value constitutes the criterion of choice for hypotheses, i.e. that of two different hypotheses which are consistent with experimental results, he should choose the weakest one (since it will be the most probable) and reject all stronger hypotheses. This criterion of choice would certainly lead to rejecting all hypotheses and theories which would go beyond the observed facts. The probabilists, however, neither propagate such a criterion nor are forced into it by the risk of inconsistency, since the problem of choice is different to the problem of justification. There is no inconsistency in the fact that a hypothesis H is accepted although it could be rejected and the acceptance of a weaker one would be sufficient. One can think, for instance, that although this weaker hypothesis is better justified than H, H is justified sufficiently.

Popper is of the opinion that this attitude cannot be explained on the basis of the view that truth is the only aim of science. However, imputation of the view that truth is the only aim of the empirical sciences to probabilists is completely groundless. If one denied the fact that the empirical sciences tend to formulate theorems which exceed the observations, or thought that such theorems are useless in science, one would not deal with the problem of inductive logic at all. The logicians who deal with the problem of induction believe that pursuit of truth is a very important goal of science (though this is not denied by Popper either), and, therefore, they think that the problem of credibility of hypotheses in science is important.

In [24] Carl Hempel writes that three phases in testing of a hypothesis should be distinguished:

(1) making appropriate experiments or observations.
(2) confrontation of the results of observations with the hypothesis.
(3) acceptance or rejection of the hypothesis.

According to Hempel, the logical theory of confirmation concerns the second phase: the confrontation consists in examination of logical relations between the hypothesis and the sentences describing the results of experiments. The first and the third phase are pragmatic in character. In particular, in the third phase we can take into consideration such qualities of hypotheses like simplicity, explanatory value, etc.

Popper seems to show a tendency to overlook the difference between the second and the third phase, or to underestimate the role of the second phase (in Hempel's understanding). He rejects the probabilistic criterion of the degree of confirmation $P(H/E)$, because it does not report on such qualities of hypotheses like simplicity, precision, explanatory value, etc., which are connected with their low probability.

However, some inconsistency is hidden in his definite criticism of probabilism. If he believes that science strives for truth (though not only for truth), and he himself states that this striving for truth implies striving for high probability of hypotheses, he should not say that the probabilistic criterion of the degree of confirmation of hypotheses is essentially inconsistent with the goals of science. He can at most say that the value of $P(H/E)$ itself does not answer the question why these and not other hypotheses are accepted in science or why very strong hypotheses are accepted in science or why very strong hypotheses are accepted if weaker ones are more probable. Going beyond the description of the observed facts involves the risk of falsity. Such risk must be explained: it must be explained by striving for goals other than truth. And so, Popper explains it with the fact that science strives for information — and this thesis of his is right. However, it does not follow from this thesis that the high probability of hypotheses relative to the results of experiments has only a negative value in science. Such a view would be justified only if we assumed the other extreme, namely, that striving for information is the only goal of science. This assumption, however, would be as groundless as the assumption that truth is the only goal of science.

The fact that Popper's criticism in the period after the publication of Carnap's book *Logical Foundations of Probability* was mostly aimed at Carnap's theory, can, to some extent, explain why Popper was so strongly opposed to probabilism. In Chapter 6.11 we saw that in Carnap's theory all non-tautological universal statements have null probabilities (when the universe is infinite). In face of this, the degree of confirmation of H by E measured by $P(H/E)$ is always null for such statements, while the Popperian degree of confirmation $C(H/E)$ need not be null; for those cases when E follows from H we get $P(E/H) = 1$, thence $W = (H/E) = (1 - P(E))/(1 + P(E))$, so if $P(H) = 0$, then $C(H/E) = W(H/E) = (1 - P(E))/(1 + P(E))$. Therefore, if $P(H) = 0$, then the degree of confirmation of H by the consequence E becomes completely independent of $P(H)$. Null values of the degree of confirmation of universal statements did not disturb Carnap because of his anti-theoretical attitude which consisted in this, that he underestimated the cognitive value of theories in empirical sciences. Popper fought against such an attitude, and, as it seems he imputed it mostly to probabilists.

In his discussion with Popper, J. Hintikka stresses the fact that this anti-theoreticism is not connected with all probabilism, but only with a special definition of probability. Hintikka cites arguments which show that certain statements possessing those qualities which Popper regards as important (simplicity, rich information content, falsifiability) can have high a posteriori probability if the probability function is appropriately defined. In [34] Hintikka expresses the view that the measure of simplicity of constituents C_w can be the number w (see Chapter 6.); the smaller is w, the simpler is the constituent C_w. Number w is the number of Q predicates whose non-emptiness is stated by the constituent C_w, the Q predicates designate various kinds of individuals, so we can say that the less various the kinds of individuals appear in the universe, the simpler it is. Let us assume that the sentence S_c (see Chapter 6.2) describes the result of observation of a certain set Z_n, where c is the number of Q predicates ascribed to the n observed objects. The constituents C_w which are consistent with this observational result can have $w = c$ or $w > c$. The constituent C_c is — according to the above-cited criterion of simplicity — the simplest description of the universe which is consistent with the experiment S_c. At the same time, it is a description which expresses the strongest universal statement which is consistent with the experiment S_c: namely, it states that all the predicates which are not represented in Z_n, are empty. This universal statement has the highest degree of falsifiability among all possible universal statements which are consistent with S_c. It also includes the greatest information, because it excludes most logical possibilities. Therefore, we can say that the constituent C_c has, according to Popper's criteria, the highest cognitive value of all constituents C_w consistent with S_c.

And so — as we know from Chapter 6.2 — if the number of observations n is appropriately high, the probability of C_c relative to S is close to one. This shows that the probabilistic criterion of the degree of justification does not exclude the possibility of good justification of those hypotheses which posses the qualities emphasized by Popper. Therefore, this criterion does not necessarily lead to the anti-theoretical vision of empirical sciences if an appropriate probability function is accepted.

The above considerations are aimed at demonstrating that Popper's conception — despite his conviction — is not fundamentally opposite to the conceptions of inductionists. This statement, however, does not mean that Popper's ideas are devoid of novelty. Popper's criteria of valuation of hypotheses in the empirical sciences are very interesting and important, and some of them are quite new in comparison with the criteria which were considered by the inductionists at the time Popper wrote *Logik der Forschung*. A great and long-lasting contribution to the methodology of the empirical sciences by Popper is, first of all, stressing the fact that the various aims which science strives for can be in conflict with one another, that there is a conflict between the pursuit of truth which values those hypotheses whose probability relative to the results of experiments is high, and the obtaining of information which makes one value such qualities of hypotheses which are connected with their small probability, like, e.g. their information content.

The theory of semantical information is now being developed by many logicians (to say the truth, they are mostly inductionists). They often refer to Popper's idea, tending accurately to define various senses of semantic information which may be interesting and useful in the theory of science. Regarding semantic information as of cognitive value, which is one of the important goals of science, and the elaboration of various numerical measures for various kinds of information has paved the way for a very interesting conception in the theory of science: namely, it allowed the possibility of using the notional apparatus of decision theory in inductive logic. And so, we can say that Popper's ideas became an inspiration for a new formulation of inductive logic. This conception of inductive logic will be discussed in Chapter 10.3.

10
The inductive rules of acceptance

In Chapter 1 it was mentioned that the concept of acceptance with reference to empirical statements exceeding the observed facts has no clearly defined meaning. Anyway, it is acceptance in a weaker sense than the acceptance of the statement that 2+2=4, because it is not, or, at least, should not be, certain and irrevocable acceptance. In the considerations concerning inductive logic one can meet two kinds of this weaker concept of acceptance: the qualitative (classificatory) concept and the quantitative (i.e. graduable) one. If we adopt the qualitative concept of acceptance, we can speak about acceptance or non-acceptance of a given statement p; if p is not accepted, either the negation of p can be accepted (and then we say that p is rejected) or its negation can be unaccepted (and then we speak about suspension of judgement).

Difficulties connected with the qualitative concept of acceptance consist of this, that it is difficult to say what such acceptance consists of, if it is not acceptance with certainty. There exist various attempts at interpretation of this concept — from a very liberal one, according to which we accept p when we are convinced that p rather than not p — to a very restrictive one, according to which we accept p if we have the so-called 'actual certainty' that p, which in turn, is explained as a state of mind consisting of this, that we do not treat the possibility of falsity of p seriously. These explanations are unsatisfactory, so the qualitative concept of uncertain acceptance has, in fact, only some intuitive sense (obviously not for everybody: some people are of the opinion that it has no sense at all).

The graduable concept of acceptance has its interpretation in the theory of subjective probability which has already been discussed. With reference to this concept the term 'belief' is used much more often than 'acceptance' probably because gradation is more compatible with the traditional meaning of the word 'belief' than 'acceptance'. The adherents of this concept express the opinion that it allows to reports about uncertain beliefs better than the qualitative concept. For uncertain beliefs, it is characteristic that they can be less or more uncertain in the way that there is no natural boundary between the kind of uncertainty which could be regarded as lack of acceptance, and the kind of uncertainty which could mean acceptance. It is demonstrated by the difficulties in interpretation of the qualitative concept of acceptance in reference to uncertain beliefs. It seems that the adherents of the qualitative concept think that at each stage of development of science one can distinguish some theorems and theories which are not questioned at this stage; despite all its drawbacks of vagueness and obscurity, the qualitative concept of acceptance allows making an account of this situation and this is what the usefulness of the intuitions connected with it consists in. It is very difficult to find out what the problem of acceptance of hypotheses and theories in the empirical sciences 'really' looks like. Hence, it is difficult to find convincing arguments which would speak in favour of one of these concepts of acceptance. Now I shall describe a few different conceptions of the rules of acceptance which are propagated in literature concerning inductive logic.

10.1 PROBABILISTIC RULES OF ACCEPTANCE

A probabilistic rule of acceptance is a rule which prescribes the acceptance of the hypothesis H on the basis of the premises E when the probability of H relative to E exceeds certain value, i.e. the rule of the form:

(RP) H must be accepted on the basis of E if and only if:
$P(H/E) \geq 1-\varepsilon$ (where $\varepsilon<0.5$).

Occurring in this formula is the value $1-\varepsilon$ which is called the acceptance threshold which depends upon the estimation of the value of ε. The condition that $\varepsilon<0.5$ is imposed because the estimation of $\varepsilon\geq0.5$ would lead to the acceptance of incompatible statements. If the rule (RP) prescribed the acceptance of H on the basis of E when $P(H/E)\geq 0.5$, it would also prescribe the acceptance of $\sim H$ on the basis of E, because then we would have $P(\sim H/E)\geq0.5$. However, the condition that ε must be less than 0.5 is very weak in the sense that it would lead to a very liberal concept of acceptance: the rule (RP) would permit the acceptance of the hypothesis H even when the probability of $\sim H$ were little smaller than the probability of H. A more restrictive version of acceptance requires an appropriately small number ε. Still, there are no natural criteria for the choice of such number ε. Besides, the fact should be stressed that the application of this rule is considered permissible only when E represents all actual observational knowledge or all knowledge important for the conclusion H.

The main objection raised against the probabilistic rules consists in this, that such rules lead to the violation of a postulate which, according to common opinion, should be satisfied by the set of theorems which are accepted in science. It concerns the postulate which was formulated by C. Hempel in [26]:

(PU) The set of all accepted statements at time t should be compatible and closed under inference.

Closure consists of this, that if a sentence p follows from the set of accepted statements Z, p must also belong to Z, i.e. it must also be accepted.

And so, the probabilistic rule leads to violation of this postulate of Hempel's because of a property of the probability of conjunction. Namely: if we take no account of the cases of a very strong dependence of statements (e.g. inference), then the probability of conjunction will be smaller than the probabilities of the individual elements of the conjunction. Therefore, if we have a sufficient number of hypotheses $H_1, H_2, \ldots, H_r$ such that $P_i(H/E) \geq 1-\varepsilon$ for each of them, then there exists a possibility that $P(H_1 \wedge H_2 \wedge \ldots \wedge H_r/E) < \varepsilon$, and hence that $P(\sim H_1 \vee \sim H_2 \vee \ldots \vee \sim H_r/E) > 1-\varepsilon$. This means that the probabilistic rule would lead to the acceptance of each of the hypotheses H_i, and, at the same time, to the acceptance of the alternation of the negations of all these hypotheses. Meanwhile, the conjunction of the hypotheses $H_1, \ldots, H_r$ follows from the set of these hypotheses, which puts us in the following situation: if we do not accept the conjunction of these hypotheses, we shall violate the postulate (PU) because it demands that we accept the consequence of a set of accepted statements; if we accept this conjunction, we shall accept incompatible statements, because this conjunction is incompatible with the accepted alternation of negations of these hypotheses. And so, we cannot behave in accordance with Hempel's postulate.

Such inconsistency was called the lottery paradox because a typical example of it is the probability of winning a prize in a lottery. Assume that the lottery has n tickets, and, exactly one of them gives the prize, while the probability of winning the prize is for each ticket equal to $1/n$. Suppose that $n = 1\,000\,000$. Let $H_1, \ldots, H_n$ designate the statements that the winning ticket will be the first one, the second one, etc., and E be a description of the above characterized conditions of the game. It can be seen from these conditions that $p(H_1 \vee H_2 \vee \ldots \vee H_n/E) = 1$, and for each ticket $P(H_i/E) = 0.000\,001$, so $P(\sim H_i/E) = 0.999\,999$. If we adopt ε a bit bigger than $1/n$, say $0.000\,002$, the threshold of acceptance will be equal to $0.999\,998$, i.e. it will be very high. The probabilistic rule will then prescribe the acceptance of the negation of each hypothesis H_i, and, at the same time, the acceptance of the alternation of all H_i. This means that with reference to each ticket we shall accept that it will not win, and at the same time we shall accept that one of them will win. But from the set of all accepted $\sim H_i$ follows their conjunction which states that no ticket will win, and is incompatible with the accepted alternation of the hypotheses H_i which states that one ticket will win. Therefore, if we accept the consequences of the accepted statements, we shall accept incompatible statements.

The views concerning this paradox and Hempel's postulate are varied. Hempel justifies his postulate in the following way [26]: the aim of the empirical sciences is to obtain a set of 'presumably true' statements which can be the basis for anticipation of events. So, if some sentences are accepted as presumably true, all their consequences should also be accepted, because every consequence of true statements is true. On the other hand, incompatible statements cannot be true at the same time, and besides, from the set of incompatible statements follows any statement together with its negation, so, the acceptance of incompatible statements would render anticipation impossible.

The acceptance of Hempel's postulate disqualifies the probabilistic rule of acceptance and forces its rejection or at least restriction of its applicability. Some people, however, believe that Hempel's postulate is too strong for the acceptance by way of induction, and it is rather this postulate which should be modified.

And so, for instance, Kyburg in [45] modifies the postulate of the acceptance of consequences in the following way:

(PK)   If we accept the statement H, and G follows from H, we must accept G.

According to this postulate we must accept the consequences of each particular accepted statement, but we need not accept all the consequences of the set of accepted statements. For instance, if we accept H and G, and the statement p follows neither from H nor from G, but it follows from the conjunction of H and G, the postulate (PK) does not demand the acceptance of p, because it does not demand the acceptance of the conjunction of H and G if this conjunction does not follow from any of the accepted statements.

Kyburg formulates the postulate of compatibility in the following way:

(PN)   If the statement H is accepted, then $\sim H$ cannot be accepted.

It is also an attenuation of Hempel's postulate, because (PN) is confined by the requirement that the set of accepted statements cannot include incompatible statements, while consistency of the set of accepted statements postulated by Hempel requires also that incompatible statements do not follow from this set.

It is easy to notice that the probabilistic rule is concordant with the postulates (PK) and (PN) and on the basis of these postulates it does not lead to the lottery paradox. If $P(H/E) \geq 1-\varepsilon$ and G follows from H, then, according to the axioms of probability, we shall always have $P(G/E) \geq 1-\varepsilon$; so the acceptance of a consequence of the accepted statement H cannot lead to the acceptance of a statement whose probability is smaller than $1-\varepsilon$. This means that the acceptance of incompatible statements is no longer possible. Now, the condition $\varepsilon < 0.5$ constitutes a sufficient protection against the acceptance of incompatible statements. The paradox of lottery does not occur, because, even if the rule (RP) prescribes to accept the statements 'the ticket(i) will not win' about each ticket, the postulate (PK) does not prescribe the acceptance of their conjunction, i.e. the statement that no ticket will win.

Kyburg himself, in [45] describes the conception of the probabilistic acceptance rule which, in some respects, is different than (RP). First, his rule refers to the 'epistemological' probability defined by him (see Chapter 7) whose values are numerical intervals. Secondly, in the set of all accepted statements (i.e. those statements which belong to science) his rule distinguishes sub-sets of statements which are accepted with different degree of 'practical certainty'. Namely, Kyburg defines the hierarchy of sets of statements which are included in science; different sets, which he calls 'rational corpora', are distinguished according to different degrees of 'practical certainty' with which they are accepted. Here we shall designate them with the symbols K_i and call every such set 'knowledge of the level i'.

Kyburg needs such a hierarchy for different reasons. First of all, it allows us to avoid a vicious circle in the definition of knowledge accepted according to the probabilistic rule, and in the definition of probability which, as we know from Chpater 7, is relativized to knowledge. The vicious circle is avoided thanks to the recursive definition of rational knowledge: the knowledge of the lower level is defined with reference to the knowledge at a higher level. Kyburg distinguished a finite number of the levels of knowledge: among the fractions r_i which satisfy the condition $1/2 < r_i \leq 1$, he chooses n fractions $r_1, r_2, \ldots, r_n$ and to each of these fractions he assigns a set K_i of sentences which belong to knowledge. The chosen numbers r_i indicate different levels of 'practical certainty'. The order $K_1, K_2, \ldots, K_n$ is parallel to the order $r_1, r_2, \ldots, r_n$, i.e. if $i \geq j$, then $r_i \geq r_j$. The choice of the numbers r_i, is quite arbitrary. Kyburg writes, that they can be for instance, the numbers:

$r_1 = 0.8, r_2 = 0.9, r_3 = 0.95, r_4 = 0.96, r_5 = 0.97$.
$r_6 = 0.98, r_7 = 0.99, r_8 = 0.995, r_9 = 0.998$ and $r_{10} = 1$.

The knowledge of the highest level K_n consists of theorems of logic and mathematics (maybe, also all analytical statements), and the so-called base F. The base is a set of empirical sentences which are accepted in some immediate way, i.e. not by way of inference (for instance observational reports). It is assumed that K_n is a set closed under inference, this set is defined without the help of logical probability, and constitutes the starting point for the recursive definition of all rational knowledge: each set K_i (where $i < n$) is defined with the help of probability relative to the set K_{i+1}.

The definition is as follows:

(DK$_i$) The statement Z belongs to K_i with the base $F(i < n)$ if and only if the probability of Z relative to W_{i+1} with the base F is equal to $(p; q)$ and $p \geq r_i$.

Kyburg's probability satisfies the condition: if the statement Z belongs to K_i, the probability of Z relative to K_i equals 1. Therefore, the sets K_i are ordered with regard to the inclusion relation $K_i \subset K_{i-1}$. So, each level K_i includes all statements which belong to higher levels, and can also include new statements, which are not 'inherited' but joined to K_i on the basis of their probability relative to the higher level K_{i+1}. The knowledge of the lowest K_1 is equal to the sum of all K_i, and constitutes all rational knowledge relative to the given base F. The number r_1 indicates the acceptance threshold below which the acceptance is irrational (invalid), i.e. the acceptance of any statement which does not belong to K_1 is irrational. Therefore, we can say that the addition of a statement to K_1 indicates its acceptance in the qualitative sense. Among these statements, however, we can distinguish statements which are accepted with different degrees of certainty, as the levels of knowledge represent different degrees of certainty. Therefore, we can agree that the definition (DK_i) is the basis for the following rule of the graduated acceptance of statements:

(RK) the degree of certainty of acceptance of the statement Z at the base F should be equal to r_i if and only if Z belongs to K_i, but it does not belong to K_{i+1} (with the base F).

In other words, the degree of certainty of the statement Z should equal r_i when the highest level of knowledge which Z belongs to is equal to r_i. The rule (RK) is probabilistic for all levels lower than K_n because the fact that statements belong to these levels is determined only by their probability relative to a lower level.

The definition (DK_i) does not guarantee that K_i is closed under deduction. If the statement p belongs to K_i and q belongs to K_i, then their conjunction need not be included in K_i because its probability relative to K_{i+1} may be too small.

Kyburg writes that we could adopt another rule of addition of all deductive consequences to K_i, but he does not want to adopt such a rule because it might cause the above-cited lottery pardox. Therefore, K_i satisfies only the weaker postulate of consequence (PK). Kyburg demonstrates that his sets K_i satisfy the following conditions:

(T.1) if the implication $p \rightarrow q$ is a theorem of logic or mathematics, then, if p belongs to K_i, q also belongs to K_i;

(T.2) if the implication $p \rightarrow q$ belongs to K_i, and p belongs to K_{i-1}, then q belongs to K_{i-1}.

In connection with this F. Schick (in [71]) remarked that Kyburg's conception leads to the lottery paradox after all, because closure takes place on lower levels. Assume that K_i includes a description of an unbiased lottery in which there are so many tickets that for each ticket the probability of not winning is greater than r_{i-1}, so K_{i-1} includes the negations of the hypotheses H which state that the ticket number 1 will win. Let us now consider the theorems of logic, of the form:

$$\sim H_2 \rightarrow (\sim H_1 \rightarrow (\sim H_1 \wedge \sim H_2)),$$
$$\sim H_3 \rightarrow [(\sim H_2 \wedge \sim H_1) \rightarrow (\sim H_1 \wedge \sim H_2 \wedge \sim H_3)], \text{ etc.}$$

Since all $\sim H_i$ belong to K_{i-1}, then, on the strength of (T.1) K_{i-1} includes also the consequents of those implications, i.e. the implications:

$$\sim H_1 \rightarrow (\sim H_1 \wedge \sim H_2),$$
$$(\sim H_2 \wedge \sim H_1) \rightarrow (\sim H_1 \wedge \sim H_2 \wedge \sim H_3) \text{ etc.}$$

Therefore, on the strength of (T.2), K_{i-2} includes all the consequents of these latter implications, i.e. all the conjunctions of the hypotheses $\sim H_i$. And so, K_{i-2} includes the statement that no ticket will win, and its negation, namely, the statement that at least one ticket will win, which was 'inherited from the set K_i which included the description of the lottery. This being so, we can see that the definition (DK_i) does not guarantee that the postulate of consistency of knowledge, even in its weaker form (PN) will be satisfied.

In his article [46] Kyburg states that the inconsistency can be avoided if 'no more than two levels of rational knowledge are considered simultaneously': the knowledge of the highest level, say K^* and the knowledge of a lower level K_r, which consists of the statements whose lower limit of probability relative to K^* is higher than r. The knowledge K_r is not closed under implication, so the contradiction does not arise. The definition of probability allows us to calculate the probability of statements relative to K_r, but such probabilities cannot be the basis for detachment (this means that statements cannot be accepted and added to existing knowledge on the basis of their probability relative to K_r).

Kyburg himself admits that this solution is not satisfactory. The conception of inductive logic which he described in [45] aimed at the formulation of the foundations for inductive acceptance of all statements which belong to the body of knowledge. He wanted to formulate the criteria of inductive acceptance of statements not only on the basis of premises which were accepted immediately (by way of observation), but also on the basis of premises which were accepted by way of induction. In [45] Kyburg writes (on p. 87)

> Why can't we simply treat the content of rational knowledge as components of F, axioms, etc., and accept that we should believe in probable statements, but they should not be included in rational knowledge.
>
> The answer is: probability must be defined in relation to rational knowledge, but the numerous statements in relation to which we must estimate probability are only probable statements. And so, for instance, in my opinion we assign the probability 1/2 (approximately) to the statement that in the next toss of a coin we shall get tails only because we have good reasons to suppose that this coin gives the tails in half of its tosses — i.e. because a certain statistical statement is highly probable. If we did not include this highly probable statement in some rational knowledge, it would be difficult for us to find in a logic of rational beliefs some justification for the assignment of such probability to this statement.

The reduction of the number of levels of knowledge to two, of which the higher one K^* consists of the theorems of mathematics and physics and the empirical statements which were directly accepted, indicates resignation from the above conception. In connection with this in [46], Kyburg suggests that the knowledge which is regarded as actually certain in a given situation or historical period, can be included in F. In his book [47], he writes that F can be a set of any statements which we decided to use as the base for induction (p. 191). However, even if Kyburg allows the inclusion of statements which were accepted into F by way of induction, he will not solve the problem which he wished to solve, namely the problem of the foundations (rules) for all inductive inferences. The statements added to knowledge K_r by way of induction will have their foundations in their probability relative to K^*; but if F (and, thence, K^*) include the statements accepted by way of induction, the acceptance of these statements will not have its base in Kyburg's probabilistic logic, because their probability will not be estimated at all because of the lack of knowledge at a higher level.

Using the term which has recently become common in works dealing with induction, we could say that, thus modified, Kyburg's conception would be a solution of 'local induction', but not 'global induction'. Local induction is understood as induction on the basis of premises which, among others, can include statements already accepted by way of induction. The problem of local induction is the problem of the validity of such inductions with the assumption that the premises (in a given situation) are not questioned. The premises of global induction cannot be statements obtained by way of induction. In his article 'Local and Global Induction' [48], Kyburg writes that the problem of global induction is the problem of the justification of the total body of knowledge on the assumption that only necessary truths (i.e. the theorems of logic and mathematics) and those empirical statements which are directly accepted (i.e. the results of immediate observation) are not questioned. The acceptance of statements in such a direct way is not induction, so the problems connected with the acceptance of such statements go beyond the range of investigations concerning inductive logic.

Kyburg's conception based on the recursive definition of the total body of knowledge (identified with the knowledge of the lowest level K_1) was intended as an attempt at a solution of the problem of global induction. The starting point was the base F which did not include any empirical statements accepted by way of non-deductive inferences, and all empirical knowledge was defined by its relation to F. The addition of sentences accepted by way of induction on F is tantamount to the rejection of this conception.

It is worth noticing that in the two-level conception of knowledge, which was described by Kyburg in [46], the definition of knowledge K_r as related to knowledge K^* does not show any essential difference from the above-cited probabilistic rule (RP). This means that if in (RP) we put K^* in place of E, r in place of $1-\varepsilon$ and interpret the probability as Kyburg does, then the set of statements accepted on the strength of (RP) will be identical with Kyburg's set K_r. And so, the reduction of the number of levels of knowledge to two, divests Kyburg's conception of its originality and attractiveness to a large extent.

Let us return for a while to Kyburg's multi-level conception. As we have seen, in some respect it appeared to be worse than the ordinary probabilistic rule because it leads to contradiction even if the postulates (PK) and (PN) which concern consequences and consistency, are weakened. We should also consider another of its drawbacks from the point of view of global induction.

Assume that the level of knowledge K_{i+1} is defined by the number $r_{i+1}=0.6$, and the next lower level K_i — by the number $r_i=0.599$. Let us further assume that we have a hypothesis H whose probability relative to K_{i+1} equals (0.61; 0.62). According to Kyburg's definition, the hypothesis H belongs (in this situation) to the knowledge K_i because the lower limit of its probability relative to K_{i+1} — i.e. 0.61 — is higher than r_i. Yet, the number $r_i=0.599$ is to represent the rational degree of actual certainty of knowledge K_i (with the base F). This means that, according to Kyburg, the acceptance of H with the degree of certainty equal 0.599 is rational (in regard to F). Meanwhile, this degree of certainty of acceptance of H could be regarded as rational (if we accept the probabilistic conception of acceptance at all) only on the assumption that the rational degree of certainty with which we accept the premises H — i.e. the body of knowledge K_{i+1} in this case — ie equal, or, at least, close to one. The probabilistic rule of acceptance (RP) is always understood in this way: it concerns the acceptance of H on the basis of E, which means that the acceptance is admissible when the premises are stated with certainty and $P(H/E) \geq 1-\varepsilon$.

However, Kyburg — for reasons which have been discussed above — wants to have a concept of acceptance which admits uncertain premises. The probability which is the basis for acceptance on the level K_i is not based on K_n but to the knowledge K_{i+1} which has already become uncertain. The realization of this, undoubtedly interesting conception, would require the imposition of more restrictive conditions on acceptance on levels lower than K_{n-1}. Kyburg's conditions are too liberal, because — as can be seen from the above-cited example — they permit the acceptance of a conclusion with a certainty which nearly equals the certainty of its premises, although the probability of the conclusion relative to the premises is comparatively low. The assumption that $r_i < r_{i+1}$ guarantees only that the degree of certainty with which an inductive conclusion can be accepted cannot be higher or equal to the degree of certainty of acceptance of the premises.

According to probability calculus, the equality $P(H)=P(E)P(H/E)+P(\sim E)P(H/\sim E)$ holds. In Chapter 8 we saw that according to R. Jeffrey's conception, the degree of belief in the hypothesis H on the basis of the uncertain premise E should be calculated in accordance with this theorem. If someone thinks, like Kyburg, that the degree of rational belief should be based on some objective probability, he has good reasons to accept this theorem as the base for the estimation of the degree of belief about H on the basis of uncertain premises.

I do not think that Kyburg simply ignored this theorem. The problem is rather in the fact that because of special property of epistemological probability, it is difficult to apply this theorem in Kyburg's system.

The lack of satisfactory acceptance criteria on the levels lower than K_{n-1} makes the whole conception of the solution of the problem of global induction questionable apart from the fact that this conception leads to acceptance of incompatible statements. The number r_i which is assigned to the knowledge of level K_i (for $i<n-1$) does not adequately represent the degree of rational certainty of acceptance of statements K_i, because it is too high.

In the field of local induction, Kyburg's achievements are confined to his

108 THE INDUCTIVE RULES OF ACCEPTANCE [Ch. 10

original conception of probability which he adopts as the base for induction. Epistemological probability has unquestionable advantages in comparison with other concepts of probability — which was discussed in Chapter 7.

10.2 RULES BASED ON THE NUMBER OF OBSERVATIONS

Adherents of Hempel's postulate of rational acceptance (PU) must either abandon the probabilistic criterion of acceptance, or restrict in some way the applicability of the probabilistic rule. The latter solution was chosen by J. Hintikka and R. Hilpinen in [30]. They introduced the rule of acceptance of H on the basis of E only when $P(H/E)$ has a high probability, and the rule requires that E should be a report on an appropriately large number, n, of observations. This rule was very broadly discussed in a later work by R. Hilpinen [29]. The rule refers to logical probability as defined by J. Hintikka (see Chapter 6.2) for languages with one-argument predicates J^k. I repeat once more that in this language, certain distinguished types of statements are defined: individual descriptions of finite n-element sets and constituents. The Hintikaa and Hilpinen rule of acceptance is confined to those cases in which the hypothesis H does not include any individual names and the premise is an individual description of an n-element set of objects.

In Chapter 6.2 I quoted theroem (T.2) which was satisfied by the probability functions from Hintikka's system: (T.2) $P(C_c/S_C)$ comes close to one when n tends to infinity (where n is the number of elements of the set Z_n whose description is S_C). From this theorem, it follows that for any small number ε the inequality

$$P(C_c/S_C) > 1 - \varepsilon$$

can be satisfied only if n is appropriately large. In connection with this, the number n_0 which is the limit above which this equality is satisfied, can be defined. This number, in a given language J^k, is dependent upon the premise S_C (in particular upon the number c) and on the value of ε; therefore, we shall designate it with the symbol $n_0(S_C,\varepsilon)$.

The definition is as follows:

(Dn_0) $n_0(S_C,\varepsilon)$ = the largest number n such that $P(C_c/S_c) \leq 1$.

Let us use the symbol G to designate an arbitrarily chosen sentence of J^k which does not contain individual names. The rule of acceptance of G on the basis of S_C states that:

(RG) G should be accepted on the basis of S_C if and only if
   (a) $P(G/S_C) > 1 - \varepsilon$, and (b) $n > n_0(S_C,\varepsilon)$

As can be seen, high probability of the hypothesis relative to the premise is a necessary but not sufficient condition of its acceptance. Apart from this, an appropriately large number of experiments is necessary (S_C must be a description of an appropriately large number of objects). This rule does not lead to acceptance of incompatible statements for the following reasons:

We must notice that, according to the definition n_0, the condition (b) of the rule (RG) can be substituted by an equivalent condition:

(b') $P(C_C/S_C) > 1 - \varepsilon$.

Since the descriptions C are disjoint, the condition (b) has the consequence:

$P(A/S_C) < \varepsilon$

where A designates the alternation of all constituents C except C_C. From Chapter 6.2, we also know that each statement G which does not contain names in the language J^k is equivalent to the alternation of all constituents which are coherent with G. Therefore, if $P(C_C/S_C)$ is larger than $1 - \varepsilon$, then $P(G/S_C)$ can be larger than $1 - \varepsilon$ only when G is coherent with C_C. Hence, for the rule (RG), we get the following equivalent formulation:

(RG') G should be accepted on the basis of S_C if and only if
    (a) G is coherent with C_C, and
    (b) $P(C_C/S_C) > 1 - \varepsilon$

As can be seen, the rule guarantees that Hempel's postulate is satisfied. If each hypothesis G which is accepted on the basis of S_C, is coherent with the constituent C_C, then the set of those hypotheses is consistent (all these hypotheses will be true in the universe described by C_C).

Consequently, each consequence of G must also be coherent with C_C, so it will also be accepted, and so the set of Statements G which are accepted on the basis of S_C will also be closed under deduction.

The above rule refers only to those hypotheses which do not contain names, i.e. to universal and existential statements. Hintikka and Hilpinen demonstrate that if a rule of this kind were applied to any individual hypotheses, it would lead to violation of Hempel's postulate. Satisfying this postulate requires that individual statements and those composed of individual ones should be accepted only when they follow from the conjunction of the premises and universal statements which were accepted on the basis of those premises. And so, for instance, if a premise has the form of S_C and the hypothesis is of the form $M(a)$, where M is an arbitrary, simple or complex predicate, and the name a does not occur in S_C, then this hypothesis can be accepted on the basis of S_C only when the statement $\bigwedge_x M(x)$ is accepted on the basis of S_C; or if, for instance, the premise has the form of $S_C \wedge B(a)$ and a does not occur in S_C, then, if the universal statement $\bigwedge_x (B(x) \to M(x))$ is accepted on the basis of this premise, the statement $M(a)$ will also be accepted. And so, the acceptance of individual statements can be done only by way of deduction if Hempel's postulate is to be satisfied.

The rule (RG) satisfies Hempel's postulate at the cost of certain restrictions; however, not all of these restrictions are necessary. In particular, the restriction to those probability functions which satisfy the theorem (T.2) of Hintikka's system and the restriction to the premises of the form S_C can be avoided by appropriate modification of the rule.

The theorem (T.2) is the base for the definition of n_0; it warrants the existence of the number n_0 which satisfies this definition. As we have seen above, if the probability function satisfies (T.2), the rule (RG) is equivalent to the rule (RG'). It is easy to see that (RG) guarantees that Hempel's postulate will be satisfied because it is equivalent to (RG'). Yet, the rule (RG') guarantees that Hempel's postulate will be satisfied irrespective of the kind of probability function which occurs in it: it can be any function defined for the statements of J^k, providing it satisfies the axioms of probability. It could be seen in the above-cited proof of the statement that Hempel's postulate is satisfied by (RG').

The restriction to the premise in the form of state descriptions S is a considerable restriction, because S is a complete description of objects of the set Z_n with regard to all predicates of the language J^k. Such a premise can be a report of an observation only if all predicates of J^k are observational, i.e. describe observable properties. This would be the second considerable reduction of the already simple language J^k. In my article [56] I discussed the generalization of the rule (RG') for the premise E which is an arbitrarily chosen report of the observation of the set Z_n, expressed in J^k.

Every sentence E which consists of simple statements describing the elements of Z_n is synonymous with the alternation of the descriptions S of this set. Let us designate this alternation with the symbol A_S. For each S in A_S there exists exactly one constituent C which states that those and only those predicates which are assigned to the elements of Z_n by S are not empty. Let us use the symbol A_C to designate the alternation of all C assigned in this way to the elements S of the alternation A_S. The generalization of the rule (RG') will have the following form:

(RG)* G should be accepted on the basis of E if and only;
         (a) G is coherent with each constituent C in A_C, and

(b) $P(A_C/E) \geq 1 - \varepsilon$

The proof that Hempel's postulate is satisfied is parallel to that for (RG') if every hypothesis G accepted on the strength of (RG)* (which does not include names) is coherent with each constituent C in A_C, then the set of these hypotheses is consistent. All these hypotheses are true in each of the universes described by the elements of A_C. Every consequence of each accepted hypothesis G will also be coherent with the elements of A_C, and so it will also be accepted.

Let us now consider an example of the application of (RG)*. Let the language J^k include any number of simple predicates. Suppose that Z_n is a set of all observed objects with the property M_1, e.g. all observed ravens. Let the sentence E which describes Z_n state that all these ravens have the property M_2 — they are black; we can also assume that the observed ravens live in various geographical, climatic and other conditions, which we state in our premise E with the help of predicates $M_3, M_4, \ldots, M_n$ (simple or compound). Our alternation of constituents A_C will consist of all and only those constituents C which state: (1) $\bigwedge_x M_i(x)$ about each property such that the statement $\bigwedge_x M_i(x)$ follows from E; e.g. the existence of black ravens follows from E, so each constituent in A_C must state that there exist black ravens; (2) $\sim \bigwedge_x M_j(x)$ for each property M_j such that for each element a of the set Z_n, $\sim M_j(a)$ follows from E; in our example such a property is $M_1(x) \wedge \sim M_2(x)$, because E states for all elements Z_n that they are black ravens. It is obvious that the hypothesis 'each raven is black' is coherent with every description which states that there are no non-black ravens, no matter what else such a description states. And so, this hypothesis will be coherent with all constituents C in the alternation A_C. Therefore, the rule (RG)* will allow us to accept the statement that each raven is black if only the probability of A relative to E exceeds $1 - \varepsilon$.

We should notice now that the rule (RG)* eliminates one more unnecessary restriction of (RG) and (RG'), namely, these rules allow accepting the statement G only when they allow acceptance of certain constituent C. This can be clearly seen in the formulation of (RG'): the acceptance of G requires that $P(C_C/S_C) > 1 - \varepsilon$, so G will be accepted only when C_C is accepted.

Each constituent C is a very strong statement, because, for every sentence G (without names) in J^k, either this sentence or its negation follows from C. This means that each constituent C axiomatizes a complete theory without names in the langauge J^k. Therefore, the rule (RG) allows acceptance of any statement only if we accept a certain complete universal theory in the given language. In particular, for instance, we cannot accept the statement 'every raven is black' if, at the same time, we do not accept the statement' every swan is white' or the statement 'not every swan is white', 'every sparrow is grey' or 'not every sparrow is grey', etc. — whenever these predicates appear in J^k.

The rule (RG)* does not require the acceptance of a complete theory for the acceptance of a given statement because it does not require the acceptance of the constituents C, and, therefore, it better suits the inductive practice. This rule does not require a high probability for any constituent C: $P(A_C/E)$ is equal to the sum of $P(C/E)$ for all elements C of the alternation A_C, so $P(A_C/E)$ can be close to one, although all $P(C/E)$ are small. However (RG)* requires high probability of accepted statements. If each statement G is synonymous with the alternation of all constituents C coherent with G, each statement accepted on the strength of (RG)* must have $P(G/E) \geq P(A_C/E)$, so $P(G/E) > 1 - \varepsilon$. The problem whether the rule (RG)* requires a large number of observations depends upon the probability function occurring in it: if this function satisfies the above-cited theorem (T.2), we can demonstrate that (RG)* requires high n. Namely: if such a function satisfies (T.2), it also satisfies the following theorem:

(T.2)* $P(A_C/E)$ comes close to one if n infinitely grows, where A_C is defined as above for any description E of the set Z_n. The proof of (T.2)* can be found in my article [56]. For such a probability function, we can define the number n_0^* as the largest number n for which $P(A_C/E) \leq 1 - \varepsilon$, and then the condition (b) of the rule (RG) can be substituted with the condition: $n > n_0^*$.

Another significant restriction of the rules (RG) and (RG)* is the confinement to the language J^k with one-argument predicates. The generalization condition of (RG)* for richer languages is quite obvious: the thing is that in such language there must exist parallel state descriptions which are pair-wise disjoint and exhaustive, and such that the statement G without names should be synonymous to one of their alternations. In his work [31], J. Hintikka defined such descriptions for a language containing all of first order logic. Therefore, the problem of application of the rule (RG)* to such languages is reduced to the problem of the definition of a probability function for them.

On the other hand, generalization of the rule (RG) for richer languages is a bit more complicated than the generalization of (RG)*. The point is that the condition occurring in (RG) $P(G/E) > 1 - \varepsilon$ is not equivalent to the condition $P(A_C/E) > 1 - \varepsilon$, because $P(G/E)$ can be higher than $P(A_C/E)$. The condition $P(G/E) > 1 - \varepsilon$ is weaker and the substitution of the condition $P(A_C/E) > 1 - \varepsilon$ with it in (RG)* can lead to the lottery paradox, if the probability does not have appropriate properties. In Chapter 7.2 of [29] Hilpinen formulates the condition, which when satisfied by the probability function, makes the application of (RG) for richer languages possible without violation of Hempel's postulate (see Also H. Mortimer [56]).

The fact that the probabilistic rule with its modification (which were described in the last paragraph) satisfies Hempel's postulate is very important because it eliminates a basic objection to the application of such a rule.

This fact itself, however, does not demonstrate the adequacy of a probabilistic rule in the sense of its coherence with the intuitive critiera of validity of induction. Such coherence, certainly depends to a great extent on the choice of the probability function that this rule will use. Hintikka and Hilpinen stress that the dependence of the acceptance of hypotheses upon their high probability and large number of observations is quite natural; in earlier chapters, however, I have already stated that validity of induction is usually dependent upon certain conditions which are not demonstrated by the probability of Hintikka's system (se e.g. the last pages of Chapter 6).

10.3 THE RULES BASED ON COGNITIVE UTILITY

The adherents of this kind of rule assume that the solution of the problem of criteria of valid, i.e. rational acceptance of statements in empirical sciences, requires determination of the aim to which these sciences tend. For every human activity can be evaluated as rational or irrational (valid or invalid) only with reference to the aim which a man (or a group of people) want to achieve. The same activity can be rational with regard to the aim whose realization it ensures, and irrational with regard to another aim. If someone prefers to get wet to carrying an umbrella, it will be rational for him not to carry this umbrella. If, however, he most of all wants to avoid getting wet, he should carry an umbrella even when the weather is fine.

The problems of the criteria of rational action are dealt with by decision theory; strictly speaking, it deals with the problem of the choice of an action from a range of actions which are possible in a given situation in the lack of certainty as to what state of affairs will take place. The basic ideas of this theory were outlined in Chapter 5. The condition of application of various criteria of choice of action propagated by the theory of decision is the existence of a measure of utility: for each action which we can choose, the utility relative to every possible state of affairs on which the effect of our actions depend must be determined.

Acceptance of statements can be treated as a kind of action. Therefore, the conceptual apparatus of decision theory can be, in fact, applied to the problem of criteria of the rational acceptance of hypotheses in empirical sciences, if we have a measure of applicability of this kind of actions which is appropriate for the aim or aims to which empirical sciences tend.

In contemporary methodological literature, we can find several attempts at defining the measure of cognitive utility of empirical hypotheses — strictly speaking, the utility of those actions which consists in their acceptance — and attempts at the formulation of rules which make acceptance dependent upon this utility. Attempts were made, e.g. by C. Hempel [25] and [26], J. Levi [50], J. Hintikka and J. Pietarinen [36]. The best developed and detailed is the conception of acceptance described in the book by Isaak Levi *Gambling with Truth*, [50] which will now be discussed.

Levi does not pretend to make his conception a completely adequate formulation of inductive inferences. He mostly aims at indicating the fundamental possibility of a decisive approach to the problem of inductive logic. He wants to show that such an approach need not mean a pragmatic formulation of the goals of science. According to Levi, science has its special cognitive, theoretical aims. Levi agrees with Popper that the aim of science is not simply the pursuit of truth; that science strives for hypotheses and theories which have informational, explanatory value and which are possibly characterized by great simplicity. He also agrees with Popper that all these cognitive values of hypotheses (except truth), which are appreciated in science are connected with the high level of their falsifiability. In connection with this Levi assumes that science strives for two basic aims: truth and information (the second aim is called 'reduction of ignorance' by Levi).

Science, however, cannot give certainty as regards truth, hence the realization of these aims is associated with a risk. If truth were the only aim of science, no risk would be rational, so induction would not be rational either. On the other hand, if information were the only aim, there would also be no risk: such an aim can be achieved without any risk and without induction. So, risk is connected with the conflict of the aims of science the rational value of risk should depend upon what relative importance we wish to ascribe to the conflicting aims. In connection with this, the cognitive usefulness of hypotheses should be determined so that it would depend — in certain proportion — both upon truth and upon information.

Levi founds his measure of the information in a sentence on the proportion of the number of logical possibilities which are excluded by H, to the number of all possibilities which come into play. So, one of the commonly accepted measures of semantic information $\text{cont}(H)$ is accepted. It is defined as $1 - P(H)$, where P is a logical probability, i.e., the values of $P(H)$ depend on the number of logical possibilities which are excluded by H and which can be distinguished in some way (see Chapter 6).

The measure $\text{cont}(H)$ has the following important properties: if H is a logical truth (tautology), then $\text{cont}(H) = 1 - P(H) = 0$; whereas if H is a logical falsehood, then $\text{cont}(H) = 1$. (Tautology does not exclude any logical possibility, while logical falsehood excludes all possibilities). So, $\text{cont}(H)$ has its maximum for logically false H and its minimum for tautologies.

Levi imposes the following conditions of rationality on cognitive utility:

$$(1) \quad U(H) \geq u(G),$$

where $U(H)$ denotes utility of a true hypothesis H — strictly speaking the utility of acceptance of H when H is true — and $u(G)$ denotes the utility of a false hypothesis G (i.e. the usefulness of acceptance of G when G is false).

And so, condition (1), says that the acceptance of a false hypothesis cannot be considered as more useful than the acceptance of a true hypothesis.

$$(2) \quad U(H) \gtreqless U(G) \leftrightarrow u(H) \gtreqless u(G) \leftrightarrow \text{cont}(H) \gtreqless \text{cont}(G)$$

The condition (2) says that in a set of true (resp. false) hypotheses the order according to the measure of utility is identical with the order according to the measure of information.

THE INDUCTIVE RULES OF ACCEPTANCE

Levi adopts the following definition of utility which satisfies the above-cited conditions of rationality:

(DU) (1) $U(H) = 1 - q \operatorname{cont}(\sim H)$, and
(2) $u(H) = -q \operatorname{cont}(\sim H)$, where $0 < q \leq 1$.

Levi interprets the parameter q as an index of relative importance ascribed to two cognitive aims: the higher q, the greater the importance is ascribed to the informational content of hypotheses. The choice of q determines — for a definite measure $\operatorname{cont}(H)$ — the choice of a definite measure of utility, i.e. it determines the values $U(H)$ and $u(H)$.

The measure of of utility thus defined has the following properties:

(a) If H is logically false, then $u(H) = 0$ (because then we have $\operatorname{cont}(\sim H) = P(H) = 0$),
(b) If H is logically true, then $U(H) = 1 - q$. Logical truths have no informational value ($\operatorname{cont}(H) = P(\sim H) = 0$); on the strength of (b) the utility of a logical truth depends upon q; i.e. upon the importance we attach to information: the greater the importance, the greater the utility of logically true statements decreases and comes close to zero, i.e. to the utility of logically false statements.
(c) $U(H) - U(G) = u(H) - u(G) = q(\operatorname{cont}(\sim G) - \operatorname{cont}(\sim H)) = q(\operatorname{cont}(H) - \operatorname{cont}(G))$.

On the strength of (c), the greater importance we attach to information, the greater the difference of utility of two hypotheses with the same logical value is reduced to the difference in their informational content.

Levi believes that it is not possible to state conclusively to what extent two conflicting cognitive aims — truth and information — can determine utility: in different scientific contexts it can be rational to attach greater or lesser importance to information. Therefore, we must not think that only one measure of cognitive utility is rational. However, we can determine the limits within which such a measure can be considered to be rational, these limits are determined in the definition (DU) by reduction to the value of q.

The admission of $q = 0$ would mean the reduction of aims of science to truth. All true hypotheses would have then the same value 1, no matter what their contents are, and all false hypotheses would have the value 0. Such a measure of utility would lead to the rejection of induction as an always irrational procedure. On the other hand, if we admitted $q > 1$, tautologies would have a negative value, that is, smaller than logical falsehood (whose value is 0). This would also be an irrational measure: the above-cited condition (1) of the rationality of the measure of cognitive usefulness would be violated. For these reasons, Levi accepts for q the limits $0 < q \leq 1$. When $q = 1$ we get the strongest permitted importance which is ascribed to the need for information: a tautology has then a null value, like logical falsehood. The lower q, the more the need for truth dominates the need for information.

Estimation of the measure of cognitive usefulness opens up possiblities of application of the decision theory criteria of rational choice of action to the problem of acceptance of hypotheses by way of induction. In his book, Levi analyses one such criterion, namely Bayes' criterion of maximal value of the expected usefulness.

The rule of acceptance formulated by Levi is relativized to certain special situations where the researcher faces the problem of acceptance — on the basis of the knowledge he possesses — of a certain hypothesis which is supposed to be the answer to a certain problem. According to Levi, such a situation is typical in science, because the aim of science is just solving problems. When the problem is clearly stated, the researcher considers various hypotheses which are possible solutions of this problem, and he makes experiments to decide which hypothesis should be accepted. The problem can be characterized as a set of possible answers which are evaluated by the researcher as good answers to the given problem, i.e. a set of hypotheses. Levi's rule is restricted to those situations in which that set of hypotheses — let us denote it by H — has a certain definite structure; namely, for the set H, there exists a finite set of basic hypotheses $B = \{B_1, B_2, \ldots, B_n\}$ which satisfy the following conditions: (1) it follows from the investigator's knowledge that exactly one of the basic hypotheses is true (2) every H_i included in H (i.e. every right answer to the problem) is equivalent — on the basis of certain knowledge — to the alternation of basic hypotheses B_j.

Levi gives the following example of such a situation. Assume that someone is interested in the results of an election and he knows that there are three candidates X, Y and Z, one of whom will win the election. Right answers to the question 'Who will win the election?' can be the hypotheses: X will win, Y will win, Z will win, and their various alternations: X or Y will win, etc. The basic hypotheses can be the first three of these hypotheses: it follows from knowledge that exactly one of them will be true.

Levi relativizes the measure cont(H) to the given problem on the assumption that the information value included in the answer to this problem depends on what information is required to solve the problem. Generally speaking, in Levi's system the information value is related to the number n of basic hypotheses. Since this number is dependent on the present knowledge E of the one who is to draw the conclusion (basic hypotheses are defined as pairwise disjoint and exhaustive on the base of knowledge E), Levi relativizes the information measure to E, and uses the symbol cont(H,E) for this measure. For basic hypotheses this measure is equal to:

$$\text{cont}(B_i, E) = (n-1)/n,$$

because each basic hypothesis excludes all the other basic hypotheses. For any hypothesis H_i from the set H we have

$$\mathrm{cont}(H_i, E) = r/n,$$

where r is the number of basic hypotheses excluded by H_i. In the above-cited example we have the following values: $\mathrm{cont}(X \text{ will win}, E) = 2/3$, and similarly for the hypotheses Y will win and Z will win. For the disjunctive hypothesis that X or Y will win, the value of information is 1/3, while for the three element alternation that X or Y or Z will win, which follows from the body of knowledge, the value is null.

As we can see, Levi assumes that all basic hypotheses have equal information values. If someone considers the information that, e.g. X will win as more valuable than the information that another candidate will win, then, according to Levi, he should formulate his problem in a different way. For instance, instead of the question of which of these three candidates will win, he can ask whether X will win, or not. The second problem would determine a different set of basic hypotheses B, and instead of three such hypotheses we would have two: $B_1 = X$ will win, and $B_2 = Y$ or Z will win. Then, the information values would change, and we would have $\mathrm{cont}(B_1, E) = \mathrm{cont}(B_2, E) = 1/2$. In his later works, Levi admits the possibility that the information values for basic hypotheses may be unequal.

Levi assumes that a scientist has at his disposal a method for assigning conditional probabilities $P(H/E)$ to hypotheses. Probability is understood as a rational estimation on the basis of knowledge E of the chances that H is true. In the very formulation of his rule of acceptance Levi does not impose on this probability any special conditions apart from the axioms of probability and the so-called postulate of regularity, which states that for any statement H coherent with E, $P(H/E)$ should be higher than zero.

Later, however, in the numerous commentaries to his rule, he expresses views concerning this probability, which, in fact, are similar to those expressed by Kyburg. He states that personalism imposes conditions on probability that are too weak; in [50] he writes that for the evaluation of inference, we need not the probabilities which are assigned, but the probabilities which should be assigned (p. 191). Levi regards the lack of criteria of choice of confirmation function as the basic shortcoming of Carnap's theory which is an attempt at a formulation of a standard method for assigning probabilities to statements. He writes that the situations in which it seems possible to assign probabilities to statements in a standard way often occur in science. Such situations occur when knowledge (total evidence) includes statistical hypotheses which determine the statistical probabilities of the results of repeatable tests (p. 191). And later, on page 209, he writes that it seems reasonable to assume that inductive probability, i.e. the probability which is to be the base for induction, of obtaining of certain result in a given experiment is equal to the statistical probability of obtaining this result in any experiment of this kind, on condition that we have no information about this experiment, apart from that it is an experiment of this kind. This objection is imposed by the condition that inductive probabilities should be assigned to hypotheses in relation to the total of accessible premises important for the conclusion.

total of accessible premises important for the conclusion.

Levi's text suggests the identification of inductive and statistical probability which would result in the empirical character of inductive probability. The whole context, however, demonstrates, that it was only an incautious formulation. The intention seems to be the same as Kyburg's: inductive probability is to be coherent with the present knowledge about statistical probability. Like Kyburg (see Chapter 7), Levi thinks that, for certain empirical statistical hypotheses, their inductive probabilities can be estimated on the basis of Bernoulli's law of large numbers (pp. 206–7).

I must also stress that in Levi's conception, the measure $\text{cont}(H,E)$ is independent of inductive probability $P(H/E)$. The measure cont used by him can obviously be defined as some probability function, say, $P_B(H/E)$ so, that $\text{cont}(H,E) = 1 - P_B(H/E)$, but this measure of $P_B(H/E)$ cannot be identical to the inductive probability $P(H/E)$: the measure $P_B(H/E)$ is dependent upon the problem, i.e. upon the set of hypotheses B, and it is determined only for the hypotheses which belong to H. On the other hand, inductive probability is independent of the problem and it is not restricted to the hypotheses from the set H. Levi's conception excludes the possibility of defining the measure cont by inductive probability. The reasons why this possibility was excluded will be obvious when I describe Levi's rule of acceptance.

This rule prescribes the scientist to choose (accept) a hypothesis which is the answer to the problem determined by a set of answers H which was characterized above. Strictly speaking, it does not concern the choice of one hypothesis H, because in the set H there are, as a rule, hypotheses H_i, H_j such that one follows from another; so, if we accept some H, we will also accept its consequences. The thing here is to choose the strongest hypothesis H which is to be accepted. Levi's rule advises that the choice be made on the basis of Bayes' criterion of maximization of the expected value of usefulness.

As we already know, Levi uses the measure of information relativized to the premise E, $\text{cont}(H,E)$, and, therefore, the measure of usefulness is also relativized to E. This means that for a given hypothesis H, the usefulness of its acceptance on the basis of E can have one of two values: $U(H,E) = 1 - q\,\text{cont}(\sim H,E)$ if H is true, or $u(H,E) = -q\,\text{cont}(\sim H,E)$ if H is false. The probabilities of these values relative to E are equal to $P(H/E)$ and $P(\sim H/E)$ respectively, so the expected value (see Chapter 5) of the usefulness of acceptance of H on the basis of E is:

$$E(H,E) = P(H/E)U(H,E) + P(\sim H/E)u(H,E) =$$
$$= P(H/E)(1 - q\,\text{cont}(\sim H,E)) - (1 - P(H/E))q\,\text{cont}(\sim H,E)$$
$$= P(H/E) - q\,\text{cont}(\sim H,E).$$

The value $E(H,E)$ of the hypothesis H is maximum for the set H if, for any hypothesis G from the set H, the inequality:

$E(H,E) \geq E(G,E)$ holds.

However, in the set H, there can be more than one such hypothesis. In order to exclude freedom of choice in such a situation, Levi defines the concept of a strong maximal value $E(H,E)$:

$E(H,E)$ is strongly maximal in the set H if and only if: (1) $E(H,E)$ is maximal in H, and (2) for every other hypothesis G from the set H: if $E(G,E)$ is also maximal, then $\text{cont}(H,E) < \text{cont}(G,E)$.

Later, Levi proves that in the set H there always exists only one hypothesis H which has the strong maximal value of $E(H,E)$; namely, it is the alternation A^* of all B_i such, that $E(B_i,E) \geq 0$.

In connection with this, Levi formulates the following rule of acceptance:

(RL) (1) all basic hypotheses B for which $P(B/E) < q \, \text{cont}(\sim B/E)$, i.e. $E(B,E) < 0$, must be rejected, and the alternation A^* of all other B, as the strongest hypothesis from the set H accepted by way of induction on the basis of E, must be accepted;
(2) all deductive consequences of $A^* \wedge E$ must be accepted.

The number $q \, \text{cont}(\sim H,E)$ is called by Levi the level of rejection of hypothesis H. For all basic hypotheses B, the level of rejection is the same, namely q/n, because $\text{cont}(\sim B,E) = 1/n$, where n is the number of all basic hypotheses. The higher q, the higher is the level of rejection. And the higher the level of rejection, the more basic hypotheses will be rejected, and the stronger statement will be accepted as the strongest.

Let us return to the above-cited example. We have three basic hypotheses there: $B_1 = X$ will win the election, $B_2 = Y$ will win, $B_3 = Z$ will win. Assume that the probabilities are as follows: $P(B_1/E) = 0.1$, $P(B_2/E) = 0.3$ and $P(B_3/E) = 0.6$. For each of these hypotheses we have $\text{cont}(\sim B_i,E) = 1/3$. If we assume $q = 0.96$, the level of rejection will be $0.96/3 = 0.32$, in face of this we will reject the hypotheses B_1 and B_2 and accept B_3. If we assume $q = 0.66$, the level of rejection will be 0.22, so we will reject only B_1, and accept the alternation $B_2 \vee B_3$ as the strongest hypothesis. If we accept $q = 0.3$, the level of rejection will be 0.1, which will not allow us to reject any B_i, so as the strongest hypothesis H, we will accept only the alternation of all B_i which is a deductive consequence of knowledge E. The alternations $B_2 \vee B_3$ and $B_1 \vee B_2 \vee B_3$ follow from the hypothesis B_3, so we can see that at the highest of these three values of q, we have accepted the strongest hypothesis. At the lowest value of q we have only accepted the deductive consequences of E, i.e. we have not accepted any hypothesis by way of induction; here judgement is suspended. As we know, maximal $q = 1$ indicates maximum need of information, so we can see that the more the need of information dominates the need of truth, the stronger statements can be accepted on the strength of (RL). It can also be seen that the lower is q, the higher is the probability $P(H/E)$ required for the acceptance of H. When $q = 0.96$ the rule prescribes the acceptance of B_3 for which $P(B_3/E) = 0.6$; when $q = 0.66$ the rule prescribes the acceptance of $B_2 \vee B_3$ as the strongest hypothesis whose probability relative to E equals 09, and when $q = 0.3$ the rule prescribes the acceptance of the deductive consequences of E, i.e. such hypotheses H for which $P(H/E) = 1$.

In connection with this, the parameter q can also be interpreted as the degree of inductive cautiousness (or rather incautiousness, inclination to risk): the higher is q, the stronger, and at the same time less probable, are the hypotheses we would be ready to accept on the basis of the same premises E. $q = 0$ indicates extreme cautiousness — relinquishment of induction; $q = 1$ indicates the highest permissible inclination to risk.

One can say that the rule (RL) is in a sense probabilistic: it subjects the positive acceptance of H to the value of $P(H/E)$, because the value of $E(H,E)$ is positively dependent upon $P(H/E)$ at the given value of $cont(H,E)$ and q. It is not, however, a probabilistic rule in the same sense as the rules discussed in previous paragraphs because for the acceptance of H, it does not require that $P(H/E)$ be higher than 0.5 (i.e. higher than $P(\sim H/E)$).

Let us take the following example: let $B = \{B_1, B_2, \ldots, B_5\}$, and $P(B_1/E) = 0.4$, while for all other hypotheses $P(B_i/E) = 0.15$. For all B_i we have $cont(B_i, E) = 1/5$, so when $q = 0.8$, we obtain the level of rejection equal to 0.16. Therefore, the rule will prescribe rejection of all B_i except B_1, i.e. acceptance of B_1 whose probability is smaller than 0.5. Still, it does not lead to the acceptance of contradictory statements, because the rule (RL) does not suggest the acceptance of negation of hypothesis B_1 (i.e. the alternation of the rejected B_i) even if the probability of this negation is very high. Therefore, high probability is, here, neither necessary nor sufficient for the acceptance of this hypothesis. For this reason (RL) does not lead to the lottery paradox. This rule excludes the possibility that of all basic hypotheses can be rejected: even if these hypotheses are extremely numerous and all their probabilities are very small, it is not possible that for all these hypotheses the inequality $P(B_i/E) < 1/n$ holds because the sum of all the probabilities must equal 1.

Therefore, even at the maximum value of $q = 1$, i.e., when the level of rejection is $1/n$, all of these hypotheses cannot be rejected. In the case when B_i are hypotheses concerning the winning of particular tickets in an unbiased lottery, all these hypotheses will have probabilities equal to $1/n$, so none of them will be rejected, and suspension of judgement will take place.

Levi is of the opinion that the decision of suspension of judgement in such situations is rational: if the lottery is unbiased, there is no reason to reject the hypothesis that for any given ticket, it will win. According to Levi, rejection of any hypothesis can be rational only when its probability is small in comparison with the probabilities of competing hypotheses which have the same information value.

From the above remarks, it can be clearly seen why using of the rule (RL) excludes the possibility of defining of the measure of information cont by inductive probability. If we accepted the definition $cont(H,E) = 1 - P(H/E) = P(\sim H/E)$, then, for each basic hypothesis, we would obtain $E(B_i, E) = P(B_i/E) - qP(B_i/E)$, so the rule (RL) would never permit the rejection of any basic hypothesis, and it would always prescribe suspension of judgement, i.e. rejection of induction.

In numerous publications which contain comments regarding Levi's conception, we can usually find the objection that his rule makes the acceptance of a hypothesis too dependent upon the problem to which this hypothesis is to be an answer.

R. Hilpinen in [29] gives the following example: assume that the person X wants to foresee the result of a race in which three horses: a_1, a_2 and a_3 take part. Let H_i denote the hypothesis that a_i will win the race. Assume the following probabilities: $P(H_1/E) = 0.44$, $P(H_2/E) = P(H_3/E) = 0.28$. If X asks the question whether a_1 will win or not, then, according to Levi's suggestion, he should have $B = \{H_1, H_2\}$. If X assumes, for instance, $q = 0.9$, he will reject H_1, because the level of rejection will be $0.9/2 = 0.45$. If, however X asks which of these three horses will win, all three hypotheses will be elements of B, which will change their informational value and, for the same number q, we shall get the level of rejection $0.9/3 = 0.3$. Then X will reject H_2 and H_3, and accept H_1. And so, according to the problem, the rule (RL) prescribes the acceptance of the hypothesis that a_1 will win or its rejection, on the basis of the same knowledge E and with the same degree of cautiousness q. Hacking [23] and R. Jeffrey [41] describe similar examples. In [47] H. Kyburg expresses a supposition that every hypothesis whose probability is not equal to zero can be accepted on the strength of (RL) if B is appropriately chosen. This supposition is quite right. It can be seen from the above-cited example of Hilpinen that the choice of such B for H consists in the division of the hypothesis $\sim H$ into so many separate hypotheses that the probability of each of them is appropriately smaller than $P(H/E)$. Only the restrictions concerning language (lack of means to express such hypotheses) can constitute an obstacle in the construction of such set B.

In this way, Levi's rule can lead to the acceptance of contradictory statements H and $\sim H$ on the basis of the same knowledge E, if only the statement H is a proper answer to the questions posed by a scientist.

I. Hacking in [23] and R. Hilpinen in [29] demonstrate that Levi's rule can avoid these consequences if the value of q is reduced to numbers smaller than 0.5. As we already know, Levi's rule never allows the rejection of all n basic hypotheses; at most $n - 1$ hypotheses can be rejected. Therefore, the sum of $P(B_i/E)$ for all rejected B_i must be smaller than $q(n-1)/n$, and if $q < 0.5$ this sum must be smaller than 0.5. So the probability of the strongest accepted hypothesis (alternation of non-rejected B_i) must be higher than 0.5 if q is smaller than 0.5. The rule (RL) modified in this way permits the acceptance of hypothesis H only when $P(H/E) > 0.5$, and since (RL) never permits the rejection of such hypothesis, it cannot lead to the acceptance of contradictory statements on the basis of the same knowledge E.

I must emphasize that such a restriction of the value of q does not turn the rule (RL) into a probabilistic rule. Although $P(H/E) > 0.5$ becomes necessary for the acceptance of H, it is not yet sufficient. If, for instance, the probabilities of two basic hypotheses are $P(B_1/E) = 0.45$ and $P(B_2/E) = 0.55$, then, if $q = 0.49$, the level of rejection will be close to 0.25, so suspension of judgement will take place. The same hypothesis B_2, however, will be accepted on the basis of the same knowledge if B, instead of B_1 includes 100 hypotheses whose probabilities will be equal to 0.0045, because all these hypotheses will be rejected at the same $q = 0.49$ (the level of rejection will be then close to 0.0049). Therefore, the acceptance of one hypothesis as the answer to one problem and its non-acceptance (suspension of judgement) in answer to another problem will be possible, but the acceptance or rejection which is contingent upon the problem will not be possible.

In [29] Hilpinen raises another objection against Levi's rule namely, that it does not satisfy the following postulate:

(PH) If hypothesis H is acceptable on the basis of E, while G is not acceptable on the basis of E, then G should not be acceptable on the basis of $H \wedge E$.

Levi expresses the view that, although the acceptance of a hypothesis may be rational, its inclusion as knowledge, i.e. adopting it as a premise for further inferences (acceptance as evidence) may be irrational. Levi does not formulate any clear conditions concerning the inclusion of hypotheses as knowledge, but from his remarks we can see that it requires the acceptance of the hypothesis when the value of q is very small, which means that great importance is attached to truth, and great cautiousness is shown in acceptance by way of induction.

Levi gives the following example [50], p. 147, 151: there are four basic hypotheses B_1, B_2, B_3, B_4 whose probabilities are respectively: $p_1 = 0.74$ and $p_3 = p_4 = 0.005$, $p_2 = 0.25$. If we accept q a little larger than 0.02 (say 0.0021), the level of rejection will be a little higher than 0.005, so the hypotheses B_3 and B_4 will be rejected, while the alternation $B_1 \vee B_2$ will be accepted. This hypothesis accepted at so high degree of cautiousness (i.e. at a very small value q) may be, according to Levi, included as knowledge. If the researcher includes this hypothesis as knowledge E, his problem will be reduced to the question of which of those two hypotheses is true which means that he will have two basic hypotheses whose probabilities, on the basis of the new knowledge $E \wedge (B_1 \wedge B_2)$ are:

$$P(B_1/E \wedge (B_1 \vee B_2)) = \frac{P(B_1 \wedge (B_1 \vee B_2)/E)}{P(B_1 \vee B_2/E)} = \frac{P(B_1/E)}{0.99}$$
$$= \frac{0.74}{0.99} = 0.7475,$$

and

$$P(B_2/E \wedge (B_1 \wedge B_2)) = \frac{P(B_2/E)}{0.99} = \frac{0.25}{0.99} = 0.2525$$

If now the researcher adopts a q which is a little higher than 0.5, the level of rejection will be a little higher than $0.5/2 = 0.25$, in face of which, the hypothesis B_2 will be rejected and B_1 accepted.

In this example, the acceptance of B_1 on the basis of E and $B_1 \vee B_2$ requires a much higher q than the acceptance of $B_1 \vee B_2$ on the basis of E. Therefore, although the hypothesis B_1 could be accepted on the basis of E and $B_1 \vee B_2$, it could not be included as knowledge if we assume that inclusion requires a very small q. If, however, the probabilities of these hypotheses were more varied — for instance $p_1 = 0.981$ and $p_2 = 0.009$, we would have $P(B_2/E \wedge (B_1 \vee B_2)) = 0.00909$, so B_1 could be accepted on the basis of E and $B_1 \vee B_2$ at the same $q = 0.021$; the level of rejection $q/2$ would be then 0.0105, and B_2 would be rejected. In this way, Levi's rule allows inclusion as knowledge even those hypothesis which could not be accepted on the basis of E, but was accepted on the basis of $E \wedge G$, although G was accepted on the basis of E by way of induction.

Levi thinks that violation of the postulate (PH) is inconsistent with the intuitions which are connected with rationality of acceptance; he believes, however, that it cannot be avoided if we decide to include as knowledge those sentences which are accepted by way of induction, and to regard them as premises for further inferences. Hilpinen does not agree with this view and as the refuting argument he quotes (in [29], p. 108) an example of a rule of acceptance which satisfies the postulate (PH). This rule is a modification of Levi's rule (RL) which consists with the change of definition of practical usefulness. Levi based this definition on the measure of information $\text{cont}(B,E) = (n-1)/n$, relativized to the premise E and the problem H, because n is the number of basic hypotheses consistent with E.

Hilpinen, after Hintikka [36], adopts the definition of usefulness which is based on the absolute measure of information $\text{cont}(H) = 1 - P(H)$, where the probability $P(H)$ is equal to the inductive probability H relative to tautology t, i.e. $P(H) = P(H/t)$. In connection with this, the definition of cognitive usefulness is not relativized to the problem H and to the premise E either, but apart from this it does not differ from Levi's definition, i.e. we have:

$$U(H) = 1 - q \, \text{cont}(\sim H) = 1 - qP(H),$$
$$u(H) = -q \, \text{cont}(\sim H) = -qP(H).$$

As can be seen, cognitive usefulness of hypotheses is here independent of the problem, i.e., choice of B, and independent of the present knowledge E. The expected usefulness value of the acceptance of hypothesis H (as the strongest one) on the basis of E is:

$$E(H,E) = P(H/E)(1 - qP(H)) - (1 - P(H/E)) qP(H)$$
$$= P(H/E) - qP(H/E)$$

With the same definition of the strong maximum value $E(H/E)$, the hypothesis with this value appears to be the alternation of all B_i for which $P(B_i,E)$ has non-negative value, i.e. for which:

$$P(B_i/E) > qP(B_i).$$

The rule of acceptance, as presented by Hilpinen states:

(RH) All B_i for which $P(B_i/E) < qP(B_i)$ should be rejected, and the alternation of all other B_i should be accepted as the strongest hypothesis accepted on the basis of E.

The proof that the above rule satisfies the postulate (PH) is based by Hilpinen on the assumption that inference on the basis of $E \wedge H$ is done with the same value of q as the inference which led to the acceptance of H on the basis of E. As can be seen from this, Hilpinen interprets the postulate (PH) in the following way:

(PH) If H is and G is not acceptable on the basis of E at the degree of cautiousness q, then G is not acceptable on the basis of $H \wedge E$ at the same (or larger) degree of cautiousness q.

Such an interpretation is quite right. If we assume at all that various degrees of cautiousness are admissible in acceptance, then, quite naturally, we must agree that the same statement on the basis of the same knowledge can be accepted or not, according to the chosen degree of cautiousness.

The proof that the rule (RH) satisfies (PH) is as follows:

Assume that on the basis of E the rule (RH) has led to the acceptance of the hypothesis $A = B_1 \vee B_2 \vee \ldots \vee B_k$, as the strongest one. This being so, for each element of this alternation we have:

(1) $P(B_i/E) \geq qP(B_i), i = 1, 2, \ldots, k$.

Let H be an hypothesis accepted on the basis of E. If A is the strongest accepted hypothesis, then H must be an alternation of at least all elements of A, and since an alternation follows from each of its elements, H satisfies the conditions:

(2) $P(H/E \wedge B_i) = 1$ and $P(H/E) \geq P(B_i/E)$ for $i = 1, 2, \ldots, k$.

Therefore, on the strength of probability calculus and (2), each element B_i of the alternation A satisfies the condition:

(3) $P(Bi/E \wedge H) = \dfrac{P(B_i\ E)\ P(H/E \wedge B_i)}{P(H/E)} = \dfrac{P(B_i/E)}{P(H/E)} \geq P(B_i/E)$

(4) In face of (1) and (3) no hypothesis which is an element of A — i.e. not rejected on the basis of E — can be rejected on the basis of $E \wedge H$ (the level of rejection is $qP(B_i)$);

(5) So, the strongest hypothesis accepted on the basis of $E \wedge H$ is still the alternation A, that is, the set of hypotheses accepted on the basis of E will be identical with the set of hypotheses accepted on the basis of $E \wedge H$.

The fact that the rule (RH) satisfies the postulate (PH) follows from the fact that Hilpinen makes the informational value of hypotheses independent from E and from B. Thanks to this, the level of rejection of basic hypotheses $qP(B_i)$ does not change because of inclusion of new premises in E. Hilpinen also shows that the effects of his rule are less dependent on the choice of B.

The above-cited example of the horse race demonstrates that Levi's rule allows acceptance of the hypothesis that the horse a_1 will win if we ask whether this horse will win or not, and the acceptance of the negation of this hypothesis if we ask which of the three horses will win. On the other hand, the rule (RH) gives the same effects to both questions. If, for instance, we assume that for all three horses the a priori probabilities of winning the race are equal (i.e. we adopt the measure cont as it is required by Levi three basic hypotheses) the rule (RH) will prescribe the acceptance of the hypothesis that the horse a_1 will win, as an answer to both these questions, only if q is higher than 0.84; if, however, $q \leq 0.84$, the rule will prescribe the suspension of judgement also for both questions.

The independence of acceptance from the problem obviously follows from the independence of the measure of information from the problem. The equality of the a priori probabilities assumed in the above-cited example is quite inessential; it is their independence from the problem which is essential.

From the two quoted examples of the rules of acceptance which are based on cognitive usefulness, we can see that such rules can have various properties, according to what measure of usefulness they refer to. The measures of cognitive usefulness found in literature differ between one another mostly in this, that they are based on different measures of semantic information (like in the above examples). Different measures of information refer to different intuitions which are connected with the concept of the value of information which we get while learning that a given statement is true. The literature devoted to this subject is abundant.

The rules which are based on cognitive usefulness show how the controversy between the probabilitists and the adherents of Popper's conception could be solved. The authors of these rules agree with Popper that truth cannot be considered as the only aim of science. They also admit that he was right in indicating other aims which science tends to, and in stressing the fact that they are parallel to the tendency towards possibly strong statements, i.e. statements with high informational value. The rules of acceptance which are based on cognitive usefulness refer to various definitions of this usefulness, but all these definitions assume that science strives both for truth and for information.

The above-cited Levi's rule of acceptance (as well as Hilpinen's one) was based on Bayes' criterion of maximalization of expected usefulness. Levi does not think that it is the only possibility for the rules of acceptance: if the measure of usefulness is definite, there is also a possibility of the application of other decision-theoretic criteria which were discussed in Chapter 5.

11

Induction of confirmation

Not all induction theorists regard induction as reasoning in the sense of a mental process which leads to the acceptance of a hypothesis on the basis of accepted premises.

Such an understanding of inductive procedure is particularly opposed by the conception, called behaviourism, which was started by Jerzy Neyman [57], [58], one of the originators of decision theory. According to Neyman's view — which is commonly accepted in contemporary statistics — statistical rules of induction are not rules of inference, but rules about deciding to act. Neyman thinks that the wrong, confusing term 'inductive inference' should be substituted by the term 'inductive behaviour'. The rules of induction, on this interpretation, do not prescribe the acceptance of any statements, but only decisions of undertaking of certain actions. Carnap introduced this view in the theory of the empirical sciences. Carnap believes that there is no need to treat these sciences as a set of accepted statements, and so there is no need to seek the criteria of rational (correct) acceptance of statements by way of induction. The procedures applied in science which lead to the confrontation of hypotheses and empirical theories with the results of observation lead to confirmation of certain hypotheses, and, thanks to this, science makes a basis for man's practical activity. The acceptance of hypotheses and theories, however, is not necessary for it. According to Carnap, the logic of induction is reduced to the theory of confirmation whose task is defining the function of logical probability (confirmation function); this function is to assign to hypotheses definite degrees of confirmation relative to the premises which report on experimental results. In his later works, Carnap relinquished the thesis that there exists one confirmation function which adequately represents the logical relations between sentences. In the article [11] Carnap writes that the task of confirmation theory of confirmation is the imposition on the confirmation function of appropriate postulates (like, for instance, the postulate of satisfying of the axioms of probability); however, the reasons why we adopt these postulates are not of purely logical character; they refer to the concept of the rationality of decisions to act which are based on the confirmation function. Inductive logic — writes the author — is not a logic of inference. By the application of inductive logic, from the statement $C(H/W) = p$ which states that the degree of confirmation of an hypothesis H relative to the initial knowledge W is p, we move to the statement $C_r(H) = p$, which states that the degree of rational credence of H equals p. The statement $C_r(H) = p$ is an analytic statement which follows from the accepted definitions and postulates of rationality. The acceptance of such a statement does not lead to the acceptance of the hypothesis H. Carnap stresses that this formulation of inductive logic is not exposed to Hume's criticism, since the statement $C_r(H) = p$ is obtained by way of deduction. The confirmation function (or the function of rational belief) can be used as a determinant of rational decisions to act, but this does not belong to inductive logic, rather to the theory of rational decisions. The decision rules formulated by this theory do not require the acceptance of hypotheses whose truth the results of actions depend upon: the values of the confirmation function for these hypothesis are sufficient here.

In this way Carnap reduces the tasks of science to tasks which directly serve practical activity. For this reason, Carnap was not disturbed by the fact that his confirmation function (see Chapter 6.1) had null values for universal hypotheses. Positive degrees of confirmation for any general hypotheses are not necessary to make a rational decision to act. We always act in a particular situation; if the results of our actions depend on whether in this situation — say s — a certain condition — say M — is satisfied, then, to make a decision to act, we shall need the degree of confirmation of an individual hypothesis $M(s)$ and not a universal hypothesis $\bigwedge_x M(x)$.

Although confirmation theory is now commonly associated with Carnap, the interpretation of induction as confirmation is not essentially connected with the anti-theoretical view of science which is represented by Carnap.

I shall use the name 'confirmative conception of science' with reference to the view that induction does not lead to the acceptance of statements but only to their confirmation. This view is compatible with various conceptions of science. In particular, it is possible to appreciate special tasks and theoretical values of science, and at the same time express the opinion that the concept of uncertain acceptance and the concept of inductive justification are so vague that a demarcation line between accepted and non-accepted statements, or between justified and unjustified ones cannot be drawn in science, and that attempts at drawing such a line of necessity are too arbitrary, and, therefore methodologically useless.

Relinquishment of inductive acceptance methods can be reconciled with the view that induction is a kind of inference on condition that reasoning will be conceived in an appropriately weak sense. For instance, I shall quote the definition of validity of uncertain inference as expressed by Ajdukiewicz in his *Pragmatic Logic* [4], p. 119:

> (Uncertain) inference is conclusive in the light of (knowledge) K if the degree of certainty with which the conclusion is accepted on the strength of a fully certain acceptance of the premises does not exceed the logical probability of the conclusion relative to the premises and the body of knowledge K.

As can be seen, inference is here understood in such a way that it need not lead to the acceptance (in a qualitative sense), i.e. as it sometimes is said, of the detachment of the conclusion; it leads only to acceptance of a statement with some degree of certainty, which can be very small. Conclusiveness of inference understood this way can be reconciled with the fact that we accept the statement Z with the degree of certainty equal to 0.3, and the negation of Z with the degree of certainty 0.7. The concept of acceptance, in this sense, is usually called 'belief'. And so, we can say that Ajdukiewicz's definition constitutes a rule of inference which is not a rule of acceptance, but only a rule of partial belief: it identifies the rational degree of belief (maximum) with the logical probability, which, in fact, is in agreement with Carnap's view on the role of the confirmation function.

Literature concerning confirmation is dominated by the view that the confirmation function, i.e. the measure of the degree of confirmation of a hypothesis by the results of experience, ought to be a probability. This view is mostly (though not exclusively) opposed by the representatives of a Popperian orientation to methodology. However, the difficulties connected with the concept of confirmation concern not only a definition of an adequate measure of the degree of confirmation; they already occur on the level of a qualitative (classification) concept of confirmation. On this conception various postulates are imposed, which are not always consistent, and this leads to the so-called paradoxes of confirmation. Inconsistency of these postulates indicates that different semantic intuitions are connected with the concept of confirmation, and that this concept is not understood univocally. I shall quote a few examples of such paradoxes, whose analysis allows the description of the divergence of those intuitions.

11.1 POSTULATES FOR CONFIRMATION — THE SO-CALLED RAVEN PARADOX

This paradox is connected with the problem of confirmation of universal statements by individual statements. On the one hand, it is thought that confirmation should satisfy the condition that logically equivalent hypotheses should be confirmed by the same statements. Therefore, e.g. the hypothesis that each raven is black should be confirmed by the same statements as the hypothesis that each non-black object is not a raven. On the other hand, however, the view which suggests that the observations of, say, white shoes confirm the hypothesis that each raven is black, is clearly considered to be inconsistent with the concept of confirmation.

G. von Wright in [87] expresses the opinion that this paradox can be avoided by an appropriate interpretation of universal statements. The statement $\bigwedge_{x}$ (if x is a raven, then x is black) can express various sentences, depending on what range of generalization we shall adopt. According to von Wright, the natural range of the above generalization is the set of ravens. If we interpret the statement that each raven is black in this way, then only observations of ravens can confirm this statement. If, however, we assume that the range of generalization is bigger, observations of non-ravens will also confirm it.

Carl Hempel (in [24] and then in [27]) rejects this solution as an unnecessary logical complication. According to Hempel, the paradox is only apparent, and arises from erroneous intuitions concerning universal statements. The sense of paradox disappears if we realize that the statements with a universal quantifier are statements about all objects. For instance, the statement $\bigwedge_{x}(P(x) \rightarrow Q(x))$ says that in the set of all objects there are no objects which are P and not-Q. In Hempel's opinion, the sense of paradox may also originate from the fact that the confirmation of the hypothesis H by E tends to become independent of those statements that were part of knowledge before obtaining the result of experiment E. Hempel gives the following example concerning the hypothesis that each piece of sodium colours the flame yellow;: we take some unknown substance and perform an experiment from which it appears that the flame does not turn yellow; then by virtue of another experiment we find out that this substance is not sodium. That we do not detect any paradox in the result of the experiment confirms a universal statement. If, however, we knew in advance that the examined substance was not sodium, we would regard the fact that the experiment showed that it did not give a yellow colour to the flame as insignificant for confirmation of the hypothesis; we would consider that this result does not confirm the hypothesis because it does not confirm it more than the previously known fact that this substance was not sodium. Yet, from the logical point of view there is no difference here, in both cases we have the same premise that the given substance is not sodium and does not colour the flame yellow.

In Chapter 9 I quoted Hempel's view concerning the distinction between three phases of testing the hypotheses. According to him, the problem of confirmation is connected with the second phase which consists in the confrontation of the hypothesis with the results of experiments. This phase has a formally logical character in contrast to the other phases in which various pragmatic metters play an important role. The confirmation of the hypothesis with the experiment consists in the examination of a formally logical relation of confirmation, which can be defined with the help of syntactic means, like the relation of logical inference.

M. Black in [7] also emphasizes the fact that the concept of confirmation is sometimes understood in a formal-logical sense and sometimes in a pragmatic sense. One can, for instance, think — writes Black — that confirmation takes place only in case of the application of a certain methodological procedure called a test; a test may consist in a random choice of a raven and examination of whether it is black. With such an understanding of confirmation — remarks Black — the statement that an object is a black raven may either confirm a universal hypothesis, or not (if it is a result of a chance observation). The examination of non-ravens, on the other hand, cannot be a test for this hypothesis at all because this 'test' would be equally good for the hypothesis that no raven is black. In effect Black states that there are two ways of avoiding the paradox:

(1) rejection of the postulate that each concordant case confirms a universal statement,
(2) acceptance of Hempel's argument that the sense of paradox of this postulate is based on an erroneous intuition.

The first solution is chosen by Popper. According to him confirmation of an hypothesis can only by a result of a test, and a test is understood as an attempt at falsification of a hypothesis. The examination of non-ravens is not an attempt at falsification of the hypothesis that each raven is black because none of its results can refute the hypothesis, therefore, it is not a test.

One of the greatest enthusiasts of Popper, J. Watkins in [85] writes that the Popperian solution of the raven paradox consists of the acceptance of the postulate that equivalent hypotheses are confirmed by the same observation results, and by the rejection of the 'instantial' theory of confirmation according to which each observation of an object which satisfies a universal statement confirms this statement.

H. Alexander (in [5]) states that it is not a solution of the paradox, because, if we accept that equivalent hypotheses are confirmed by the same observations, the Popperian concept of test cannot eliminate the paradox; if something is a result of an attempt at falsification of the hypothesis, it will also be a result of the attempt at falsification of an equivalent hypothesis.

It is not clear to me why Alexander thinks that Popper's conception does not eliminate the paradox. Given that certain observations, i.e. of black ravens confirm both the hypothesis that each raven is black and the hypothesis that no non-black object is a raven, there is nothing paradoxical. The raven paradox consists in the acceptance of the three following postulates simultaneously:

(1) Every observation of objects with properties A and B confirms the hypothesis that each A is B.
(2) No observation of objects with properties non-A and non-B confirms this hypothesis.
(3) Equivalent hypotheses are confirmed by the same observations.

The postulates (1) and (2) constitute the so-called 'Nicod's Criterion' for confirmation, which was introduced by J. Nicod in [59]. The acceptance of those postulates together with (3) is clearly paradoxical, because it leads to contradiction: all cases of non-A and non-B confirm and at the same time disconfirm the hypothesis that each A is B. However, Popper rejects both the postulate (1) and (2). His attitude should be understood in the following way: if the observation of black ravens is a result of the test of the hypothesis that each raven is black, it confirms both this hypothesis and each equivalent hypothesis; if, however, it is not the result of a test, it confirms neither of these hypotheses. The same refers to the observation of non-black non-ravens: from the fact that examination of non-ravens is not a test of the hypothesis that every raven is black, it does not follow that, for instance, the sentence 'this bird is not a raven' cannot be a result of a test. Let us assume that some white birds whose shape resembles that of a raven were observed. The examination of these birds is a test in Popperian sense, because it may lead to falsification of this hypothesis if it appears that these birds are ravens. Therefore, if, in effect of this examination, we find that those birds are not ravens, we shall get confirmation of the hypothesis. Hempel's example with sodium was similar to this one.

And so, the pragmatic concept of confirmation in the above sense does not lead to the view-that instances of black ravens always confirm, while the instances of non-black non-ravens never confirm the hypothesis that each raven is black. Popper's attitude, when it is understood in this way, leads to elimination of the paradox a effectively, as the formal-logical attitude of Hempel, which consists in the rejection of postulate (2) and acceptance of a reverse hypothesis: all instances of objects which are neither A nor B confirm the hypothesis that each A is B.

One could say that Popper's view is more coherent with the common intuitions concerning confirmation: I think that anybody can be easily convinced that the result of the observation which consists in the statement that certain objects are neither A nor B can sometimes confirm the hypothesis that each A is B, if we describe an appropriate example of a test (certainly, if one does not reject the view that any individual statement can confirm a universal statement). On the other hand, the thesis that each incidental observation of an object non-A and non-B confirms such an hypothesis is greatly discordant with common understanding of both universal statements and the concept of confirmation.

However, from the fact that Popper's solution is more coherent with common intuitions it does not follow that Hempel's solution should be rejected. We can, and probably should, accept both concepts of confirmation the formal-logical one and the pragmatic one, as useful. I shall discuss it further, particularly in section 11.5. The most reasonable way of avoiding this paradox seems to be not confusing these two concepts, each of which avoids the paradox in its own way.

Another solution, or rather another explanation of the paradox, is described by J. Hosiasson-Lindenbaum [37] and H. Alexander [5]. They reject postulate (2) like Hempel, but they explain the sources of the intuitions connected with the postulate quite differently. The explanation consists of a justification of the following thesis:

(4) the observations of objects non-A and non-B confirm the statement that each A is in a weaker fashion than observations of objects A and B, if objects A were fewer than objects non-B.

Hosiasson-Lindenbaum and Alexander express the opinion that the source of eroneous intuitions which lead to the acceptance of (2) is the fact that the hypotheses explicitly formulated in science of the form 'each A is B', refer as a rule to cases in which the number of objects A is smaller than the number of objects non-B. In connection with this the instances of non-A and non-B confirm these hypotheses to such a slight extent, that it becomes the source of belief that they do not confirm them at all.

The justification of thesis (4) certainly requires a quantitative or at least comparative concept of confirmation. Hossiasson-Lindenbaum (in [37]) proves the thesis (4) on the assumption that the degree of confirmation is a conditional probability. Hosiasson-Lindenbaum's proof, however, is vague and unnecessarily complicated. She formulates the thesis (4) as follows [37]:

(4) Statement E_1 of the form 'x is A and x is B' confirms the hypothesis of the form 'each A is B' (and the equivalent hypothesis 'each non-B is non-A) better than the statement E_2 of the form 'x is non-A and x is non-B' if the number of objects A is smaller than the number of objects non-B (assuming that $0 < P(H) < 1$).

In the proof of this thesis, the author makes use of the following theorem on probability:

(T) if statement E follows from the statement H, and $0 < P(H) < 1$ then the lower $P(E)$, the higher $P(H/E)$. However, neither E_1 nor E_2 follows from H.

Hosiasson-Lindenbaum does not explicitly accept any assumption concerning probabilisitc dependence of statements E_1 and E_2 from H, which is necessary for the proof of her thesis, because the value of

$$P(H/E) = \frac{P(H)P(E/H)}{P(E)},$$

when $P(H)$ is given, is dependent not directly upon $P(E)$, but on the proportion of $P(E/H)$ to $P(E)$. Probably because of the obscurity of the proof described by the author (*Note*: Alexander's argument is also obscure), M. Black in [7] rejected this way of solving the paradox. He expressed the view that the thesis (4) is impossible to maintain because $P(H/E)$ depends not only on $P(E)$, but also on $P(E/H)$.

However, Hosiasson-Lindenbaum's thesis is right, if probabilistic independence of the statements 'x is A' and 'x is B' from H is assumed (she assumes it implicitly).

Namely, the author proves the following lemma:

(L) If the number of non-B objects is not larger than of non-A objects for any hypothesis G_i which concerns probabilistic dependence of A upon B: $P(x$ is B/x is $A) < P(x$ is not A/x is not $B)$.

In the proof of this lemma (which, in fact, is not necessary for the proof of her thesis), the author assumes that the statement of the form 'x is a A' and 'x is B' are probabilistically independent from each of these hypotheses G_i.

Something which is crucial for the proof follows from the assumption that the statements 'x is A' and 'x is B' are probabilistically independent of the hypothesis H that each A is B. This hypothesis is equivalent to the statement that 'x is A and $B \leftrightarrow x$ is A' for any x, so that $P(x$ is A and $B) = P(x$ is $A)$ for any x, i.e. to a hypothesis about probabilistic dependence of statements 'x is A' and 'x is B'. If the probabilistic independence of statements 'x is A' and 'x is B' from the hypothesis H is assumed, the proof of Hoisasson-Lindenbaum's thesis can be conducted in an extremely simple way. Besides, this assumption is natural, as these statements are logically independent of H.

To shorten the record, I shall adopt the following symbols: A — is an abbreviation of the statements of the form 'x is A', B — 'x is B, $\bar{A}$ — x is not A, AB — x is A and x is B, etc., H — each A is B. Later, I shall assume the following designations of the a priori probabilities (relative to the initial body of knowledge):

$$P(AB) = p_1, \quad P(A\bar{B}) = p_2, \quad P(\bar{A}B) = p_3, \quad P(\overline{AB}) = p_4$$

The assumptions are:

(1) $0 < P(H) < 1$,
(2) $P(A/H) = P(A)$ and $P(B/H) = P(B)$ (independence of A and B from H),
(3) $P(A) < P(B)$ (instead of the assumption concerning the number of objects).

From assumption (3) it follows that $p_1 < p_4$ (because $P(AB) = P(A) - P(A\bar{B})$), and $P(\overline{AB}) = P(\bar{B}) - P(A\bar{B})$. Since H excludes $A\bar{B}$ we get $P(AB/H) = P(A/H)$ and $P(\overline{AB}/H) = P(\bar{B}/H)$ and therefore, on the strength of the assumption (2) we get

$$P(AB/H) = P(A) \quad \text{and} \quad P(\overline{AB}/H) = P(\bar{B}) \ .$$

Compare now the conditional probabilities of H relative to $E_1 = AB$ and $E_2 = \overline{AB}$.

$$P(H/AB) = \frac{P(H)P(AB/H)}{P(AB)} = \frac{P(H)P(A)}{P(AB)} = P(H)\frac{p_1 + p_2}{p_1}$$

$$P(H/\overline{AB}) = \frac{P(H)P(\overline{AB}/H)}{P(\overline{AB})} = \frac{P(H)P(\bar{B})}{P(\overline{AB})} = P(H)\frac{p_2 + p_4}{p_4}$$

It can be seen that

$$\frac{p_1 + p_2}{p_1} > \frac{p_2 + p_4}{p_4}$$

if $p_1 < p_4$ and $p_2 > 0$. The inequality $p_1 < p_4$ follows from the assumption (3), while $p_2 > 0$ from the assumption (1) (if $p_2 = P(A\bar{B}) = 0$, we would have $P(H) = 1$). Therefore, Hosiasson-Lindenbaum's thesis is right if an additional assumption (2) is made.

H. Alexander in [5] formulates a slightly different thesis, namely: if we are to choose among two hypotheses: H = each A is B, and $G = A$ and B are probabilistically independent (i.e. $P(AB) = P(A)P(B)$), then the instances of AB confirm the hypothesis H better than the instances of $\overline{AB}$. It is not clear, however, how Alexander understands this 'better confirmation'. His reasoning is as follows: If we take a random sample from an n-element set of objects A, and obtain the result E_1 = all objects in the sample are B, then the probability of this result when the hypothesis G is assumed (i.e. independence of A from B) is very small, namely, $P(B/A)^n = P(B)^n$. If, however, we take a n-element random sample from the set of non-B objects, then the probability of the result E_2 = all objects in the sample are non-A is, on the assumption of G, equal to $P(\bar{A}/\bar{B})^n = (P(\bar{A}))^n$. So, if $P(A) < P(\bar{B})$, then, obviously $P(B) < P(\bar{A})$ hence $P(B)^n < P(\bar{A})^n$.

On this basis, Alexander states that the observations of AB better confirm H than the observations $\overline{AB}$. However, he does not clearly formulate a criterion of better confirmation. We can suppose that he does not adopt probability $P(H/E)$ as the measure of the degree of confirmation of H by E, because in such a case he would not need to assume the alternation of the hypotheses H or G; I have just demonstrated that for the proof of the inequality $P(H/AB) > P(H/\overline{AB})$, it is enough to make the above cited assumptions (1), (2) and (3). Alexander's text suggests that the problem concerns the differences between the probabilities of the results of experiments when H and G are assumed. Since, when H is assumed, both results have probabilities equal to one, so this difference is much bigger for E_1 than for E_2. It must be stressed, however, that in Alexander's reasoning E_1 is not identical to the statement AB; E_1 is a conjunction of n statements of the form a_i is B, about the objects $a_1, \ldots, a_n$, while the conditional probability E_2 is estimated relative to the hypothesis H (or G) and the knowledge that the set of objects $a_1, \ldots, a_n$ is a random sample from A.

It is not the fact that AB confirms H better than $\overline{AB}$, which follows from the dependences revealed by Alexander, but the fact that if A and $H \lor G$ are assumed, B confirms H better than A when $\bar{B}$ and $H \lor G$ are assumed, if the degree of confirmation is understood not as $P(H/E)$, but as the result of the subtraction $P(E/H \land K) - P(E/H)$ where the body of knowledge K includes the above assumptions.

J. Mackie in [53] adopts this result of subtraction, i.e. the Popperian measure of severity of a test (see (T) in Chapter 9) as the measure of confirmation. Mackie states that the degree of confirmation of the hypothesis that each A is B, which is understood in this way, is higher for the premise AB than for $\overline{AB}$ if $P(A) < P(\bar{A})$. Mackie accepts the above-mentioned assumption about the independence of A and B from H, i.e. $P(AB/H) =$

$P(A)$ and $P(\overline{AB}/H) = P(\overline{B})$. His thesis, however, appears to be false, because, according to the probability calculus and the above assumption, the equalities:

$$P(AB/H) - P(AB) = P(A) - P(AB) = P(A\overline{B}),$$

$$P(\overline{AB}/H) - P(\overline{AB}) = P(\overline{B}) - P(\overline{AB}) = P(A\overline{B}) \text{ hold.}$$

So it can be seen that $P(AB/H) - P(AB) = P(\overline{AB}/H) - P(\overline{AB})$, i.e. the degree of confirmation of H understood as the Popperian severity of the test is quite the same in both cases. I have omitted here the relativization to the body of knowledge K which appears in Mackie's system because it does not assume anything concerning knowledge which would change these equalities. Namely, he makes an assumption that A and B are probabilistically independent relative to knowledge, and that $P(A/K) < P(B/K) < P(\overline{B}/K)$ which, however, has no influence on the above-cited equalities.

The situation changes fundamentally if instead of the conjunction of premises AB and $\overline{AB}$, we adopt in the first case the premise B, adding A to the body of knowledge, and in the second case, the premise A, adding B to the body of knowledge, i.e. doing as Alexander does. Simplifying Alexander's considerations we can consider the following situations: we know that something is A, and then, because of a test we state that this something is B, in the second case we know that something is $\overline{B}$ and then it appears that it is $\overline{A}$. Now, we ask what is the degree of confirmation of H by the result of the test B on the basis of knowledge A and by the result of the test A on the basis of knowledge B. To realize the difference between these situations and the situations in which the premises are the conjunctions AB and $\overline{AB}$ it is better to quote an example of some properties which are not so immediately perceivable as black ravens — for instance Hempel's hypothesis that each piece of sodium colours the flame yellow. Assume that we know that a certain substance is sodium and we investigate whether it makes the flame turn yellow. The situation is quite different if we know that a substance colours the flame yellow and we ask whether it is sodium, because the result of the second test cannot falsify the hypothesis.

Now we shall accept Hosiasson-Lindenbaum's assumptions as above, i.e.

(1) $P(A) < P(\overline{B})$,
(2) $P(A/H) = P(A)$ and $P(B/H) = P(B)$,
(3) $P(A\overline{B}) > 0$ (instead of $P(H) < 1$)

and Mackie's additional assumption, which in this arrangement of premises plays a significant role:

(4) $P(B) < P(\overline{B})$.

The assumption (4) is as natural as (1) for the general-affirmative statements which are usually formulated in science and natural language: there are fewer black objects than non-black ones, there are fewer substances which colour the flame yellow than substances which do not do it, etc. To conceive the results better, we shall adopt definite probabilities, e.g.:

$$P(AB) = 0.001, P(A\bar{B}) = 0.009, P(\bar{A}B) = 0.099, P(\bar{A}\bar{B}) = 0.891.$$

Hence: $P(A) = 0.01$ and $P(B) = 0.1$.

Let us now compare the degrees of confirmation of the hypothesis $H =$ each A is B, in several different cases, accepting as their measure the result of subtraction:

$$P(E/H \wedge K) - P(E/K)$$

(1) The body of knowledge includes A, while B is a result of the test:

$$P(B/A \wedge H) - P(B/A) = 1 - \frac{P(BA)}{P(A)} = \frac{P(A\bar{B})}{P(A)} = 0.9$$

(2) The knowledge includes $\bar{B}$, and $\bar{A}$ is the result of the test:

$$P(\bar{A}/\bar{B} \wedge H) - P(\bar{A}/\bar{B}) = 1 - \frac{P(\bar{A}\bar{B})}{P(\bar{B})} = \frac{P(A\bar{B})}{P(\bar{B})} = 0.01$$

As can be seen, the difference between the degrees of confirmation is now very large. Large us now see what the values of the degrees of confirmation measured by $P(H/E \wedge W)$ will be

(a) $P(H/BA) = \dfrac{P(H)P(BA/H)}{P(BA)} = \dfrac{P(H)P(A)}{P(BA)} = P(H) \cdot \dfrac{0.01}{0.001} = 10P(H)$

(b) $P(H/\overline{AB}) = \dfrac{P(H)P(\bar{B})}{P(\bar{A}\bar{B})} = P(H) \ P(H)0.9/0.191 \approx P(H)$

Here, the difference of the degree of confirmation is also very large.

The differences between these two measures, however, will become evident when we take into consideration the instances of examination of those objects about which we already know that they are B or that they are $\bar{A}$.

(3) The knowledge includes B while the result of the test is A. The measure $P(E/H \wedge K) - P(E/K)$ gives the result:

$$P(A/BH) - P(A/B) = \frac{P(AB/H)}{P(B/H)} - \frac{P(AB)}{P(B)} = \frac{P(A)}{P(B)} - \frac{P(A\bar{B})}{P(B)}$$

$$= \frac{P(A\bar{B})}{P(B)} = 0.09$$

(4) The knowledge includes $\bar{A}$, while the result of the test is $\bar{B}$:

$$P(\bar{B}/\bar{A}H) - P(\bar{B}/\bar{A}) = \frac{P(\bar{B}\bar{A}/H)}{P(\bar{A}/H)} - \frac{P(\bar{B}\bar{A})}{P(\bar{A})} = \frac{P(\bar{B}) - P(\bar{B}A)}{P(\bar{A})} =$$

$$= \frac{P(A\bar{B})}{P(\bar{A})} \approx 0.0091$$

As can be seen, the measure $P(E/H \wedge W) - P(E/W)$ gives a much smaller degree of confirmation in situation (3) than in (1), and a much smaller degree in the situation (4) than in (2); whereas the measure by the conditional probability of the hypothesis is the same in the cases (1) and (3) and in the cases (2) and (4). This result is quite obvious in the face of the formulation of the function $P(H/E \wedge K)$: E and K are here treated symmetrically. On the other hand, function $P(E/H \wedge K) - P(E/K)$ does not treat the premises E and K symmetrically, which permits distinguishing the influence of the premise included in the initial body of knowledge, and later results of experiments on the degree of confirmation.

In connection with this, I could risk the statement that the result of subtraction $P(E/H \wedge K) - P(E/K)$ manifests the property of confirmation in the sense which M. Black called pragmatic (see above) better than conditional probability $P(H/E \wedge K)$. However, it does not do it absolutely well: the examination of the objects B whether they are or are not A is not a test in the pragmatic sense for the hypothesis that each A is B; neither is the examination of object $\bar{A}$ a test of this kind. So, if someone wants — like, for instance, Popper — to have the measure of confirmation parallel to the value (severity of test), then, in the cases (3) and (4) such a measure would give equal values; whereas the measure accepted by Popper gives significant differences. Still, the examination of objects $\bar{B}$ can falsify the hypothesis, although the chances of its falsification are smaller than in case (1), because $P(A) < P(\bar{B})$; however, the value of Popperian measure is larger in case (3) than in case (2), so this measure gives a lower degree of confirmation of H by the positive result of the test which could falsify the hypothesis, than by the result of examination which is not a test for this hypothesis at all.

I must stress that this result is not an effect of the particular values of a priori probabilities chosen here; they are chosen so that they satisfy the condition of probabilistic independence of statements A and B, i.e. $P(AB) = P(A) \cdot P(B)$. It can be seen, however, that no a priori probabilistic dependences of these statements (except $P(A\bar{B}) = 0$) will change the order which exists between the values of this measure in the situations 1, 2, 3 and 4, because this order results from the assumed general assumptions concerning $P(A)$ and $P(B)$, i.e. from the assumed order: $P(A) < P(B) < P(\overline{B}) < P(\overline{A})$.

The difference between values of $P(E/H \wedge K) - P(E/K)$ in the other two cases in which no experimental results contradict H are not intuitive either.

(5) The knowledge includes $\overline{A}$, while the result of observation is B:

$$P(B/\overline{A} \wedge H) - P(B/\overline{A}) = \frac{P(A\overline{B}) - P(A)}{P(\overline{A})} = \frac{P(A\overline{B})}{P(\overline{A})} = -0.0091$$

(6) The knowledge includes B, while the result is $\overline{A}$:

$$P(\overline{A}/B \wedge H) - P(\overline{A}/B) = \frac{P(AB) - P(A)}{P(B)} = -\frac{P(A\overline{B})}{P(B)} = -0.09$$

In both cases, the values are negative which, in Popper's interpretation, means that the results of observation shake the hypothesis, though they are not the results of a test which could falsify the hypothesis. Besides, the result of the observation (6) shakes the hypothesis more than the result of (5).

However, we could not raise the objection against Popper that he accepted a wrong measure of severity of the test because he always emphasizes the fact that this meaure cannot be fully formalized.

J. Mackie in [53] expresses the view that the pragmatic concept of confirmation which makes the degree of confirmation of a hypothesis by certain premises dependent upon the temporal order in which they were stated, is a paradoxical concept. I think that its paradoxicality depends on how one understands confirmation; anyway, if someone wants to understand confirmation so that it is independent of the order of statement of premises, he should not accept the result of the subtraction $P(E/H \wedge K) - P(E/K)$ as the measure of confirmation; for this measure treats the premises in a non-symmetrical fashion. Meanwhile Mackie himself accepts a measure like this.

11.2 POSTULATES FOR CONFIRMATION — CONFIRMING INCONSISTENT HYPOTHESES BY THE SAME EXPERIMENTS

N. Goodman in [20] noticed that what leads to the acceptance of inconsistent hypotheses is, as a rule, the occurrence of the so-called 'unforseeable' predicates in hypotheses. I mentioned this fact in Chapter 7 in connection with Kyburg's definition of the relation of randomness. Goodman believed that the discrepancy can be avoided if these predicates are eliminated from the language. However, Hempel in [25] demonstrates that the range of confirmation of discrepant hypotheses is much broader. Hempel gives the following example: Assume that we investigate the relation between the values of X and of Y and we have the following results of measurements of these values for three objects: (1) $X = 0$, $Y = -1$, (2) $X = 1$,

$Y = 0$, (3) $X = 2$, $Y = 1$. Assume that we have different hypotheses concerning the relation between the values of X and Y, and that these hypotheses are inconsistent, e.g.: H_1: $Y = X - 1$, H_2: $Y = (X-1)^3$, H_3: $Y = \cos \pi(1 - X/2)$ etc.: these results of measurements in all three cases satisfy each of these hypotheses, so, if we assume that each result which satisfies a hypothesis confirms this hypothesis (such a criterion of confirmation was accepted, i.e. by Hempel — see the previous paragraph), we must accept that the same results confirm inconsistent hypotheses.

Hempel states that Carnap's theory of confirmation does not avoid this kind of paradox because it reduces inductive logic to the estimation of the degree of confirmation whose measure is $P(H/E)$. Hempel writes that confirmation of inconsistent statements is here impossible because it is impossible that two inconsistent statements have high probability relative to the same premises. Hempel seems to assume that Carnap accepts the following definition of the classification a concept of confirmation.

$$E \text{ confirms } H \leftrightarrow P(H/E) > 0.5$$

Carnap, however, has never explicitly accepted such a definition. In his foreword to the second edition of *The Logical Foundations of Probability*, Carnap writes that the quantitative concept of confirmation, whose measure is the confirmation function $P(H/E)$ corresponds to the following classificational concept:

(DP)$_1$ E confirms $H \leftrightarrow P(H/E) > k$,

where k is a constant.

In the text of [9], one can find remarks that k may be, for instance, equal to 0 or 0.5. Carnap thinks that the classificational concept of confirmation is not very important. In §87 of [9], he speaks against the acceptance of a postulate of coherence of a set of statements confirmed by a premise E. The question whether Hempel interprets Carnap in the right way is not important here, the fact is that the definition (DP)$_1$, when $k = 0.5$, really excludes the confirmation of inconsistent statements by the same sentence because, if $P(G/E) > 0.5$ and G is inconsistent with H then $P(G/E) < 0.5$.

I must stress, however, that the definition (DP)$_1$ makes accepting the postulate of deductive closure of a set of sentences confirmed by E impossible. The acceptance of (DP)$_1$ together with the closure postulate leads to a similar paradox as in the case of probabilistic rule of acceptance: if $P(H/E) > k$ and $P(F/E) < k$ but $P(h \wedge F/E) < k$, then $H \wedge F$ will be confirmed and unconfirmed at the same time.

The acceptance of the second variant of the definition (DP)$_1$ suggested by Carnap, namely, the acceptance of $k = 0$, in fact indicates the rejection of the classificational concept of confirmation. The concept of confirmation in a formal respect becomes similar to such purely quantitative concepts as, for instance, length or weight. Confirmation — in this quantitative sense — of inconsistent statements is obviously possible, even to the same extent.

In the first edition of *The Logical Foundations of Probability*, Carnap formulated a completely different definition of the qualitative concept of confirmation which identifies confirmation with the positive probabilistic dependence:

(DP)$_2$ E confirms $H \leftrightarrow P(H/E) > P(H)$.

This definition was also accepted by Popper in [60]. In fact, this definition is incompatible with the Carnapian measure of confirmation $P(H/E)$, but this will be discussed in section 11.5.

Although, the definition (DP)$_2$ excludes the confirmation of contradictory statements, i.e. statements of the form H and $\sim H$ by the same premise E — because if $P(H/E) > P(H)$, then $P(\sim H/E) < P(\sim H)$ — it does not exclude confirmation of inconsistent hypotheses. Here is an example: let E be a statement that in a throw of a die, the result was an even number, H — a hypothesis that the result was a six and G — a hypothesis that the result was a four. We have $P(H) = P(G) = 1/6$, and $P(H/E) = P(G/E) = 1/3 > 1/6$. This means that both hypotheses are confirmed to the same degree.

In my opinion, confirmation of inconsistent hypotheses by the same premises is not paradoxical at all, if and only the confirmation of H by E (in the classificational sense) or any definite degree of confirmation of H by E is not treated as a base for the acceptance of H on the basis of E, but only at most, as a base for a definite degree of conviction about H on the basis of E.

A paradox arises when the postulate of coherence is imposed on the set of statements confirmed by E (or statements confirmed by E to the same degree). The postulate of coherence of a set of accepted statements can be treated as one of the very natural postulates of rationality of acceptance. We cannot see, however, why rationality of (uncertain) beliefs should require the postulate of coherence. Just the contrary: if, for instance, knowledge does not give us any base for belief that it is hypothesis H which is true, and not $\sim H$ (or vice versa), then, on the basis of such knowledge, the same degree of belief as regards these two contradictory hypotheses will be rational. In the above-cited example of inconsistent hypotheses, one of which states that a six was obtained in a throw of a die, while a second states that a four was obtained, the degree of belief as regards the truth of these hypotheses on the basis of the information that the result was an even number seems to be completely rational.

11.3 POSTULATES FOR CONFIRMATION: THE TRANSITIVITY PARADOX

Transitivity is here understood as confirmation of consequences or justification of the confirmed statement.

C. Hempel in [24] considers the so-called predicative criterion of confirmation which, like Nicod's criterion (see section 11.1) was widely discussed at that time. The criterion is as follows:

(Pred) The set of statements E confirms the hypothesis E if E can be divided into two disjoint subsets E_1 and E_2 in such a way that each statement which belongs to E_2 follows from E_1 and H, but it does not follow from E_1 alone.

An example: H is of the form $\bigwedge_x (P(x) \to Q(x))$, and E has the form $P(a) \land Q(a)$. E confirms H, because $Q(a)$ follows from H and $P(a)$, and $Q(a)$ does not follow from $P(a)$. Hempel shows that the confirmation understood according to (Pred) satisfies the following condition of transitivity:

(P1) If E confirms H and H is a consequence of G, then E confirms G.

The condition (P1) follows from (Pred), because the inference relation is transitive: if a statement E_2 follows from E_1 and H, and H follows from G, then E also follows from E_1 and G. Therefore, confirmation in the sense of (Pred) has the property which consists of the fact that if a statement E confirms H, then E confirms also each logical justification of H.

Later, Hempel states that confirmation — according to intuition — should satisfy another transivity condition, namely:

(P2) If E confirms H and G is a consequence of H, then E confirms G (i.e. if E confirms H, it should also confirm each consequence of H).

This condition should be accepted for the reason that if H is true then all consequences of H are true.

However, confirmation cannot satisfy conditions (P1) and (P2) at the same time, because it leads to a paradoxical consequence:

(K) If a statement E confirms a statement H, then E also confirms any arbitrarily chosen statement G.

The proof is as follows:

Assume that E confirms H, hence, on the strength of (P1), E confirms the conjunction $H \land G$ — where G is any arbitrarily chosen statement — because H is a consequence of $H \land G$, but G is also a consequence of $H \land G$, so, if E confirms $H \land G$, then it also confirms G on the strength of (P2).

Therefore, (K) cannot be maintained because the confirmation relation which satisfies this postulate must be either universal or empty. This being so, Hempel states that the criterion (Pred) must be rejected together with the postulate (P1), because otherwise we would have to reject the highly intuitive postulate (P2).

However, (Pred) is also deeply rooted in intuition: the view that hypotheses and empirical theories are confirmed by their observable consequences is very common. According to Hempel it is so because (Pred), and therefore (P1) as well — is true in many cases. For instance, when the hypothesis H is a specialization of G (i.e. a consequence of G), it is just to accept that if E confirms H then it also confirms G. However, the condition (P1) cannot be imposed on confirmation as a general principle, i.e. for any hypothesis G which H follows from, because then we get such absurd consequences as, for instance, the confirmation of Hook's law by the statement 'a is a raven'.

In connection with this, R. Toumela in [84] proposes to weaken both these postulates of transitivity by substitution of the deductive relation by the explanation relation. Tuomela assumes that the inference of H from G is a necessary condition of explanation of H by G, but not a sufficient one. It would be difficult to maintain that the conjunction $H \wedge G$ explains H although H follows from this conjunction. The definition of explanation introduced by Toumela tends to exclude such trivial instances of deduction, as giving no explanation. However, Toumela does not quote any definition of confirmation which would satisfy these two modified postulates together; he confines himself to the statement that such a proof of (K) as was conducted by Hempel cannot be conducted on the basis of the modified postulates (P1) and (P2).

Toumela admits that the most commonly adopted probabilistic definitions of confirmation, namely, the definitions $(DP)_1$ and $(DP)_2$ which were quoted above, do not satisfy these postulates together. Confirmation in the sense $(DP)_1$ satisfies the postulate (P2), but not (P1); while confirmation in the sense $(DP)_2$ does not satisfy any of these postulates. However, confirmation in the sense of $(DP)_2$ satisfies the following two other postulates on condition that $0 < P(H) < 1$ and $0 < P(E) < 1$:

(P3)   If E follows from H, then E confirms H
(P4)   If H follows from E, then E confirms H.

The inference of H from E or vice versa is an extreme case of probabilistic dependence: then we have $P(H \wedge E) = P(H)$ or $P(H \wedge E) = P(E)$.

Confirmation in the sense $(DP)_1$ satisfies (P4), because $P(H/E) = 1$, when H follows from E, but it does not satisfy (P3), even if $k \approx 0$, because the inference of E from H does not exclude $P(H/E) \leq k$.

As can be seen, confirmation in the sense $(DP)_2$ is a symmetrical relation, while $(DP)_1$ does not give symmetry. According to Toumela, it testifies to equivocal application of the term 'confirmation' in methodology: the definitions $(DP)_1$ and $(DP)_2$ give an account of meaning of two different concepts of confirmation.

Hempel in [24] did not refer to any probabilistic definitions of confirmation; his work was published ten years before Carnap's book *Logical Foundations of Probability* which directed the investigations concerning inductive logic towards a probabilistic interpretation of the validity of induction. The definition of confirmation introduced by Hempel in [24] referred to the concept of satisfying hypothesis by objects whose names occur in E. Carnap in §88 of [9] demonstrated that this definition was too narrow, because it excluded, e.g. confirmation of statistical hypothesis by statements about the observed frequencies in a sample, and the confirmation of statements of the form $Q(a)$ by statistical statements about the frequency of Q in the population.

It is worth emphasizing that the postulates which Hempel formulated for confirmation in the same work [24] are (except one) satisfied by confirmation in the sense $(DP)_1$ when $k = 0.5$, i.e. in the sense: $P(H/E) > 0.5$. Namely Hempel accepted there the postulates (P2), and (P4), and the following postulates:

(P5) A set of hypotheses confirmed by E is consistent.
(P6) If E confirms H and confirms G, then E confirms the conjunction $H \wedge G$.

Satisfaction of the postulate (P5) follows from the properties of probability: if $P(H/E) > 0.5$, and H excludes G, then $P(G/E) < 0.5$, whereas (P6) is not satisfied, because the probability of conjunction can be much smaller than the probability of each of its elements. So, from among Hempel's postulates, only the postulate of deductive closing of a set of statements confirmed by E is not satisfied by confirmation in the sense of $(DP)_1$ when $k = 0.5$. Confirmation in the sense of $(DP)_2$, on the other hand, satisfies neither (P2), not (P5), nor (P6), because:

The fact that (P2) cannot satisfy this postulate is quite obvious, at least for the reason that a logically true statement T is a consequence of any statement H, for the logically true statement T, the equality $P(T/S) = P(T) = 1$ holds, in spite of which T cannot be confirmed by any statement in the sense of the definition $(DP)_2$. Lack of confirmation of the consequence G of a confirmed hypothesis H may occur also in case when G is not a logically true statement, for instance when $P(H \wedge E) = P(G \wedge E)$ but $P(G)$ is appropriately bigger than $P(H)$.

In the previous paragraph it was demonstrated that the definition $(DP)_2$ excludes confirmation of contradictory statements, i.e. the statements of the form H and $\sim H$ by the same premise E. Hence, the set of statements confirmed by E satisfies the weaker postulate of coherence (PN) formulated by Kyburg (see Chapter 10.1). However, from the previous paragraph, we also know that $(DP)_2$ permits confirmation of inconsistent statements. So, the set of sentences confirmed by E in the sense of $(DP)_2$ does not satisfy the postulate (P5).

The fact that postulate (P6) is not satisfied also follows from the possibility of confirmation of inconsistent statements by the same statement E. The conjunction of such statements H and G will have $P(H \wedge G/E) = 0$, so it will not be confirmed, although its elements will.

11.4 THE PARADOX OF THE SO-CALLED STATISTICAL 'SYLLOGISM'

We find considerations concerning this paradox in Hempel's works [25] and [27]. Statistical 'syllogism' is described as an inference of the form:

a is A
$P(B/A) \approx 1$
therefore it is highly probable (nearly certain) that a is B.

Hempel notices that an object a as a rule belongs to different sets $A_1, A_2, \ldots$ for which $P(B/A_i)$ are different. For instance, the conditional frequency of Catholics — B — in a set of Swedes A_1 is, say, lower than 0.02, while the frequency of non-Catholics in the set of pilgrims going to Lourdes is, say, also lower than 0.02. If a is a Swede who went on pilgrimage to Lourdes — A_2 — then for the statement 'a is a Catholic' we obtain:

a is A_1	a is A_2
$P(B/A_1) < 0.02$	$P(B/A_2)$ 0.02
it is highly improbable that a is B	it is highly probable that a is B

The paradox consists in this, that various true premises lead to contradictory conclusions.

According to Hempel paradoxicality follows from the fact that the expression 'it is highly probable' (or 'nearly certain') which appears in the conclusion is understood as referring to the statement 'a is B' while it should be understood as referring to the relation between premises and the conclusion, i.e. to the relation of confirmation of the statement 'a is B' by premises. According to Hempel, the expressions 'probably p' or 'certainly p' in the contexts of inference are in this way understood in natural langauge.

If, for instance, in connection with the deductive syllogism we say:

a is A
Each A is B
so, certainly, a is B,

then, using the expression 'certainly' we characterize the relation between the premises and the conclusion, and not the conclusion alone. In the statistical syllogism, probability appears in the second premise in one sense, and in the conclusion in another $P(B/A)$ has a statistical sense, while in the conclusion it has the sense of a logical relation, like, for instance, in Carnapian theory: it is not a relation which permits detachments of the conclusion.

As can be seen, Hempel interprets the statistical syllogism in the following way:

a is A
$P(B/A) \approx 1$
$C(a$ is B/a is A and $P(B/A) \approx 1) \approx 1$,

where P is the statistical probability, and C logical probability, i.e. a confirmation function other than P. Obviously, such an interpretation eliminates the paradox.

According to Hempel there is one more problem which requires solution: if we have different $C(H/E_i)$ for different (true) premises E_i, we have a base for making the decisions to act, whose results depend upon the truth of H. In Hempel's and in Carnap's opinion, this problem, is methodological, not logical; logic confines itself to attention to estimation of degrees of confirmation relative to different possible premises. As regards the way of solving this methodological problem, Hempel also agrees with the view of Carnap (and numerous logicians who deal with inductive logic) that the base for estimation of the degree of confirmation in the applications of logic to definite situations should be constituted by the total body of knowledge. This means that decisions to act should be based on the value of $C(H/E_i)$ on condition that E_i constitutes the total body of knowledge of the decision-maker, or such part of this knowledge which gives the same degree of confirmation of H as the total knowledge.

Kyburg's conception gives a similar solution to this paradox; the difference is that logical probability is there relativized to the total body of knowledge, and not to arbitrary premises. If the body of knowledge includes the statements 'a is A' and '$P_S(B/A) = p$', then the value of the logical probability of the statement 'a is B' equals p only when, on the basis of this knowledge, a is a random element of A relative to B. So, if on the basis of knowledge K, a is a random element A relative to B, and this knowledge includes the statements 'a is A' and '$P_S(B/A) = 0.02$', then $P_L(a \in B) = 0.02$. If, on the other hand, on the basis of the body of knowledge K, a is a random element of A_2 relative to B, and the knowledge K includes the statements '$a \in A_2$' and '$P_S(B/A) = 0.98$', then $P_L(a \in B) = 0.98$. However, these are probabilities relative to different bodies of knowledge, so their difference is not paradoxical. The definition of P and of the relation of randomness, on the other hand, excludes the possibility that on the basis of knowledge K the logical probability of any sentence can have some different value: if K includes the above-cited statistical statements, then, on the basis of K the object a will be neither a random element of A_1 nor of A_2 relative to B (an exception to this rule may occur when we know that A_1 is included in A_2, or vice versa, in such a case, however, a may be a random element of one of these sets, but not of both of them at the same time).

For Kyburg, there is no problem of the choice of premises which are to be our basis, since logical probability is already relativized to the total body of knowledge. Still, in his conception there exists a problem of finding of a proper class of reference for the relation of randomness.

P. Suppes in [76] concerns himself with the problem of statistical syllogism. He adopts subjective interpretation of probability, but the solution of the syllogism in fact goes in the same direction: two different probability functions appear in the promise and in the conclusion. The author states that a natural rule of inference is:

$$P(A) = 1$$
$$P(B/A) = r$$
$$\overline{P(B) = r}$$

where A is B are statements saying, e.g. that someone is a Swede, that someone is a Catholic, etc., $P(A) = 1$ means that we are sure that A is true, and $P(B/A)$ designates the conditional degree of belief, e.g. belief that someone is a Catholic relative to the fact that he is a Swede. In the situation when $P(B/A_1) = r$, $P(B/A_2) = s$ and $P(A_1) = 1$, we can prove that $r = s$, and there is no contradiction in it, on condition that we use the same measure of belief, P, which satisfies the axioms of probability. Therefore, the total body of knowledge is not necessary to avoid the paradoxes, while in the examples like the one which was quoted by Hempel, the syllogism is simply incorrect because the conditional measure P which is used in the second premise is based on some absolute measure P from the time preceding the statement that A has happened. The correct formulation should be as follows:

$$P_1(B/A_1) = r$$
$$\underline{A_1 \text{ has occurred, i.e., } P_2(A_1) = 1}$$
$$P_2(B) = r$$

$$P_1(B/A_2) = r$$
$$\underline{A_2 \text{ has occurred, i.e. } P_3(A_2) = 1}$$
$$P_3(B) = s$$

P_1, P_2, P_3 are different measures (of beliefs from different points in time) so the paradox does not exist here, either.

Suppes's solution suggests that if we have found out both that someone is a Swede and that he went on a pilgrimage to Lourdes, i.e. our beliefs are $P_2(A_1) = P_2(A_2) = 1$, then we should not identify the degree of belief that he is a Catholic with the belief concerning the conditional frequency of Catholics in the set of Swedes, nor with the belief concerning their frequency in the set of pilgrims going to Lourdes. So, how are we the determine our degree of belief $P_2(B)$ in this situation?

Suppes states that the postulate of relativization of beliefs to the total body of knowledge is alien to deduction. Hempel, to the contrary, states that it is trivially satisfied by every deductive inference: if the conclusion follows from the premise E, it also follows from the total body of knowledge. Hempel adds, however, that the application in practice of the rule which prescribes relativization of the degree of confirmation of a hypothesis to the total body of knowledge is extremely difficult because of the immensity of knowledge. According to Suppes, this postulate cannot be imposed on beliefs, if it is unrealistic. However, Suppes accepts a weaker version of this postulate, namely, he says that in order to estimate the degree of belief, the $P(B)$ premise must be constituted by the total body of this knowledge which the author of the inference regards as important for the occurrence of the event B. And yet, the question of in what way the new experience is to change the function of belief P is, according to Suppes, and extremely difficult problem. Anyway, the author rejects the view that the function P_2 at time t_2 should be deduced from P_1 in the previous time t_1 by conditionalysing (see Chapter 8); in his opinion this view is impossible to maintain, because we continuously receive milliards of new pieces of information.

11.5 CONTROVERSY OVER THE MEASURE OF CONFIRMATION

In contemporary literature the following measures of the degree of confirmation of hypothesis H by premises E are most often propagated:

(A)   Conditional probability $P(H/E)$
(B1)   The result of subtraction of probabilities $P(H/E) - P(H)$, or
(B2)   the result of subtraction $P(E/H) - P(E)$.

The results (B1) and (B2) as a rule have different values, but because of symmetry of probabilistic dependences the equivalence

$$P(H/E) \gtreqless P(H) \leftrightarrow P(E/H) \gtreqless P(E) \text{ holds;}$$

this being so the results increase or decrease simultaneously and they have null value under the same conditions.

In the appendix IX to his *Logik der Forschung* (p. 322) Popper accepts the measure of degree of confirmation based on (B2), namely, the measure (C) which was discussed in Chapter 9. He regards (B2) as the measure of severity of the test and (C) as the measure of degree of confirmation. He states, however, that (C) is in fact only a form of normalization of (P2) or (P1). Indeed, the measure (C) has properties which are so similar to those of (B1) and (B2) that everything what will be said about these measures, will also refer to (C).

Popper is absolutely against the measure (A); his objections against acceptance of this measure were discussed in Chapter 9. In Appendix IX to *Logik der Forschung*, Popper raises another objection concerning formal incorrectness of this measure. Namely, he states that this measure leads to the following paradox: there are instances when E confirms H and shakes G, but at the same time E confirms H in a smaller degree than G. So, the following statement is paradoxical: x has the property A, and y does not have property A, but x has the property A to a smaller extent than y.

Popper's argument is as follows: the classificational concept of confirmation should, in his opinion, satisfy the definition $(DP)_2$ (see section 11.2) which is based on probabilistic dependence. Popper remarks, that this definition was accepted by Carnap in [9]. At the same time Carnap, assumes that (A) is the measure of the degree of confirmation which leads to paradoxical consequences. Popper gives the following example: H is a statement that the result of a throw of an unbiased die was a six, and E is a statement that the result of this throw was an even number, the probabilities are as follows: $P(H) = 1/6$, $P(E) = 1/2$ and $P(H/E) = 1/3$. In this situation, according to the definition $(DP)_2$ E confirms H, because $P(H/E) > P(R)$, and at the same time E shakes $\sim H$, because $P(\sim H/E) < P(\sim H)$. But $P(H/E) < P(\sim H/E)$ so, according to the measure (A), the degree of confirmation of H by E is smaller than the degree of confirmation of $\sim H$ by E. This being so, Popper states that identification of the degree of confirmation with probability is absurd both from the formal and intuitive point of view — because it leads to contradiction (p. 115).

Popper's conclusion, however, is too far-reaching: his arguments prove only that the measure (A) is inconsistent with the definition $(DP)_2$, i.e. it cannot be the measure of confirmation understood according to $(DP)_2$. In his foreword to the second edition of *The Logical Foundations of Probability* from 1962, Carnap explains that the definition $(DP)_2$ refers to the concept of increase of firmness, and the measure (A) — to the concept of firmness: Carnap defines the classificational concept of firmness, whose measure is (A), by a certain threshold of value $P(H/E)$ (see section 11.2) $(DP)_1$. On the other hand, firmness in the sense of $(DP)_2$ corresponds with the measure (B1). The paradox results from the confusion of two concepts, neither of which is inconsistent. Let me add that the measures (B2) and (C) are also consistent with the concept of confirmation $(DP)_2$ in the sense that they do not lead to the above paradox. In the same Appendix IX to *Logik der Forschung*, Popper expresses the opinion that Carnap's elimination of the paradox by way of rejection of the definition $(DP)_2$ is an *ad hoc* solution to save his theory.

It is doubtless that this controversy about the measure of confirmation is, as a matter of fact a controversy concerning the concept of confirmation. Carnap and Bar-Hillel, who in [6] defend the Carnapian theory of confirmation against the accusation of inconsistency, quite justly distinguish these two concepts of confirmation. The rejection of $(DP)_2$ for the concept of confirmation whose measure is to be (A) is not *ad hoc* at all, it is simply the elimination of an error which arose from confusion of two different concepts. It is difficult to understand why Popper does not want to agree with the fact that $(DP)_2$ and (A) refer to two different concepts, since the difference in senses of these concepts is very distinct.

The concept of confirmation whose measure is to be $P(H/E)$ is commonly associated with the intuition that the degree of confirmation of H by E is to be the measure of credence of the hypothesis H (rational degree of justificaiton, rational belief or trust in H) on the basis of the premises E. To see that the measures (B) cannot be the measure of the degree of confirmation in this sense, we shall return to the example of the throw of a die, which was used by Popper as an argument against identification of the degree of confirmation with conditional probability. In this example, according to the measures (B), the information E (that the result was an even number) gives a higher degree of confirmation of the hypothesis H that the result was a six than of the hypothesis that the result was not a six. However, it is obvious that if we have only the information that the result was an even number and the die is unbiased, it would be irrational to have greater belief concerning the hypothesis that the result was a six than the hypothesis that the result was not a six, i.e. that the result was a two or a four. Although the information that the result was an even number increases the degree of belief concerning H and decreases the degree of belief concerning $\sim H$, it does not do it to such extent that H can become more credible than $\sim H$.

Therefore, the measure (B1) cannot be used as an indicator of the degree of confirmation in the sense of credence. The same applies to Popper's measures (B2) and (C). On the other hand, these measures can be the indicators of the increase of credence in a hypothesis with regard to the degree of credence before acquiring the information E, to ensure that (A) is an indicator of the degree of credence.

The question whether $P(H/E)$ is a good indicator of credence of H on the basis of the premises E (on assumption of lack of other information significant for H), is obviously an open question. It depends to a great extent upon which function $P(H/E)$ we use, but it also depends greatly upon the general formal properties of probability. In Chapter 3, I indicated certain properties of probability which are good from the point of view of this application. The property which consists of the fact that $P(H/E)$ has maximum value in the cases of inference of H from E is undoubtedly good. For no premises can give a higher degree of credence to H than those which give the guarantee of truth of P if they are true.

On the other hand, the measures (B) and (C) do not have this property. These measures also have 1 as the upper limit of their value but in the case of inference of H from E these measures give very different values which are negatively dependent on the value of $P(H)$. Namely, the measures (B1) and (C) give, in such a case, the value $1 - P(H)$, and (B2) gives the value $(1 - P(H))(P(E)/P(H))$. Therefore, if H follows from E, and a certain weaker than H hypothesis follows from H (e.g. a precisation of H), then $P(H) \leq P(G)$, so the stronger hypothesis can have a higher degree of confirmation than the weaker one. These measures give a higher degree of confirmation to the stronger hypotheses not only in those case when they follow from the premises. According to Popper, it is an advantage of these measures, since the stronger measures are more valued in science because of their rich contents, informational value, etc. This, however, speaks against the application of these measures, if one wants to measure the degree of credibility of hypotheses on the basis of premises. For it is clearly irrational to assign higher credibility to the hypothesis H than the hypothesis G if G follows from H, and, consequently G must be true if H is true.

It is not clear whether Popper's intention was to make the degree of confirmation of H by E the measure of the degree of credibility of H on the basis of E. Popper does not always express univocally his view as regards this problem. And, so, for instance in Appendix IX to *Logik der Forschung*,

p. 334, he writes that the measure (C) can be interpreted as the degree of rationality of our belief in H in the light of tests of the assumption that E is a report on the results of genuine attempts at the falsification of H. On the next page, however, he writes that the degree of confirmation is nothing other than the measure of the degree to which the hypothesis H underwent tests and in which it resisted these tests.

Therefore, it must not be interpreted as the degree of rationality of our belief in the truth of the hypothesis H, we know that $C(H,E) = 0$ whenever H is logically true. It constitutes rather the measure of the degree of rationality of the temporary acceptance of a doubtful speculation — which is known to be a speculation — but which undergoes a detailed examination.

Anyway, no matter what the intentions of Popper might be, the measures (B) and (C) cannot be interpreted as measures of the degree of credibility or of rational belief because they admit the higher level of confirmation for the hypotheses than for their consequences.

Let us now ask, in turn, whether the interpretation of these measures as the measures of the degree of rationality of acceptance is possible. If the degree of confirmation of the hypothesis H by E is lower than the degree of confirmation of the hypothesis G by E were to be understood simply in the way that, on the basis of E, it is more rational to accept G and H, then the measures (proposed by Popper) for the same reason violate the intuitions connected with the rationality of acceptance (even of temporary acceptance). The statement that the acceptance of G is more rational than the acceptance of H, when H is a consequence of G is paradoxical. However, the statement that the acceptance of certain weaker consequences of G is more rational than the acceptance of certain weaker consequences of the hypothesis G is not paradoxical any more. It seems that Levi ascribes such intentions to Popper, when in [50] he states the expected value of utility of acceptance of the hypothesis can be regarded as an interpretation of the Popperian degree of confirmation of an hypothesis.

In Chapter 10.3, we saw that Levi's rule prescribes the acceptance of the hypothesis H with maximum value of $E(H, E)$ not because this hypothesis derserves acceptance more than all other hypotheses in the set H — since this rule prescribes also the acceptance of all concequences of H — but because the hypothesis H, being the strongest one, deserves the acceptance more than all the others. Levi thinks that the major shortcoming of Popper's work is that he does not explain the relation between aptly determined goals of science and his method of testing, and that he does not introduce any theory which could prove that the tendency to maximalization of the degree of confirmation as defined in his works is a good means to achieve these goals. In his book [50], Levi wanted to demonstrate that such a role may be played by decision theory.

The relation between the expected utility value of a hypotheses and the Popperian degree of comfirmation of a hypothesis is probably not very explicit in the definition of the expected value of utility of a hypothesis accepted by Levi, because Levi defines the informative value of a hypothesis with the help of the measure cont which is independent of inductive probability. However, in the version of this definition modified by Hilpinen (see Chapter 10.5) this relation is clearly visible). It is so because Hilpinen defines the measure cont by inductive a priori probability, so the expected value of utility of acceptance of H is $P(H/E) - qP(H)$. So, we can see that the measure (B1) is a special case of the measure $E(H, E)$ accepted by Hilpinen: these measures become identical when $q = 1$, i.e. at the greatest 'inductive incautiousness' admitted by Levi (when the greatest importance is attached to the informative value of hypotheses).

These two concepts of confirmation,, which are discussed here, should not be regarded as competitive concepts. Each of them can be methodologically useful. The concept of confirmation in the sense of credibility better coresponds to the measure (A), while the concept of confirmation in the sense of value of acceptance — on assumption that the value of acceptance of a hypothesis is positively dependent upon the informative value of an hypothesis — better corresponds with the measures (B) or (C). It is obvious that the adequacy of both these measures depends upon what will be possessed by the probability function of statements occurring in them. In this chapter, I have confined myself to the discussion of properties of these measures with regard to the formal properties of probability. The properties of various probability functions connected with their special interpretations were discussed in Chapters 4, 6, 7 and 8.

Let us now return again to the problem of interpretation of the measure (A) as the measure of the degree of credibility of hypotheses on the basis of premises. In this section I have discussed certain advantages of (A) as the measure of the degree of credibility. This measure, however, has also certain formal properties which are not intuitive in such an interpretation.

They are mostly concerned with a priori probabilities which at the applications of probability calculus to sentences are identified with conditional probabilities relative to tautologies. If T is a tautology and H is an empirical hypothesis, then $P(H/T)$ becomes the measure of credibility of this hypothesis on the basis of exclusively tautological premises. And because the sum of $P(H/T)$ and $P(\sim H/T)$ must equal 1, we obtain the consequence that tautologies confirm certain empirical hypotheses to a comparatively high degree. Anayway, it is incompatible with the empiricist view, according to which only experience can confirm or falsify an empirical hypothesis.

Measures (B) do not have this drawback: if in place of E we put a tautology, these measures will always give null value for any hypothesis H and for the negation of H. For then we have $P(H/T) = P(H)$ and $P(T/H) = P(T)$.

From the inevitable inequalities of a priori probabilities for certain empirical hypotheses, it follows that the inequalities of conditional probabilities $P(H/E) < P(\sim H/E)$ must hold for certain hypotheses H in the case of their logical independence from E. In Chapter 6.1 I quoted Salmon's view that inductive probability should satisfy the condition of probabilistic independence of statements which are logically independent. However, the fact that this condition is satisfied by some probability functions does not prevent the occurrence of the above-cited inequalities. Satisfying this condition would ensure that occurrence of the following equalities: $P(H/E) = P(H)$ and $P(\sim H/E) = P(\sim H)$ in the cases of logical independence of the statements H and E, but the inequalities of a priori probabilities $P(H)$ and $P(\sim H)$ would give the inequalities of $P(H/E)$ and $P(\sim H/E)$. The interpretation of $P(H/E)$ as the degree of credibility of H on the basis of E must lead to the fact that for certain logically independent statements H and E, H will be more credible on the basis of E than $\sim H$.

We can see, then, that the measure (A) as the measure of credibility has certain non-intuitive properties which are independent of the choice of the probability function occurring in it, but are connected with the property of every such function. They are connected simply with this, that such a function must have some a priori values, and no such values are intuitive on the interpretation of the measure (A) as the degree of credibility of statements on the basis of premises.

Theories of logical probability in Carnap's or Hintikka's style try to explain the values of a priori logical probabilities by the logical properties of statements. It is accepted that the more logical possibilities exclude the statement, the smaller its a priori probability. This assumption, however, is too weak for estimating the values of a priori probabilities. In Chapters 6.1 and 6.2, we saw that equally probable possibilities can be chosen in many ways. The theory of subjective probability does not try to justify any choice of probability function at all. Any degrees of a priori belief are regarded there as rational, since rationality of beliefs is understood only as satisfaction of the axioms of probability.

Now, I wish to return for a moment to Kyburg's conception of probability which was discussed in Chapter 7. His probability is also a measure of a degree of conformation in the sense of credibility, but it is always relativized to the body of knowledge and not to particular premises. Kyburg's conception avoids the above-mentioned drawback of the measure (A), because it avoids — as we already know — assuming any a priori probabilities. However, probability in Kyburg's sense is not strictly speaking a probability because the values of functions $P(H)$ are not numbers but numerical intervals. In [45], p. 225, Kyburg writes that the value of a priori probabilities for empirical statements are simply all numerical intervals of possible values of probability, i.e. (0;1). So a priori we always have for empirical hypotheses $P(H) = P(\sim H) = (0;1)$. Reduction of this interval can be caused only by empirical knowledge.

Kyburg's conception is doubtless the most reasonable conception of inductive probability. It avoids abitrariness in estimation of values of probability, which occurs both in the conceptions of logical probability in the Carnapian style and in the theory of subjective probability. At the same time Kyburg's probability has the above-mentioned advantages of the measure (A): in the case that a statement follows from the body of knowledge, the probability of this statement relative to knowledge has maximum value 1, and in the cases when a statement H follows from a statement G, the probability of the consequence H is not smaller than the probability of the cause G. The fact that Kyburg's probability does not satisfy the axioms obviously causes various practical and theoretical complications. For this reason probably Kyburg's conception stands aside the main current of works and discussions concerning induction.

12

Machine learning and induction
IAIN D. CRAIG,
Department of Computer Science, University of Warwick, Coventry
CV4 7AL, UK

1. INTRODUCTION

The previous chapters of this book have been concerned with the theoretical aspects of the problem of induction. The present chapter is an attempt to describe some of the more representative work in machine learning that has been undertaken in the last two decades and to relate it to the theoretical material that appears elsewhere.

When faced with this task, there is an immediate problem: machine learning work, although it employs terms like *induction* (for example, as in *inductive* concept formation), is not easily relatable to work in Philosophy and Logic. One does not, for instance, find *explicit* attempts to construct learning programs that work using a Popperian refutation method. Equally, probability theory is not used all that much by learning programs because they are essentially symbolic, and not numeric, in content. Instead of working from the basis of the degree of support afforded by evidence that some newly formed hypothesis is (currently considered to be) correct, machine learning tends to concentrate on the processes of generalization, specialization and analogy, and the techniques these processes employ are almost entirely symbolic.

For example, a concept learning program will attempt to from a generalization of a concept on the basis of symbolic descriptions of examples and non-examples of the concept. The symbolic descriptions are often highly structured, and the components of each description form the basis for the generalization process: in other words, machine learning research is based very much on the use of the *semantics* of highly specific concepts (often expressed as structures similar to predicates) and not on a general conception of inductive process — indeed the idea of an inductive process in machine learning is rather more a pragmatic mixture of Hempel's confirmation and Popper's refutation.

There is another complication: machine learning is typically concerned with the development or acquisition of individual concepts and not on the development of theories (Amarel's work (1986) and Hayes-Roth (1983), are exceptions to this). The literature on induction is, on the contrary, concerned with the status of entire theories and of the predictions that they make — that is, on the hypotheses they support. The Raven Paradox is about the ways in which we are justified in making statements about the colour of the ravens that we might observe in the future — clearly, this is based on the theory that 'all ravens are black'. When an albino raven is observed, it reduces the status of the theory about raven colour to one which admits of exceptions (one might only be able to say 'some ravens are black').

In inductive terms, one might say, in general, that learning programs make hypotheses about what might be the correct form of the concepts they are acquiring. A problem is, though, that once a concept has been completely formed, it is retained thereafter — two exceptions to this are Lenat's AM and EURISKO programs (see below). Humans, on the other hand, continually revise their beliefs and hypotheses in the light of experience: an inductively formed concept may be retained, even though it is believed to be incorrect, until further evidence is available.

The inductive processes of machine learning are not concerned with theory formation for the most part: they are concerned with learning descriptions (concepts), rules, action sequences and so on. One could argue that machine learning operates at a level that is considerably lower than that of the entire theory, although they do maintain hypotheses about very limited things. The various approaches to concept formation that are discussed in the next section can be described as vaguely Popperian because any inductively formed hypothesis remains in force until there is evidence that it is no longer valid: a similar comment can be applied to heuristics learning. In addition, as will be noted very shortly, one could describe the actual inductive concept formation method as being an example of Hempel's confirmation theory. The problem is, though, that these issues are never brought out by workers in the machine learning field.

It is, of course, possible to ask questions such as those about the validity of a structure that has been learned by a program. This amounts to questions about properties such as over-generalization and over-specialization: if a concept is too general, it has too many examples of low utility and so is not particularly useful (the converse applies to overly specific hypotheses). However, it is usually the experimenter who determines these questions and not the program: in other words, learning programs do not, typically, contain any representation of a learning theory — a theory of induction, one might say. Given the controversies inherent in the subject of induction in general, this does not seem surprising; also, given the difficulty of articulating a theory of learning (let alone one based on a theory of induction), there is the purely practical problem of how to represent the theory in a way that is going to be of use to the program — after all, if a program is to reason about something, it must have a representation of it and that representation must be such that reasoning is facilitated.

A question that must be addressed when considering the relation between machine learning and induction is this: why is it that learning programs are not concerned too much with the development of entire theories? One might argue that any learning program is actually developing a theory, as, indeed, it has been argued (e.g. Wilensky, 1983) that any knowledge-based program embodies a theory. For example, it has been claimed that the development of R1 (McDermott, 1982) enabled a theory of VAX configuration to be developed. Here, I believe, one is on shaky ground and the relationship between inductive theories and Artificial Intelligence becomes confused. A theory of VAX configuration is not a theory in the sense that General Relativity is a theory, for General Relativity makes predictions which can be tested empirically; a theory of VAX configuration is rather more like a recipe and makes few (if any predictions). This leads directly to the reason that I believe is behind the discrepancy between theory in machine learning and theory in terms of induction. The current generation machine learning program has access only to a highly limited world, whereas people have access to the external world. It is very hard so see how one can improve matters for learning programs because the natural world is intensely complex and one would expect any complete representation to be at least as complex.

Machine learning is *not* about theory formation in the large, then. What it is about is the formation of rather smaller hypotheses about data: for example, Winston's (1970) arch-learning program and Mitchell's version space technique (see below) could be thought to be operating using an inductive principle similar to Hempel's (1965) confirmation theory. Given the examples, 'Fido is a dog', 'Fido barks'. 'Rover is a dog' and 'Rover barks', these programs will form the generalization 'If X is a dog, X barks'. Confirmation theory seems to be the machine learning technique most closely related to the philosophical literature, even though, as has been mentioned above, the overall structure can be related to Popper's work. It might be argued that programs such as Quinlan's ID3 (see below) and Michalski's work on Conceptual Clustering (1983b) operate on lines closer to inductive probabilism. Quinlan's approach is to construct decision trees based on the properties of features. Michalski's work on classification is similar. The clearest reference to induction in the machine learning literature is Langley's (Langley *et al.*, 1983) sequence of BACON programs. The BACON programs are intended as experiments in scientific theory formation and their workings are modelled on the theory of scientific method outlined by Bacon. The fundamental idea behind Baconian induction is that theory formation is data driven: empirical evidence is gathered, and, from this, theories are developed.

There is no real discussion of the bases for the various kinds of induction in the machine learning literature, however: there are fleeting references (e.g. Michalski, 1983a), but nothing particularly solid. As a result, the reader must make his or her own connections.

2. AN OVERVIEW OF MACHINE LEARNING TECHNIQUES
2.1 Introduction
This section contains a fairly brief overview of the major approaches to machine learning that have been followed over the past few years. The

technique that is closest, at least in spirit, to the theories of induction discussed elsewhere in this book are those concerned with learning from examples. As is to be expected, machine learning has developed a number of quite different approaches, not all of which are directly related to induction: indeed, explanation-based learning (DeJong, 1986; Mitchell, 1986) is a deductive technique that performs a generalization task based on only one example. In addition to these techniques, there has also been considerable interest in learning by analogy and in learning by discovery. All of these techniques will be described in this section. The section ends with a description of learning in connectionist models.

2.2 Learning from examples

The basic problem for programs that learn from examples is as follows. Given a set of examples and non-examples of a concept, form the most general description of the concept on the basis of those examples. This problem is one of the most extensively studied learning problems in Artificial Intelligence, and, despite its simplicity, it has generated a number of different approaches and solutions. Learning from examples is fundamentally construed as being about learning and refining concepts.

One of the most famous learning programs that falls within the learning from examples paradigm is Winston's (1970) program. This program learned the concept of an arch from a number of structural descriptions of examples and non-examples of the arch concept. The program was presented with examples from which it could produce generalized descriptions and their production was constrained by the presentation of non-examples. A non-example of an arch (in the blocks world) is two blocks standing upright and a third on the table-top next to them. If a generalized description merely required there to be three blocks in close proximity, it would be rejected on the basis of this non-example.

When new positive instances of the concept (examples) are not covered by the current definition, the current definition is too specific and has to be generalized. When non-examples are covered by the current definition, it is too general and has to be specialized. Most algorithms that learn from examples operate in this way and require positive and negative examples on which to work, although the actual use made of positive and negative information varies with the algorithm.

Learning from examples can be considered to be a variety of search process (Mitchell, 1982; Dietterich and Michalski, 1983). Under this interpretation, the points in the search space represent concepts. When considered in this way, each concept can be thought of as consisting of a number of different features and the particular combination of features for any given point in the space determines whether the concept is correct, overly general or too specific. When construed in these terms, the ordering on the points in the concept space is partial: in other words, although some concepts are related by the generalization/specialization relationship, others are not. Within a space such as the one under consideration, there are clearly two basic operations that are to be performed: generalization and specialization, and they suggest two fundamental ways in which the space can be searched.

The first way is to search for more general concepts; the second is to search for more specific ones. When searching for more specific descriptions, the algorithm begins with the most general possible concept description and attempts to refine it. When searching for more general concept descriptions, the starting point is the most specific possible description which is modified by a generalization process. It is, of course, possible to combine the two search methods so that the algorithm sometimes moves towards more general, sometimes towards more specific concepts.

Given the fact that the conception of the search space has been defined in terms of its points and its operators, it is necessary to say how it can be searched. Clearly, it is possible to employ a more-or-less brute force method such as depth-first or breadth-first search, but for any search space of a reasonable size (and most problems of any interest generate large search spaces), these strategies entail that the learning process will take a very long time. Some researchers (e.g. Michalski, 1983a) have employed heuristic methods to assist convergence.

Since the concept space can be searched in specific-to-general, general-to-specific and in a combination of these ways, it seems useful to give a brief outline of each method, beginning with the specific-to-general one. Only an outline of the general principles will be given: it is possible to instantiate each scheme in a variety of different ways.

Specific-to-general methods begin with the most specific description of the concept to be learned. This description, as with most of the methods considered here, can be thought of as being in some variety of predicate calculus. The basic idea is that the most specific description is to be generalized as a result of examining the instances and non-instances of the concept presented to the program.

When positive instances are encountered, the algorithm checks them against the current best description (hypothesis). If the positive instance is not covered by the current best description (if the current best hypothesis fails to classify the example as an instance of the concept), the current best hypothesis must be generalized so as to classify the positive instance correctly. The goal of this process is to find the description that will correctly recognize all positive instances presented to the learning program as instances of the target concept, and to find the description which will also recognize all non-examples as falling outside the concept.

Quite clearly, when the current best hypothesis classifies a non-example as falling within the concept, some adjustments must be made. For an algorithm that operates in both a specific-to-general and general-to-specific manner, when a negative instance is classified as falling within the concept, a specialization must be undertaken. When generalization is the sole operation, as it is for the specific-to-general method (specialization is the sole operation for the dual case), some way must be found of changing the current best hypothesis so that it correctly classifies non-examples. This can most easily be solved by maintaining a partially ordered set of current best descriptions or hypotheses. When a non-example is encountered, all of those elements of the best hypothesis set that admit the non-example as falling within the concept are rejected — all those which reject the non-example are retained.

The general-to-specific algorithm, in its most abstract form, is clearly the dual of the above description. The current best hypothesis set has elements which are the currently most specific descriptions that cover positive and negative instances with varying degrees of accuracy. When positive instances of the concept are encountered, these hypotheses which do not admit them to the concept are rejected as overly specific. In general, the roles of positive and negative instances of the concept (examples and non-examples, in other words) are used in precisely the opposite sense to that in which they are employed when using the specific-to-general method.

At this point, it is worth stepping back a little from the two fundamental and abstract algorithms outlined above so that the question of what a learning algorithm needs to know can be addressed. First, it is necessary for the algorithm to be informed explicitly that it has been supplied with a positive or negative instance. This is necessary because the algorithm has to decide what to do in the case of a match or non-match (that is, it has to decide whether to generalize/specialize as a result of the classification of the instance). Second, it has to know what the important features of each description are. This is usually done in an implicit way by constraining the representation language to contain *only* the important features of a description: this move introduces tacit knowledge into the algorithm. Third, each algorithm must start with an initial description of the concept to be learned. No matter how inaccurate this starting point may be, it must be such that learning is possible using it as a basis. In a sense, each algorithm is provided with a description of the concept it is to learn — in other words, each algorithm begins by knowing what it is looking for.

The first point is important if one wishes to claim some psychological plausibility about one's algorithm (many workers in machine learning do not do this, although Anderson (1983) certainly does). In the natural environment, the learner does not usually know which instances of a concept are positive and which are negative: this is the raven paradox, for any non-black object will support the inductive hypothesis — that is what makes it a paradox. Most, if not all, machine learning algorithms avoid the paradox by having the relevant information explicitly supplied to them.

With these observations expressed (and I think they are important to the whole machine learning enterprise), let us now consider two ways of combining the two basic approaches to learning from examples: these are Anderson and Klein's method (1979) and Mitchell's version space (Mitchell, 1982).

The combination of moving from specific to general *as well as* from general to specific has some advantages — one of which was alluded to above: the combined method can be thought of as allowing a kind of backtracking so that the concept space can be searched more effectively. It can also converge more rapidly in some cases.

Anderson and Klein (1979) employed a combined scheme that starts with specific hypotheses and generates more general hypotheses as new positive instances are encountered; as negative instances are encountered, more specific hypotheses are created. This scheme has the advantage that it can generate *disjunctive* descriptions, whereas the simpler methods create only conjunctive ones. That is, the simpler methods can create concept descriptions that are composed *only* of conjunctions of predicates and relations (feature specifications). Combined methods can create descriptions that contain conjunctions and disjunctions of feature specifications.

Mitchell's version space (1982) differs from Anderson and Klein's approach to the combined method. The version space method relates two sets of hypotheses: the most specific set of descriptions that covers the input data and the most general set of descriptions. When new positive instances are encountered that are not covered by any of the most specific descriptions, the set of specific descriptions is transformed (using the specific-to-general method described above) into a set of more general descriptions. In a similar fashion, when a negative instance is encountered, the most general descriptions are modified so that they do not classify the new instance as falling within the concept.

If one thinks of the version space as consisting of the set of generalizations at the top and the specializations at the bottom, the idea is that new positive, but unclassified, instances move the specialization set up towards the generalization set, and when negative instances that are classified are encountered, the version space moves the generalization set down.

Termination occurs when the generalization and specialization sets are both singleton and identical: i.e. termination occurs when the version space contains one and only one description. Because of the way the version space operates, it can be thought of as a constraint satisfaction process which terminates with the most constrained single element of the space. An idea similar to the version space, but less computationally expensive is described by Bundy *et al*. (1985).

The example-learning algorithms considered so far have depended entirely upon the existence of a representation composed of structured descriptions which can be thought of as predicate calculus formulae. An alternative method has been adopted by Quinlan (1983, 1986), for example. This alternative is based on the idea of constructing decision trees from the example sets. Quinlan refers to this method as *TDIDT* (*Top-Down Induction of Decision Trees*): it was pioneered, amongst others, by Hunt *et al*. (1966). Quinlan's ID3 (1983, 1986) is the most widely known of the TDIDT systems, so the description below will concentrate on it.

The input to ID3 is a list of positive and negative examples of a concept. Each example is represented as a list of attribute-value pairs. The output of the ID3 algorithm is a decision tree containing tests at each node which sort instances along alternative branches. The leaf nodes of the tree contain the class of objects that have been sorted by walking the tree: the classes at the leaves are not further discriminable.

Quinlan's method begins with the top node (the root) of the tree and it grows its decisions one branch at a time towards the leaves. For each decision, ID3 uses an information-theoretic evaluation function to discover the most discriminating attribute. The rating derived by the algorithm is based on the number of positive and negative examples of the concepts to be discriminated associated with each attribute's values. The idea is that the values for each attribute which is eventually chosen provide the best way to determine whether the attribute can be used to determine whether an example or non-example has been presented. This process is applied recursively until the leaf nodes are reached.

The TDIDT method differs from the purely symbolic methods described above because it can represent disjunctions at any level in the tree. Systems like ID3 can generate disjunctive concepts far more easily than can any of the methods discussed above. Noise is a severe problem for the purely symbolic methods, and this, too, can be handled easily by TDIDT systems; also, TDIDT systems require very little search — this contrasts strongly with the extensive searches made by systems using the other methods, for example the version space technique. On the other hand, the TDIDT approach suffers from the disadvantage that, once a tree has been learned, the only way to add concepts or attributes is to rebuild the tree completely from scratch with the new objects added to the training set.

TDIDT methods might be thought of as just a set of discrimination methods and not learning processes. The concept definitions are given to the algorithm which then, basically, sorts the attributes according to their relatedness to the positive examples. TDIDT methods cannot be used, as has been observed, to build or derive concepts in an incremental fashion for the methods need an adequate set of attribute-value pairs, together with annotations concerning the relevance to the concept, in order to construct a discrimination tree.

The approaches to learning from examples discussed so far can all be classed as more-or-less inductive. This is so in the sense that there is no a priori guarantee that exactly the right concept will be learned. For example, by skewing the training set (the set of positive and negative instances of the concept that is to be learned), it is possible to force the learning algorithms to generate either something nonsensical or else to learn a very peculiar version of the concept. For methods other than TDIDT, the initial description can also impact upon what is learned. This has prompted an alternative set of methods for concept acquisition. This alternative set is sometimes referred to as the *analytic approach* (another term is *Explanation-Based Generalization* or *EBG* — this term will be preferred below) (DeJong, 1986; Mitchell, 1986).

The analytic approach requires considerable domain knowledge because it is based on the idea of constructing proofs based on formal axioms and rules of inference. The fundamental idea is that an EBG system constructs *explanations* of why an object satisfies a functional definition: the explanation is used to construct a structural description of the concept. Although the goal of EBG is still to form intentional descriptions of objects, as do the other methods, only a single positive example is ever required (this contrasts with the case for the more inductively-oriented methods described above which require many examples — both positive and negative — and which often require a special ordering on the presentation of examples). In place of the myriad data presented to the inductive methods, EBG systems employ a *domain model* or *domain theory*: this model is stated as a set of domain-specific axioms and inference rules which are used to explain how an instance satisfies the concept to be learned. In addition, an EBG system needs some test for determining when an operational definition has been formulated: this involves restating an initial functional definition in terms of structural features that are present in the training example.

EBG, basically, uses two steps. In the first step, the domain model is used to construct an *explanation* that proves that the training example is a positive instance of the concept to be learned. The explanation is really a deductive proof of correctness of a specific solution to a problem, given the domain theory's axioms. The second step involves transforming the leaf nodes of the proof tree into a set of sufficient conditions under which the explanation will hold. That is, the step consists in finding the most general version of the existing proof that is consistent with the domain theory. This can be accomplished by goal regression: the goal concept (the concept to be learned) is regressed through the explanation tree, replacing constants with variables when unifying variables are required to match against the same term.

Although EBG has advantages over the more inductive methods (principally, it requires only one example — it is a 'one shot' method), it suffers from the disadvantage that considerable domain knowledge must be available before any learning can take place. This suggests immediately that EBG cannot form a basis for any learning system that will bootstrap its knowledge in significant ways from an initially very small basis. EBG can also be thought of as a *transformational* method in which a general, functional description is transformed into a structural description. EBG is also a deductive and not an inductive method. In a sense, it relates to Popper's beliefs that science is an entirely deductive enterprise and that there can be neither an inductive logic nor an inductive method (for the latter must, he believes, rest upon some logical foundation for it to entitle us to make sensible statements about the world). It should also be noted that EBG is also a refutation method for negative examples and a constructive/confirmation method for positive ones.

2.3 Learning heuristics

The discussion has so far concentrated on learning static concepts. One might argue that there is very little point in merely acquiring concepts unless one can actually use them for some practical purpose — e.g. planning or problem-solving. Indeed, Wittgenstein (1953) argued that one can only be said to understand a concept if one can show that one can be seen to use it correctly. As a result of this consideration and as a result of the need for practical problem-solving systems, such as expert systems (McDermott, 1982), heuristics learning has become a major area for machine learning research. The fundamental intuition behind heuristics learning is that operators are used to guide search through a space from some initial state to a goal state.

One immediate consequence of this intuition is that heuristics learning can be thought of as the learning of heuristic conditions that determine the applicability of some operator to any given state. A second approch is the learning of macro-operators that collect together many smaller operators to increase the size of the steps taken when an operator is applied. The third major approach is the learning of analogies between previously encountered problems and a newly posed one.

A fundamental idea in the problem-solving literature (e.g. Nilsson, 1980) is that problems can be decomposed into states which can be reached via the application of operators. Each problem is specified in terms of an *initial state*, a *goal state* and a set of *operators* that are used to transform the inital into the goal state. A search has to be undertaken whenever more than one operator applies to any particular state: this requires that alternatives must be considered and evaluated in terms of the likelihood that they will lead in fewer steps to the goal state. Some constraints on operator application are given by the legal conditions on each operator which are seldom sufficient to reduce search by very much. In order to reduce the amount of search, *heuristic relevance conditions* must be associated with each operator: the acquisition of these conditions is the aim of heuristics learning. The idea is that the heuristic relevance conditions determine when an operator might be applicable — they are more general than the legal conditions which just state the conditions under which an operator *can* be applied.

The task of learning heuristics is simplified by the assumption that operators are independent of each other.

This suggests that *problem reduction* (Nilsson, 1980) can be used to learn heuristics. Problem reduction works by first dividing the task into a number of sub-problems (i.e. defining its sub-goals), one per operator; secondly, the heuristic conditions under which each operator is useful are formulated; finally, the rules are recombined into a complete heuristic search system. Nearly all work on learning heuristics has taken this three-part approach to the problem which divides the problem of learning heuristics into a variation of the learning from examples problem. The problem becomes, for each operator, one of formulating heuristic conditions on the basis of examples of situations in which they do and do not hold. In order to do this, positive and negative examples must be provided for each operator. Usually, the examples are computed because no tutor is provided to the system.

The problem of producing positive and negative instances is closely related to the *credit assignment problem* (see Samuel, 1963). The problem occurs in situations in which the learner receives feedback from its environment and has to decide whether it has made a good or a bad move. In the case of problem-solving, this amounts to deciding whether an operator application was such that it tended to move the overall solution towards or away from the goal state. For operator and heuristics learning programs, the problem is that sequences of operator applications are at issue and not the application of a single operator in isolation. It is rarely the case that the effects of applying an operator can be determined at the time that it is actually applied. Instead, the program must wait until some other operators have been applied (thus forming a sequence of operator applications) before the worth or utility of any particular operator application can be determined. Quite obviously, this can be an extremely expensive process, computationally. The aim of such an analysis is, though, to award credit to positive instances of operator application (those applications in which progress has been made towards the goal state) and assigning no credit for negative instances (those applications in which no progress or a regression has been made).

Learning from examples can be thought of in terms of credit assignment because it represents a situation in which there is only one operator (either the generalization or the specialization operator) and in which the solution path has a length of one (the step from the initial description to the final one). Within the heuristics learning paradigm, there are three fundamental approaches to the credit assignment problem: the simplest is the solution path approach, which will now be briefly described. This approach is the simplest because it relies on the intuitive notion of the application of operators forming a path from the initial state to the goal. The other techniques are learning while doing (Anzai, 1978; Langley, 1983) and the learning apprentice approach (Mitchell, 1986). The solution path approach also relates heuristics learning to concept learning in a conceptually clear manner.

The solution path approach relies on waiting until a complete solution path has been found. In some situations, there may never be such a path (for example, the operator set may be incomplete and will, thus, never lead to a solution). All moves along the solution path are desirable because they make progress from initial to goal state, whereas all moves that diverge from the solution path are undesirable because they do not lead to the solution (goal) state. In the case in which there is more than one solution path, some measure must be applied to choose one — if only one is chosen — for example, one might decide that the least-cost path be chosen (this is the alternative used in Mitchell's LEX (Mitchell *et al.*, 1983)).

The method of learning from the solution path involves two steps. First, each move along the solution path is marked as a positive instance of the responsible operator. Secondly, each move that leads directly off the solution path is marked as a negative instance of the responsible operator. It should be noted that only moves that lead *directly* off the solution path are so marked: moves two or more steps away from the path are considered to be consequences of the original divergence.

A limitation of this method, it should be noted, is that it is difficult to apply in domains in which solution paths are long. Techniques for learning while doing have been developed to support learning in such domains.

Once credit has been assigned, it is possible to move into the learning phase proper. As has been stated, the marking of the solution graph generates positive and negative instances of operator application. Once this has been completed, the markings can be used to learn heuristic conditions for the operators in question, and the learning problem has been reduced to a form of concept acquisition. There will exist, therefore, a space of concept descriptions for each operator in which the concepts to be learned are 'those states for which the operator should be applied'. This space is partially ordered by generality and can be searched using any of the methods for concept learning described above.

The method used for learning heuristics does place some restrictions on the learning method that is actually used. The learning system *must* be able to generate positive and negative instances of the operators it contains. This poses problems for general-to-specific systems because they begin with overly general descriptions. Specific-to-general methods are inherently conservative and make errors of omission rather than of commission. Clearly, mixed approaches seem to be the best choice for heuristics learning programs (Mitchell's (Mitchell *et al.*, 1983) LEX system used the version space approach (Mitchell, 1978), for example).

The approach used by Anderson (1983) in the ACT* system is similar in some respects to the credit assignment approach used by LEX: however, ACT*'s learning methods are rather different. ACT* learns a new production rule in a goal-directed fashion. Whenever a production appears as an operator in a goal tree on the solution path, a number of operations can be performed on it. One operation is *proceduralization*.

Proceduralization is based on the idea on specializing knowledge from a combination of a declarative knowledge base and a set of production rules. Some of the production rules are very general and contain variables. The production can only be instantiated by retrieving matching items from the knowledge base. The proceduralization process basically works by creating new rules on the basis of their instantiations in the goal tree. It works, basically, by taking a copy of the instantiated rule and storing it in production memory. The result of proceduralization (often referred to, also, as *knowledge compilation*) is that fewer knowledge base accesses are required so the task performed by the production rule is accomplished in considerably less time.

The second learning process used by ACT* is *rule composition*. Composition is a mechanism which takes two or more productions as input and combines them into a single, new production rule which accomplishes the task-performed by the input set in one step. This reduces the time taken to perform a task because it reduces the number of problem-solving steps required.

It should be noted that the generation of new rules by ACT* in no way alters the contents of production memory other than by addition. When new rules are created, they augment the existing set and do not cause the previous rules to be erased.

A completely different approach to heuristic learning was adopted by Lenat in his EURISKO program (1983a, 1983b, 1983c). EURISKO was the successor to AM (Lenat, 1982) and was primarily concerned with learning by discovery: its main interest for present purposes is the way in which it would create new heuristics. Both AM and EURISKO were based on Polyá's (1945) ideas on mathematical invention. Before describing the heuristics learning mechanisms, it is necessary to digress and consider the discovery task performed by EURISKO and AM.

The task assigned to AM was the discovery of concepts in set and number theory. The program started out with a fairly small number of basic concepts (115) and a slightly larger number of heuristic rules (250). With this initial corpus, AM examined its knowledge base of concepts to find interesting tasks to perform. The idea was that a task consisted in some mutation of one of the concepts present in the knowledge base and that interestingness could be defined in terms of a numeric measure. AM did not work in a goal-directed fashion, but merely engaged in generalization and specialization. When a task was taken from the program's agenda (a queue of tasks to be performed) and executed, it could cause other tasks to be added and, at some later stage, executed to cause either new concepts to be formed or old ones to be altered. Some alterations to concepts decreased their interest level (which was determined in part by the number of references to the concept from other concepts, in part by the reasons for the concept's existence, and in part by other factors — see Lenat, 1982), others caused the interest level to increase which caused other tasks to be executed using the same concept or its descendants.

AM was successful in deriving a number of interesting concepts, given its starting point. In this context, 'interesting' means 'interesting' to a human. For example, AM discovered prime numbers for itself. (see Lenat, 1982, for details).

Although AM was judged to be a success, it had a number of shortcomings, the principal one of which was that its set of heuristics was fixed. AM contained no mechanisms for operating on its heuristics in a manner similar to the way in which it could modify its concepts. The initial choice of heuristics was, therefore, crucially important to AM's operation.

The EURISKO program (Lenat, 1983a, 1983b) was designed as an extension to AM. EURISKO was designed to explore a concept space, mutating existing concepts to form new omes, again using an interestingness measure. EURISKO was applied to a number of domains — the application to a new domain required the extension (not replacement) of the program's knowledge base — including: mathematical concept discovery, LISP programming, game playing and VLSI design. In each case, the program discovered new concepts and, in the game playing domain, became a champion player in a space fleet design and war game (Lenat, 1983b). As Lenat remarked in his IJCAI-83 keynote address on machine learning, the success of EURISKO was due to a synergistic relationship in which the program would generate new concepts and Lenat would examine them himself, removing those *he* considered to be of low utility. Despite the fact that EURISKO worked in combination with Lenat, it is still worth briefly considering what the program did.

For any domain, EURISKO started out with a collection of concepts and heuristic rules, very much as AM had. A major difference between EUR-

ISKO and its predecessor was that heuristic rules (henceforth: *rules* or *heuristics*) were represented as individual concepts. This representation of rules differed from the one used for AM. AM's heuristics were represented as comparatively large pieces of LISP code (the program was implemented in LISP) and, while each heuristic covered a considerable amount of ground, it was not amenable to inspection and modification (the fundamental way in which AM and EURISKO both worked). For AM, there were two fundamental organizational structures: concepts, which were modifiable, and heuristics which were not. In EURISKO, the relative size of each heuristic was considerably reduced: instead of a few pages of code, each heuristic could easily be accommodated by one page of paper. Instead of one large heuristic, as had been the case in AM, EURISKO used collections of smaller heuristics which were combined using operators such as functional composition (which were themselves represented as concepts).

The representation of each heuristic was the same as for the concepts in EURISKO: heuristics were considered to be 'active' concepts — that is, concepts which could be executed as programming language code to cause some change to the program and its repertoire of concepts (including the rules themselves). This change in representation entailed that the concept mutation operators found in AM could be applied to heuristics *as well* as to static domain concepts: this entailed that any heuristic that EURISKO possessed could be modified as a result of the discovery process.

The reasoning behind this change to the structure and representation of the program was that, as a domain develops, new heuristics emerge to guide future discoveries. In order to escape the problem with AM that, after a certain time, no new interesting discoveries were made, it was considered necessary to be able to mutate and to augment the total set along with any changes to the conceptual structure of the domain.

In both cases, the learning process was construed as a process of discovery which was guided by the idea of interestingness. Learning was performed as a result of tasks being placed on the agenda. A set of learning operators which performed little 'tricks' (e.g. replacing constants with variables, replacing references to specific concepts with those to more general ones, etc.) was provided. A task on the EURISKO agenda might specify that a given concept should be generalized and give a set of reasons for this, together with a rating of the importance of the change.

As has been observed above, neither AM or EURISKO engaged in goal-directed activity. The discovery process was guided only by the concept of interestingness represented by the worth of individual concepts and heuristics and by the priority value assigned to each task on the agenda. Both programs appeared at times to engage in random mutations, then to emerge with a fairly coherent set of modifications and generate interesting and useful concepts and heuristics. This aspect of the behaviour has been noted by Lenat as reflecting the progress of science. Science does not always progress smoothly with new discoveries being made on a regular basis: instead, there are long periods during which little or no progress seems to be made. Although this similarity is interesting, I believe that it should not be pushed too far.

In addition to generalization and specialization, EURISKO contained methods for generating concepts by analogy. AM's concepts contained slots for recording analogies, but it did not exploit them to any significant extent. EURISKO's use of analogy was somewhat greater than its predecessor's, but still falls short of the use which is made in CYC (Lenat, 1986), a project to construct an intelligent encylopaedia using a derivative of the representation language RLL (Lenat, 1980) developed by Lenat for EURISKO. Mention of learning by analogy leads us to the last part of this brief review of machine learning: learning by analogy.

2.4 Learning by analogy

Analogy has, for a long time, been considered a powerful reasoning method. For example, an early Artificial Intelligence program reasoned by analogy (Evans, 1968). For learning, the importance of analogy is as follows. Once a problem has been solved, humans find solving similar problems less difficult: they are able to use their previous experience as a guide to solving new problems which may appear unrelated at first sight to anything previously encountered. For example, given the problem of focusing two X-ray beams on cancerous tissue, a solution will be found with greater difficulty without prior information about pincer movements in battles. With this prior knowledge, the focusing problem can be solved by analogy (it might be argued that this example exploits a deeper analogy between medical treatment and war). There is considerable evidence in the literature (e.g. Clements, 1982) that analogy is a very powerful tool.

In machine learning terms, it clearly amounts to learning from previous experience. More specifically, it amounts to using the solutions generated for previous problems as a guide to the solution of newly presented ones. There are two main approaches to learning by analogy: *traansformational* and *derivational* analogy. Of these two, transformational analogy is the more direct method.

Transformational analogy consists in transforming the solution to a previously solved problem in such a way that it can be used to solve a new one. It operates using a basically four-step method.

In step one, episodic memory is searched for instances of past problems that closely match the current problem description.

In step two, the previous solution is recalled: this may lead to the recall of a set of solutions, it should be noted. In the third step, the recalled solution is transformed by an incremental process which reduces the differences between the way in which the recalled solution achieves its goal and the steps which the new problem requires. This transformation process involves perturbing the recalled solution in a variety of ways — for example mapping operators in the recalled solution into the operators required by the new problem. The typical method for transforming the recalled solution is to employ a *means-end analysis* procedure in the solution space (rather than in the space of possible world-states): more details can be obtained from Carbonell, 1983). The means-end analysis procedure reduces differences between corresponding points in the solution space by a sub-goaling process (see Ernst, 1969, for more details).

The final step is taken only when the transformation step fails. If no solution to the current problem is generated from the recalled solution, a new candidate analogue problem can be selected from episodic memory and the process repeats from step two; alternatively the attempt to recall an analogous problem as a basis for the solution to the current problem can be abandoned in favour of an attempt directly to solve the problem. If a direct atempt is made which succeeds, the solution can be remembered for future use.

The effectiveness of transformational analogy depends upon the existence of a measure of similarity between present and previous problems. If the memory for previously solved problems is large (there have been many problems solved in the past, that is), transformational analogy will only reap dividends if those problems that are most directly related to the current one can be recalled: otherwise, the recall of problems can amount to no more than an iteration over *all* previously solved problems which results in a great many failures of analogy. It remains to be seen whether such measures can be found that are applicable to more than a few, very closely related problems.

Derivational analogy (Carbonell, 1986) relies on the information that is generated while searching for a solution to a problem. Sub-goal structures are frequently developed by AI problem-solving systems: these are typically discarded once the problem has been solved so that the alternatives that were considered cannot be accessed once the solution has been completed. The transformational analogy process outlined above ignores the additional information and operates only on the direct solution. As a consequence, where a new problem requires that an alternative decision be followed up, transformational analogy will be of no use. Transformational analogy, then, concentrates only upon the solution path and not, for example, on the reasons why a particular decision was made while deriving the solution. Derivational analogy makes direct use of this additional information to reason from experience.

The derivational process concentrates on *how* a solution was derived, and not just on what the solution *is*. The information that is used in derivational analogy is about the justifications for each decision that was taken in finding a solution to a problem: in other words, it is concerned with the justifications for applying any given operator. The idea is that the analogical transfer process should continue *as long as* the justifications for each step in a previous solution hold for the solution of the problem currently being attempted. It has the advantage that it allows more distant analogies to be drawn because the same justifications might hold for very different problems. The additional book-keeping information is handled by a Truth Maintainance System (Doyle, 1979) which is basically concerned with determining which justifications hold at any given point in the solution process.

There has been considerable interest in analogical reasoning in Artificial

Intelligence over the last few years. Analogical reasoning has also become a growth area in machine learning as the section in Michalski *et al.*'s (1986) second volume on machine learning shows. The analogical reasoning literature is particularly confusing if one wants to try to find some relationship between the work there and theories of inductive inference because it concentrates either on case studies (such as the one mentioned above about X-ray beams) or else on the computational mechanisms that are employed. Indeed, it is particularly hard to see any relationships between learning by analogy and conventional inductive reasoning — analogy is a phenomenon that has been largely ignored in the induction literature, although Polyá (1945) makes extensive use of it. Analogy appears to be a process of mapping one set of structures into another, whereas induction is concerned with the generation of hypotheses and with their predictive power. In a review of machine learning, learning by analogy cannot be omitted because it has become an important branch of the field. However, the reader is again left to figure out the connections between induction and analogy.

2.5 Connectionist learning

Connectionism represents a revival of a very old line of AI research. It is concerned with the functioning of brain at a more-or-less cellular level and not with the operation of high-level symbolic systems. Connectionist models are *sub*-symbolic and not symbolic. Another difference between learning in connectionist models and the symbolic approach to learning is that the former are *numeric* and *not* symbolic in form. In addition, connectionist networks operate basically in parallel, whereas most symbolic learning programs are sequential.

A connectionist model consists of a number of elementary processing elements (called *units*) which are connected via links to form a network; each link has a weight which determines the amount of activation that is passed along it. Units are thought of as operating in parallel. The activation that is passed along a link is determined by the processing unit whose output is connected to the link. The pattern of weights across the network determines what the network represents. Each processing unit represents a 'micro-feature' and the links between units determine how much of the micro-feature represented by the unit which supplies it with input will be found in the pattern of weights across the network: this is what activation represents, to an approximation. Rather than combining entire symbols by logical or heuristic processes, a connectionist model represents information by 'blending' micro-features together.

Connectionist networks are basically pattern-recognition devices and their history goes back to McCulloch and Pitts (1943) and to the Perceptron (Rosenblatt, 1959; Minsky, 1969). However, it is possible for connectionist network to have an internal structure that is far richer than the structure of a network of Perceptrons. Furthermore, the majority of the problems with learning that were encountered by workers in the Perceptron area have now been overcome (Rumelhart, 1986), so it is possible for a connectionist network to learn even when it has a rich structure — this was the problem with the Perceptron: there was no convergence theorem for multi-layer Perceptron networks.

Connectionist networks operate by propagating activation values along the links which form the network. The activation values come, in the first instance, from patterns that are presented to the network. Now, although a connectionist network is, essentially, a pattern-recognition device, it is also capable of computing functions such as Exclusive-Or. Patterns are usually represented as numeric vectors — this is where activation values ultimately come from. When a network is presented with a pattern, the values for each component are passed to the corresponding unit. Each unit performs some internal computation and sends the result along links to other units. The activation generated by the input pattern is spread across the network until it reaches the units that are designated as the network outputs. The activation values on the output units are the components of the output vector generated by the network as a whole. The output vector can be transformed in arbitrary ways because of the influence of the link strengths and the computations performed by individual units.

Given these basic facts about how connectionist netwoks function in general, it is possible to see how learning procedures can be developed. There are different ways in which learning can be undertaken: one dimension being whether the learning procedure is supervised or not. Supervised learning is the simplest case and is the most commonly found learning procedure type. For these reasons, it will be discussed first.

In supervised learning, the basic idea is that a training pattern is presented to the network. The aim is that the network learns the output pattern as a function of an input pattern. The simplest way in which a training pattern is employed is that the componentwise difference between the output generated by the network for the given input pattern and the training pattern is computed. That difference gives the error for the network. The error represents the amount by which the actual output differs from the desired output represented by the training pattern. Once the error has been determined, the value is propagated back through the network and all link strengths are recalculated. This process is repeated until the error generated by the network falls within some tolerance. The crucial portion of this learning process is that the weights on the links between units are adjusted. The weights determine how much of each unit's output is blended to form the output of the network.

It should be noted that it is not necessary for patterns to be stored explicitly in a connectionist network: the weights between units do the job of holding the information that is stored. Indeed, one aim of one formulation of connectionism (Rumelhart, 1986) is that there should be no units at all that represent a complete entity (pattern). Instead, entities are stored in the form of a distributed representation that is spread across the network as a whole. This approach has one advantage over the approach (the so-called *localist* approach) in which units represent definite entities (such as cars or items of furniture): it is possible to store considerably more patterns in a distributed representation than it is using a local representation (a semantic network — e.g., Fahlman, 1979 — is an example of a local representation, as is first order logic). Also, distributed representations greatly facilitate the generalization of patterns (Rumelhart, 1986, ch. 3).

The basic learning algorithm for supervised learning works by adjusting link strengths, which, in turn determine what the micro-feature blend currently stored in the network is. By presenting patterns to a network which differ only in some respects, but not in others, it is easily possible for the network to acquire a representation of the set of patterns such that whenever one pattern is presented, the output represents the generalization of the entire set (see Rumelhart, 1986, ch. 17). The kind of generalization that is developed is, though, quite different from the generalizations produced by symbolic learning programs. A symbolic learning program usually develops a description that is a generalization of previously encountered descriptions. In a connectionist generalization network, the generalization is much closer to a statistical property: the network generates the statistically most general output vector.

In addition to the formation of generalizations, connectionist networks are able to display other kinds of learning behaviour when using the kind of algorithm described above. They are, for example, able to produce at the output the same pattern as they were presented as input, but without storing the pattern explicitly (so no simple look-up procedure is employed). They are also able to learn associate totally different patterns with those presented as input.

Supervised learning is the simplest learning procedure for a connectionist network. Other schemes include unsupervised methods. In unsupervised learning, there is no teaching pattern from which to generate an error signal. As a result of this, the network has to use other means for generating the distribution of connection strengths. One form of unsupervised learning is described by Rumelhart (1986, ch. 5): this procedure operates by trying to generate clusters of units which discriminate features in the input patterns. The clusters are generated by means of a competition between units in the network, with the winners being given additional activation (this technique is similar in spirit to that employed by Holland *et al.*'s (1986) classifier systems).

Learning in connectionist networks is a very different process than it is in purely symbolic learning programs. The fact that these networks can learn a variety of different processes and structure gives them enormous power. Indeed, the relative ease with which these networks can learn has contributed to the increase in interest in them over the past few years. The major problem with connectionist models is that they always seem to be very low level and appear suited to perceptual rather than to cognitive tasks: this is a research challenge, as is the fact that most learning algorithms take enormous amounts of time to converge on a solution. The major difference between learning in connectionist networks and learning in symbolic systems is that, in the former, the learning process is very much closer to an approximation process and, in the latter, it is frequently a process of assembling and modifying symbolic descriptions.

The problems in relating connectionist models to induction are many. In particular, the sub-symbolic nature of connectionist models makes it very difficult to reconcile them with the high-level descriptions of inductive processes to which we are used. Indeed, we simply do not know enough about these models to make any real assessment of them. The best we can do with these models, at least with the models that are not simply re-interpretations of symbolic processes using a connectionist vocabulary, is to try to find analogies and to reason inexactly. The fact that we do not have a developed conceptual framework for reasoning about connectionist models is, at present, a severe disadavantage, but it does represent an important and intensely exciting challenge and could, possibly, lead to a new framework within which to make genuine progress towards a computational theory of mind and brain.

3 CONCLUSIONS

This chapter has been concerned, for the most part, with an overview of the primary techniques and concerns of machine learning. The chapter has outlined learning from examples, learning heuristics and learning by analogy: these are areas that are either historically important or areas of current activity. Learning from examples, and, to a certain extent, learning heuristics, can be construed as inductive processes, at least given an informal definition of induction. It seems worthwhile to consider for a moment the relationship between machine learning and theories of inductive inference.

As was advertised in the introduction, the relationships between machine learning and induction are very hard to see with any clarity. There are clear threads which relate machine learning to the theories produced by Hempel and Popper; the relationship with Carnap's work is, it would appear, almost wholly absent. In addition, there is comparatively little work on the development by programs of theories in a scientific sense — Langley's (1983) BACON programs have been mentioned briefly, but they are intended to represent Baconian induction and is not particularly clear how they actually follow the Baconian method other than by simply detecting regularities.

There has been little or no effort expended on building programs that explicitly embody theories of learning (the reasons for this were alluded to in the introduction), or which develop large-scale theories about the world. Because machine learning is, in the end, concerned only with computational techniques, the issues that are addressed are limited in coverage. Connectionist learning methods are very different from symbolic ones and are aimed at a very different level. For this former class of learning mechanism, the lack of vocabulary (e.g. how can one really talk about a sub-symbolic induction process while keeping the intentions of all theoretical terms invariant?) means that one can only say that the status of these models is essentially statistical (and possibly, although I am reluctant to admit it, closer in spirit to inductive probabilism than to any other theory).

In conclusion, I believe it fair to say that machine learning is a technology which has achieved some fairly interesting results, but which cannot truly be said at the moment to be directly based on the problem of induction as understood by philosophers and logicians. Whether one sees this as a genuine lack depends upon one's view of Artificial Intelligence and its role.

MACHINE LEARNING REFERENCES

Amarel, S. A. (1986) Program synthesis as a theory formation task: problem representation and solution methods, in Michalski *et al.* (1986), pp. 499–569.

Anderson, J. R. and Klein, P. J. (1979) A learning system and its psychological implications, *Proc. IJCAI-7*, pp. 16–21.

Anderson, J. R. (1983) *The Architecture of Cognition*, Harvard University Press, 1983.

Anzai, Y. (1978) Learning strategies by computer, *Proceedings of the Canadian Society for Computational Studies of Intelligence*, pp. 181–190.

Bundy, A., Silver, B., and Plummer, D. (1985) An analytical comparison of some rule-learning programs, *Artificial Intelligence Journal*, **27**, 137–181

Carbonell, J. G. (1983) Learning by analogy: formulating and generalizing plans from past experience, in Michalski *et al.* (1983), pp. 137–161.

Carbonell, J. G. (1986) Derivational analogy: a theory of reconstructive problem solving and expertise acquisition, in Michalski *et al.* (1986), pp. 371–392.

Clements, J. (1982) Analogical reasoning patterns in expert problem solving, *Proc. Fourth Annual Conference of the Cognitive Science Society*.

DeJong, G. (1986) An approach to learning from observation, in Michalski *et al.* (1986), pp. 571–590.

Dietterich, T. G. and Michalski, R. S. (1983) A comparative review of selected methods for learning structural descriptions, in Michalski *et al.* (1983), pp. 41–81.

Doyle, J. (1979) A truth maintenance system, *Artificial Intelligence Journal*, **5**, 231–272.

Ernst, G. and Newell, A. (1969) *GPS: A Case Study in Generality and Problem Solving*, Academic Press, New York.

Evans, T. G. (1968) A program for the solution of geometric-analogy intelligence test questions, in *Semantic Information Processing*, Minsky, M. (ed.), MIT Press, Cambridge, MA.

Fahlman, S. E. (1979) *NETL: a system for representing and using real-world knowledge*, MIT Press, Cambridge, MA.

Hayes-Roth, F. (1983) Using proofs and refutations to learn from experience, in Michalski *et al.* (1983), pp. 221–240.

Hempel, C. (1965) *Aspects of Scientific Explanation*, The Free Press, New York.

Holland, J. H., Holyoak, K. J., Nisbett, R. E., and Thagard, P. R. (1986) *Induction*, MIT Press, Cambridge, MA.

Hunt, E. B., Marin, J., and Stone, P. J. (1966) *Experiments in Induction*, Academic Press, New York.

Langley, P. (1983) Learning effective search heuristics, *Proc. IJCAI-8*, pp. 419–421.

Langley, P., Bradshaw, G. L., and Simon, H. A. (1983) Rediscovering Chemistry with the BACON System, in Michalski (1983), pp. 307–329.

Lenat, D. B. and Greiner, R. D. (1980) RLL: a representation language language, *Proc. First Annual Meeting of the American Association for Artificial Intelligence*, Stanford, CA.

Lenat, D. B. (1982) AM: discovery in mathematics as heuristic search, in Davis R. and Lenat, D. B. *Knowledge-Based Systems in Artificial Intelligence*, McGraw-Hill, New York.

Lenat, D. B. (1983a) Theory-formation by heuristic search. The nature of heuristics II: Background and examples, *Artificial Intelligence Journal*, pp. 31–60.

Lenat, D. B. (1983b) EURISKO: A program that learns new heuristics and domain concepts. The nature of heuristics III: Program design and results, *Artificial Intelligence Journal*, **21**, pp. 61–98.

Lenat, D. B. (1983c) The role of heuristics in learning by discovery: three case studies, in Michalski *et al.* (1983), pp. 243–306.

Lenat, D. B., Prakash, M., and Shaw, M. (1986) CYC: using common sense knowledge to overcome brittleness and knowledge acquisition bottlenecks, *Artificial Intelligence Magazine*, **6**, pp. 65–85.

McCulloch, W. S. and Pitts, W. (1943) A logical calculus of the ideas immanent in nervous activity, *Bulletin of Mathematical Biophysics*, **5**, 115–133.

McDermott, J. (1982) R1: A rule-based configurer of computer systems, *Artificial Intelligence Journal*, **19**, 39–88.

Michalski, R. S. (1983a) A theory and methodology of inductive learning, in Michalski *et al.* (1983), pp. 83–134.

Michalski, R. S. (1983b) Learning from observation: conceptual clustering, in Michalski *et al.* (1983), pp. 331–363.

Michalski, R. S., Carbonell, J. G., and Mitchell, T. M. (1983) *Machine Learning: An Artificial Intelligence Approach*, Tioga Publishing Co., Palo Alto, CA.

Michalski, R. S., Carbonell, J. G., and Mitchell, T. M. (1986) *Machine Learning: An Artificial Intelligence Approach*, Volume 2, Morgan Kaufmann, Los Altos, CA.

Minsky, M. and Pappert, S. (1969) *Perceptrons*, MIT Press, Cambridge, MA.

Mitchell, T. M. (1978) Version Spaces: An Approach to Concept Learning, PhD dissertation, Stanford University.

Mitchell, T. M. (1982) Generalization as search, *Artificial Intelligence*, **18**, pp. 203–226.

Mitchell, T. M. (1983) Generalization as search, *Artificial Intelligence Journal*, **18**, pp. 203–226.

Mitchell, T. M., Utgoff, P. E., and Banerji, R. B. (1983) Learning by experimentation: acquiring and refining problem-solving heuristics, in Michalski *et al.* (1983), pp. 163–190.

Mitchell, T. M., Keller, R. M., and Kedare-Cabelli, S. T. (1986) Explanation-based generalisation: a unifying view, *Machine Learning,* **1**, pp. 47–80

Nilsson, N. J. (1980) *Principles of Artificial Intelligence*, Tioga Press, Palo Alto, CA

Polyá, G. (1945) *How To Solve It*, Princeton University Press, Princeton, NJ.

Quinlan, R. (1983) Learning efficient classification procedures and their application to chess end-games, in Michalski *et al.* (1983), pp. 463–482.

Quinlan, R. (1986) Induction of decision trees, *Machine Learning,* **1**, pp. 81–106.

Rosenblatt, F. (1959) *Principles of Neurodynamics*, Spartan Press, New York, 1959.

Rumelhart, D. E., McClelland, J. L., and the PDP Research Group (1986) *Parallel Distributed Processing: Explorations in the Microstructure of Cognition*, MIT Press, Cambridge, MA.

Samuel, A. L. (1963) Some studies in machine learning using the game of checkers, in *Computers and Thought*, ed. Feigenbaum, E. A. and Feldman, J., McGraw-Hill, New York.

Wilensky, R. (1983) *Planning and Understanding*, Addison-Wesley, Reading, MA.

Winston, P. H. (1970) Learning Structural Descriptions from Examples, Tech. Report AI-TR-231, Massachusetts Institute of Technology, 1970.

Wittgenstein, L. (1953) *Philosophical Investigations*, tr. G.E.M. Anscombe, Blackwell, Oxford.

Bibliography

[1] Achinstein, O. Variety and analogy in confirmation theory, *Philosophy of Science*, **30**, 1963.
[2] Ajdukiewicz, K. Zarys logiki, Warszawa, 1957.
[3] Ajdukiewicz, K. Zagadnienie racjonalności zawodnych sposobów wnioskowania, in: *Język i poznanie II*, Warszawa, 1958.
[4] Ajdukiewicz, K. *Logika pragmatyczna*, Warszawa, 1965.
[5] Alexander, H. The paradoxes of confirmation, *British Journal for the Philosophy of Science*, **9**, 1958–59.
[6] Bar-Hillel, Y. Comments on 'Degree of confirmation' by Professor K. R. Popper, *British Journal for the Philosophy of Science*, **6**, 1955–56.
[7] Black, M. Notes on the paradoxes of confirmation, in [88].
[8] Braithwaite, R. *Scientific Explanation*, Cambridge, 1953.
[9] Carnap, R. *The Logical Foundations of Phobability*, 1950, 2nd edn, Chicago, 1962.
[10] Carnap, R. *The Continuum of Inductive Methods*, Chicago, 1952.
[11] Carnap, R. The aim of inductive logic, in [91].
[12] Cramer, H. *The Elements of Probability Theory*, New York, 1955.
[13] Czerwiński, Z. Zagadnienie probabilistycznego uzasadnienia indukcji enumeracyjnej, *Studia Logica*, V, 1957.
[14] Czerwiński, Z. Enumerative induction and the theory of games, *Studia Logica*, X, 1968.
[15] Feigl, H. De principiis non disputandum . . . ?, in Black (ed.) *Philosophical Analysis*, 1950.
[16] Feigl, H. On the vindication of induction, *Philosophy of Science*, **28**, 1961.
[17] Finetti, B. de La prevision: ses Lois logiques, ses sources subjectives, *Annales de l'Institut Henri Poincare*, **7**, 1937, English translation in [93].
[18] Fischer, R. *Statistical Methods and Scientific Interference*, New York, 1956.
[19] Fisz, M. *Rachunek prawdopodobieństwa i statystyka matematyczna*, Warszawa, 1958.
[20] Goodman, N. *Fact, Fiction, and Forecast*, Cambridge, 1955.
[21] Hacking, I. Guessing by frequency, *Proceedings of the Aristotelian Society*, **64**, 1963–64.

[22] Hacking, I. Slightly more realistic personal probability, *Philosophy of Science*, 34, 1967.
[23] Hacking, I. Gambling with truth. A review, *Synthese*, **17**, 1967.
[24] Hempel, C. Studies in the logic of confirmation, *Mind*, **54**, 1945.
[25] Hempel, C. Inductive inconsistencies, *Synthese*, **12**, 1960.
[26] Hempel, C. Deductive-nomological versus statistical explanation, *Minnesota Studies in the Philosophy of Science*, III, ed. Feigl, 1962.
[27] Hempel, C. Confirmation, induction, and rational belief, in [88].
[28] Hesse, M. Analogy and Confirmation Theory, *Philosophy of Science*, **31**, 1964.
[29] Hilpinen, R. Rules of Acceptance and Inductive Logic, *Acta Philosophica Fennica*, 21, Amsterdam, 1968.
[30] Hintikka, J., Hilpinen, R. Knowledge, acceptance, and inductive logic, in [88].
[31] Hintikka, J. Distributive normal forms in first-order logic, in Crossley (ed.) *Formal Systems*, 1965.
[32] Hintikka, J. A two-dimensional continuum of inductive methods, in [88].
[33] Hintikka, J. Induction of enumeration and induction by elimination, in [94].
[34] Hintikka, J. Towards a theory of inductive generalization, in [92].
[35] Hintikka, J. Surface information and depth information, in [89].
[36] Hintikka, J., Pietarinen, J. Semantic information and inductive logic, in [88].
[37] Hosiasson-Lindenbaum, J. On confirmation, *Journal of Symbolic Logic*, **5**, 1940.
[38] Hume, D. *Treatise on the Human Nature*, Polish translation, Warszawa, 1963.
[39] Jeffrey, R. *The Logic of Decision*, New York, 1965.
[40] Jeffrey, R. Probable knowledge, in [94].
[41] Jeffrey, R. Gambling with Truth. A review, *Journal of Philosophy*, **65**, 1968.
[42] Keynes, J. *A Treatise on Probability*, London, 1952.
[43] Kolmogorov, A. *Foundations of the Theory of Probability*, New York, 1950.
[44] Kotarbińska, J. *Kontrowersja: dedukcjonizm — indukcjonizm*, in *Logiczna teoria nauki*, Warszawa, 1966.
[45] Kyburg, H. *Probability and the Logic of Rational Belief*, Middletown, 1961.
[46] Kyburg, H. Probability, rationality, and a rule of detachment, in [92].
[47] Kyburg, H. *Probability and Inductive Logic*, London, 1970.
[48] Kyburg, H. Local and global induction, in [90].
[49] Kyburg, H. The Rule of Detachment in Inductive Logic, in [94].
[50] Levi, I. *Gambling with Truth*, New York, 1967.
[51] Levi, I. On indeterminate probabilities, *Journal of Philosophy*, **13**, 1974.
[52] Loś, J. Podstawy analizy metodologicznej kanonów Milla, *Annales*

UMCS sec. F, Vol. II, 1947.
[53] Mackie, J. The Paradox of Confirmation, *British Journal for the Philosophy of Science*, **13**, 1962–63.
[54] Mill, J. *System logiki*, Warszawa, 1962.
[55] Mises, R. von *Probability, Statistics, and Truth*, New York, 1957.
[56] Mortimer, H. Rule of acceptance based on logical probability, *Synthese*, 26, 1973.
[57] Neyman, J. *First Course in Probability and Statistics*, New York, 1950.
[58] Neyman, J. Inductive Behavior as a Basic Concept of Philosophy of Science, *Review of the International Statistical Institute*, **25**, 1957.
[59] Nicod, J. *Foundations of Geometry and Induction*, New York, 1950.
[60] Popper, K. *Logik der Forschung*, Vienna, 1934; Polish translation *Logika odkrycia naukowego*, Warszawa, 1977.
[61] Popper, L. *Conjectures and Refutations*, London, 1963.
[62] Popper, K. The Propensity Interpretation of Probability, *British Journal for the Philosophy of Science*, **10**, 1959–60.
[63] Putnam, H. Probability and Confirmation, in: *Philosophy of Science Today*, 1967.
[64] Ramsey, F. *The Foundations of Mathematics*, London, 1950.
[65] Reichenbach, H. *The Theory of Probability*, Berkeley and Los Angeles, 1949.
[66] Salmon, W. *The Foundations of Scientific Inference*, Pittsburgh, 1966.
[67] Salmon, W. Carnap's Inductive Logic, *Journal of Philosophy*, **64**, 1967.
[68] Salmon, W. The justification of inductive rules of inference, in [94].
[69] Savage, L. *The Foundations of Statistics*, New York, 1954.
[70] Savage, L. Implications of personal probability for induction, *Journal of Philosophy*, **58**, 1966.
[71] Schick, F. Rationality and consistency, *Journal of Philosophy*, **60**, 1963.
[72] Shimony, A. Coherence and the Axioms of confirmation, *Journal of Symbolic Logic*, **20**, 1955.
[73] Smokler, H. The equivalence condition, *American Philosophical Quarterly*, **4**, 1967.
[74] Steinberg, D. Recenzja z książki Poppera 'Logik der Forschung', *Przegląd Filozoficzny*, **38**, 1935.
[75] Strawson, P. On justifying induction, *Philosophical Studies*, **9**, 1958.
[76] Suppes, P. Probabilistic inference and the concept of total evidence, in [88].
[77] Suppes, P. A Bayesian approach to the paradoxes of confirmation in [88].
[78] Szaniawski, K. The value of perfect information, *Synthese*, **17**, 1967.
[79] Szaniawski, K. Wnioskowanie czy behawior, *Studia Filoficzne*, **6/9**, 1958.
[80] Szaniawski, K. O. induckcji eliminacyjnej, in: *Fragmenty filozoficzne*, 1st series, Warszawa, 1959.
[81] Szaniawski, K. Dwie koncepcje indukcji, in: *Fragmenty filozoficzne*, 3rd series, Warszawa, 1967.

[82] Szaniawski, K. Współczesne ujęcie procedur indukcyjnych, *Zagadnienia Naukoznawstwa*, **2–3**, 1965.
[83] Toulmin, S. *The Uses of Argument*, Cambridge, 1958.
[84] Toulema, R. Confirmation, explanantion and paradoxes of transitivity, in [90].
[85] Watkins, J. Between analytic and empirical, *Philosophy*, **32**, 1957.
[86] Wright, G. von. *A Treatise on Induction and Probability*, New York, 1951.
[87] Wright, G. von. The paradoxes of Confirmation, in [88].

COLLECTIONS OF ARTICLES ON INDUCTION

[88] *Aspects of Inductive Logic*, Hintikka, Suppes (eds), Amsterdam, 1966.
[89] *Information and Inference*, Hintikka, Suppes (eds), Amsterdam, 1970.
[90] *Local Induction*, Bogdan (ed.), Amsterdam, 1976.
[91] *Logic, Methodology and Philosophy of Science*, I, Nagel, Suppes, Tarski (eds), Stanford, 1962.
[92] *Logic, Methodology and Philosophy of Science*, II, Bar-Hillel (ed.), Amsterdam, 1964.
[93] *Studies in Subjective Probability*, Kyburg, Smokler (eds), 1964.
[94] *The Problem of Inductive Logic*, Lacatos (ed.), Amsterdam, 1968.

Index

a posteriori probability, 96
a priori probability, 21, 65, 78, 133, 137, 151, 152
absolute probability, 21
ACT*, 165
AM, 155, 165, 166, 167
anti-inductionism, 17, 90
anti-probabilism, 90
artificial intelligence, 157, 174
asymmetry, 70

BACON, 156, 173
Baconian induction, 156, 173
Bayes' criterion, 44
Bayes' criterion of choice, 43
Bayes' criterion of maximal value of the expected usefulness, 116, 118, 125
Bayes' model, 84, 87, 88
Bayes' theorem, 22, 26, 83, 84
belief functions, 80
Bernoulli's formula, 23
Bernoulli's law, 118
Bernoulli's law of large numbers, 23, 118
Boolean algebra, 19, 20, 25
Boolean field, 19

characteristic function, 58
cognitive utility, 113, 115, 125
conceptual clustering, 156
conditional belief, 84, 88
conditional probability, 21, 25, 53, 55, 66, 83, 84, 88, 117, 133, 147, 148
conditionalysing, 84, 85, 86
confirmation functions, 10, 55, 56, 64, 117, 126, 128, 139
connectionist learning, 170
connectionist model, 170
connectionist models, 157
cont, 114, 115, 118, 123, 151
credance function, 86
credit assignment problem, 163, 164
CVC, 168

decision theory, 42, 150
decision trees, 156
definition of utility, 115
derivational analogy, 168, 169
descriptive methodology, 16

EBG, 161, 162
eliminative induction, 15
empirical probability, 35, 89
enthymematic deductions, 15
epistemological probability, 102, 107
estimated probabilities, 37
estimation of parameters, 40
EURISKO, 155, 165, 166, 167, 168
explanation-based generalization, 161
explanation-based learning, 157

Finnish school, 71
first-order error, 40, 41
first-order logic, 112
frequential probability, 24, 35, 38, 73, 76, 78, 89

generalization, 158, 160
global induction, 106

heuristic methods, 158
heuristic relevance conditions, 163
heuristic rules, 167
heuristics learning programs, 163
hypothetico-deductive method, 91

ID3, 160
induction behaviour, 126
induction by elimination, 17
induction by enumeration, 17, 28, 29, 30, 31, 32, 68, 69
inference by analogy, 17, 32, 33
inprojectible properties, 74
inprojectible sets, 74

knowledge compilation, 165

l-system, 60
Laplace's criterion, 43
law of large numbers, 23, 77
learning apprentice approach, 164
learning by analogy, 168, 170
learning from examples, 157
learning heuristics, 162
LEX, 164, 165
local induction, 106, 107
logical interpretation of probability, 35
logical probability, 24, 38, 47, 53, 72, 73, 75, 76, 86, 128, 145, 152
lottery paradox, 101, 102, 104, 112, 120

machine learning, 154
means-end analysis, 168
measure of confirmation, 28, 93, 147
measure of utility, 115
minimalization of average loss, 45
minimalization of maximum risk, 45
minimax, 43

numerical intervals, 73, 152

objective probability, 89

paradox of the so-called statistical 'syllogism', 144
partial interpretation of probability, 35
pattern-recognition, 170
perceptrons, 170
personalism, 80, 85, 86, 89, 117
postulate of coherence of beliefs, 88
postulate of compatability, 102
postulate of consequence, 104
postulate of genuineness, 93
postulate of rational acceptance, 108
postulate randomness, 36
postulates of rationality, 45
postulates of transitivity, 142
power of a test, 41
principle of indifference, 47
principle of minimalization of maximum risk, 43
principle of minimizing the average loss, 43
probabilism, 94, 96
probabilistic independence, 60
probabilistic rules of acceptance, 100, 107, 139
probability calculus, 11, 20, 54, 71, 82, 84, 107, 151
probability confirmation function, 53
probability function, 20
problem reduction, 163

proceduralization, 165
propensity interpretation, 38

Q numbers, 50, 51, 54, 57
Q numbers N, 57
Q predicates, 51, 56, 57, 60, 62, 65, 66, 68, 69
Q sets, 50, 51, 52, 54, 62, 63
qualitative concept of acceptance, 99
qualitative statements, 27
quantitative concept of acceptance, 99
quantitative statements, 27

randomness, 36, 72, 73, 74, 75
rational corpora, 102
rational knowledge, 105
rational risk, 82
rational sets, 73, 74
raven paradox, 128, 130, 155
reductive inference, 17
relative frequencies, 38
RLL, 168
rule composition, 165
rules of acceptance, 10, 99

second-order error, 41
simple rule, 38
simple rule of confirmation, 58
specialization, 158, 160
statistical induction, 40
statistical probability, 24, 35, 38, 73
Str, 52, 54
strong maximal value, 119
subjective interpretation of probability, 35
subjective probability, 24, 38, 80, 83
subtraction of probabilities, 147
supervised learning, 172
symmetry, 70, 147

TDIDT, 160, 161
testing of hypotheses, 40
theorem of complete probability, 87
theorem of full probability, 22
top-down indiction of decision trees, 160
transformational analogy, 168, 169
transitivity paradox, 140
truth maintenance system, 169

variety of instances, 30, 31, 68, 69
version space, 156, 159, 160